ENDING TERRORISM IN THE UNITED STATES:

GOD HAS WARNED U. S.

Elmore Richmond Jr.
A Prophet of God

Victory Publishing Company
P. O. Box 2935
Jackson, Tennessee 38302-2935
Visit Web Site at: www.america-america.org

Victory Publishing Company
P. O. Box 2935
Jackson, Tennessee 38302-2935
Printed in the United States of America

International Standard Book Number:
ISBN-10: 1-886636-52-4
ISBN-13: 978-1-886636-52-1

Library of Congress Catalogue Card Number:

Edited By: Linda Broadous Miles
               Darlene Richmond

ACKNOWLEDGEMENTS

I praise God for calling and choosing me to be one of His servants, a Prophet of God, to do this work.

I give special thanks to my brother and Pastor, Elder Robert L. Richmond and his wife Darlene; he is Pastor of Bible Way Full Gospel Church in Oak Ridge, Tennessee. Moreover, I thank my brother Major and his wife, Iva Dean, for their support and encouragement. I also give thanks to Bishop William C. Latta for support and encouragement. And I give thanks to my dear friend and prayer partner, Sharon L. Almendarez.

I thank each and every one of you who love the Lord and call on the Lord God in this time of crisis. And I thank God for answering our prayers.

I give thanks to men and women around the world who have been called to preach the word of God, for using this work to ensure the body of Christ is properly fed, as we work together in seeking the Kingdom of God and His righteousness.

I give thanks to all who will read this book and receive this message from the Spirit of Truth. Then work to end the rush to shed the blood of the innocent and turn from their wicked ways, pray, and then serve the Lord in a more perfect way.

FOREWORD

Shall a trumpet be blown in the city, and the people not be afraid? Shall there be evil in a city, and the Lord hath not done it? Surely the Lord God will do nothing, but revealeth his secret unto his **servants** the **prophets.** (Amos 3:6-7)

I will raise them up a Prophet from among their brethren like unto thee, and will put my words in his mouth; and he shall speak unto them all that I shall command him. And it shall come to pass, that whosoever will not hearken unto my words which he shall speak in my name, I will require it of him. But the prophet, which shall presume to speak a word in my name, which I have not commanded him to speak, or that shall speak in the name of other gods, even that prophet shall die. And if thou say in thine heart, How shall we know the word which the Lord hath not spoken? When a prophet speaketh in the name of the Lord, if the thing follow not, nor come to pass, that is the thing which the Lord hath not spoken, but the prophet hath spoken it presumptuously: thou shall not be afraid of him. (Deuteronomy 18:18-22)

"And it shall come to pass in the last days, saith God, I will pour out of my Spirit upon all flesh: and your sons and your daughters shall prophesy, and your young men shall see visions, and your old men shall dream dreams: And on my **servants** and on my **handmaidens** I will pour out in those days of my Spirit; and they shall prophesy." (Acts 2:17-18)

"And he gave some, apostles; and some, **prophets**; and some evangelists; and some, pastors and teachers; for the perfecting of the saints, for the work of the ministry, for the edifying of the body of Christ: Till we all come in the unity of the faith, and of the knowledge of the Son of God unto a perfect man, unto the measure of the stature of the fullness of Christ: That we henceforth be no more children, tossed to and fro, and carried about with every wind of doctrine, by the sleight of men, and cunning craftiness, whereby they lie in wait to deceive; But speaking the truth in love, may grow up into him in all things, which is the head even Christ: From whom the whole body fitly joined together and compacted by that which every joint supplieth, according to the effectual working in the measure of every part, maketh increase of the body unto the edifying of itself in love." (Ephesians 4:11-16)

The Word Of God

INTRODUCTION

The Church has a great responsibility as the light of the world. To be that light we must continue to seek the righteousness of God in faith. Today, however, the Church has failed to have the godly influence on governments and our society because the Church is out of step in seeking the righteousness of God. History has shown us how Judah was out of step with the righteousness of God and God sent Isaiah unto Judah to warn of the consequences of their actions. Likewise, God is warning the United States today.

Therefore, we need a check-up to see where we are and then make the most needed adjustments. It is imperative that this check-up be conducted now in the midst of this crisis that confronts the world.

God has blessed America for over two-hundred years because of the covenant that was made with the founding fathers through the Declaration of Independence. When they wrote these precious words, **"We hold these truths to be self-evident, that all men are created equal, that they are endowed by their Creator with certain unalienable rights, that among these are life, liberty and the pursuit of happiness,"** God was with them and God blessed this land because they sought His righteousness. God continued to bless America as long as the heart of America was seeking His righteousness.

Today, however, there is trouble in the land. Our leaders must seek the counsel of God. Terrorist attacks on America have been very destructive and the threats for further attacks continue to grow. We must work to end these attacks and to return peace back to our land. Can this be done with our military might? No it cannot. Isaiah 48:18 says, "If we hearkened to His commandments, we would have His peace as a river, and God's righteousness as the waves of the sea." Through this work, God will show us how we can experience His peace, and the righteousness of God, as the waves of the sea, as God has promised us in His word.

Through this work, God provides counsel to the President of the United States of America and our leaders that will lead to peace, while the leaders are studying war. Moreover, it shows leaders around the world, answers to bringing healing and peace from God to their land.

In respect to the terrorist attacks on America on September 11, 2001, God has provided answers to your questions through this work. The book of Amos, Chapter 3, verses 6-7 says, "Shall a trumpet be blown in the city, and the people not be afraid? Shall there be evil in the city, and the Lord hath not done it? Surely the Lord God will do nothing, but he revealeth his secret unto his servants, the prophets." On September 10, 2001, God revealed the terrorist attacks and our preparation for war to me. Moreover, thirty days prior to this revelation, God gave me the task of preparing my first book on this subject, "America, America: A check-up for the Body of Christ, The Church."

The book was published within three weeks of 9/11. On October 6, 2001, a copy of the manuscript was sent to President George W. Bush. Moreover, copies of the book were sent to leaders around the country. However, who believed our report. Besides the book, other communications were sent to President Bush of various revelations from God. These revelations have come to fruition. Contained herein is a reprint of "America, America, A Check-up For The Body Of Christ and copies of the communications that were sent to President Bush and other leaders.

Besides giving answers to our current crisis, this work gives every believer a real opportunity to strengthen his/her relationship with God and shares revelations regarding the righteousness of God that all must understand. Moreover, it provides clarity for Christians on how to build their relationships with the Holy Spirit in order to serve God in a more perfect way.

Besides this work, God has given me another work titled, "Edifying The Body Of Christ: Unbinding The Strong Man." Besides providing wisdom and knowledge to the Christians, it serves as a means of healing for the Jews and the Muslims. It shows how many Christians have been deceived and the impact of this deception on the Muslims. Moreover, it brings the Spirit of Truth to the Jews to help them understand who Jesus is and it helps them discover God's rest for them.

The ones who truly love God, their eyes will be opened and then they will receive the Spirit of Truth. They will be able to enter into God's rest and then experience God's peace as a river; and God's righteousness as the waves of the

viii

sea.

Before reading this book, I ask you to pray this short prayer that is taken from Psalm 139:23-24, "Search me, O God, and know my heart: try me, and know my thoughts: And see if there be any wicked way in me, and lead me in the way everlasting." Remember to ask our heavenly Father in the name of Jesus.

With love in Christ Jesus

Elmore Richmond Jr.
A Prophet of God

TABLE OF CONTENTS

Chapter One

Personal Testimonies and

The Revelation of America Preparation for War

On or about August 11, 2001, I commenced reading the Book of Isaiah; I read it over, and over, and over. It came clear to me what God was calling me to do. God wants me to bring His word on righteousness to help equip the church to provide counsel to leaders around the world. I am one of God's prophets. This is an uphill battle for me because most people to include Christians do believe that God has prophets, today. In addition, in Luke 4:24, Jesus said, "No prophet is accepted in his own country." However, God is a faithful God. God has equipped me with everything I need for true believers to understand that God has sent me.

However, it was not until September 11, 2001 when it became clear to me what God was calling me to do today. I am charged with bringing a rebirth to the prophecy of Isaiah regarding God's righteousness and to warn God's people of the destruction to come if we fail to hearken to His word. I will explain in detail later in this chapter concerning God's call for my life regarding the world crisis that we face today. However, first let us review a few scriptures regarding prophets.

Ephesians 4:11 says, "And He gave some, apostles, and some prophets: …" I am one of God's prophets. Although the word is clear, some Christians do not believe that God has prophets today. This has occurred because they failed to allow the Holy Spirit to teach them. Luke 16:16 says, "The law and the prophets were until John: since that time the kingdom of God is preached, and every man presseth into it." This does not say God does not have any more prophets, as some suggest. However, it says before John, the gospel was not preached, but people were guided by the Law of Moses and the prophets. However, John preached the gospel and today the gospel is preached.

Prophets are servants of God. Amos 3:7 says, "Surely the Lord God will do nothing, but he revealeth his secret unto His servants the prophets." I am one of God's prophets; I know that God reveals some of his secrets to me; therefore I speak with much confidence that the foregoing is referring to the writing of the prophets. Now let us listen to the Spirit of Truth as scriptures are rightly divided, precept on precept, precept on precept, and line on line, and line on line.

Let us look at a similar statement that was made in another text. Acts 24:14, "But this I confess unto thee, that after the way which they call heresy, so worship I the God of my fathers, believing all things which are written in the law and in the prophets." Now let us look at more scriptures, "Matthew 5:17, Jesus said, "Think not that I am come to destroy the law, or prophets: I am come not to destroy but to fulfill." Jesus did fulfill the prophets that were written about the gospel because they were talking about Him. John 5:39 says, "Search the scriptures; for in them ye think ye have eternal life: and they are they which testify of me."

This scripture should resolve this matter. Mark 1:2 says, "As it is written in the prophets…" Here we can clearly see in this text the word "prophets" is not referring to people, but their writings. Was John, the Apostle who wrote the book of Revelation a prophet? Did he come after John the Baptist? We can clearly see how the unlearned could have made this conclusion, that today there are no prophets. However, there is no excuse for the learned who have love for the truth.

Scriptures do not support the conclusion reached by some that there are no prophets. Amos 3:6-7 says, "Shall a trumpet be blown in the city, and the people not be afraid? Shall there be evil in a city and the Lord hath not done it? Surely the Lord God will do nothing, but he revealeth his secret unto His servants the prophets." Has God stopped doing things? God is. Does God reveal His secrets today? Yes God does, I am a witness. Let's examine some other scriptures.

In Matthew 23:34, Jesus says, "Wherefore, behold, I send unto you prophets, and wise men, and scribes: and some of them, ye shall kill and crucify; and some of them shall ye scourge in your synagogues, and persecute them from city to city." Here Jesus is not only talking about prophets of the past but prophets that he will send in the future.

I did not make myself a prophet. God chose me. Acts 2:17-18 says, "And it shall come to pass in the last days, said God, I will pour out of my Spirit upon all flesh: and your sons and your daughters shall prophesy, and your young men shall see visions, and your old men shall dream dreams: And on My servants and on my handmaidens I will pour out in those days of my Spirit; and they shall prophesy." **Prophets are God's servants**. (Amos 3:7)

Every Christian must develop a personal relationship with the Holy Spirit in order to use the gifts in a more perfect way that the Holy Spirit has given unto each Christian. I have developed a very strong relationship with the Holy Spirit. To develop a personal relationship with the Holy Spirit, first you must want it, ask for it in prayer, listen, and then seek it with your actions and continual prayers. Ask our Heavenly Father, in the name of Jesus, to renew your mind daily by the power of the Holy Spirit. Each day, and some times more often than once a day, I use a form of prayer taken from Psalms 139:23-24, "Search me, O God, and know my heart: try me, and know my thoughts: (24) And see if there be any wicked way in me, and lead me in the way everlasting." Remember you must ask the Father to grant this request in the name of Jesus.

Before I close this section, allow me to share more about this calling and I pray that my personal testimonies will serve to edify the body and to help increase your faith that God is true to all of His promises. First, let me share some of my observations that I made regarding my personal relationship with the Holy Spirit.

3

The relationship is so personal; the Holy Spirit gives me confirmations when I ask questions. The Holy Spirit hits my body when he gives me these confirmations. It is hard to explain. However, when I asked the Holy Spirit about it, His answer was simple, "As I touched John while he was in His mother's womb and caused him to leap, like wise, I will touch you." The Holy Spirit directs me to scriptures and wakes me up, whenever I ask. I can say please wake me up in one hour or wake me up at 5:00 A.M. The Holy Spirit has never failed. This happens over and over.

I receive revelations on a daily basis. The Holy Spirit reveals future events to me. The Holy Spirit shows me ahead of time, who needs healing and for what reason. I can ask the Holy Spirit to give me a better understanding of a problem or circumstance, and the Holy Spirit provides clarity. Sometimes when the Holy Spirit shows me things to come, the Holy Spirit takes me on trips and allows me to see these events before they happen. This occurs often when I am asleep. However, there have been some exceptions. I have also received revelations even while I have been wide-awake. Often the events are news-making occurrences. However, sometimes they are not.

Often I am an observer, and sometimes I am an actual participant. I have learned that when you are an actual participant, you must have on your whole armor of God. Let me explain one of my experiences.

Sometimes my dreams are more than dreams. They are visions. When this occurs they appear to be real, very real. Once I dreamed I was in a strange place. I was just observing the various things that were going on, and then I spoke to this woman. She replied to me, "I thought you were a ghost." I told her, "No I am not a ghost," and then I woke up immediately. As I sat there wide-awake in my bed, I could still hear the background noises that were in my dream. Then the noises just faded away. I will never forget that experience.

God reveals so much to me… fires, earthquakes, accidents, floods, storms,

4

people being healed, and the list goes on and on. I actually saw the bombing of our barracks in the Mid-East before it happened, the ambush of our troops in Central America, the crew on our submarine before it hit the Japanese fishing boat, the prison outbreak in Afghanistan, our planes being shot down, the attempted theft of money by our soldiers in Iraq, the sexually perverse acts of our soldiers in Iraq, the escape of Sadam Hussein and his sons from the building that was bombed at the beginning of the war, the large protest against the war in Europe in 2003, internal problems within our military, the apartment that exploded in Los Angles in 2002, the destruction of the bridge on interstate 40 in 2002, the loss of command and control in 2004, internal problems within the military in 2004, lack of trust and lack of unity of command, the loss of control of command and control of a natural disaster in 2004 and the chemical leak in Oak Ridge in 2004. The list continues to grow as God reveals these things to me.

Besides, God giving me revelations of what is to come, through the power of the Holy Spirit in the name of Jesus, God heals when I lay my hands on the sick under the authority of our Lord and Savior Jesus Christ. This gift is available to every believer. What set me apart from most is that I have confidence that God will heal. I am not afraid to call on the name of the Lord to heal people that need blessings from the Lord. Through the laying on of hands, God has used me as His vessel to heal individuals that have been stricken by strokes, cancer and brain tumors. The dumb were able to speak and healing was brought to the broken-hearted. God has used me to cast demons out of individuals in the name of our Lord and Saviour Jesus Christ. Moreover, God has given us supernatural powers.

Recently, I made a discovery about this power that is unknown to most people. In fact, I found that all whom I have approached with it knew nothing about this power. I am not sure if everyone has this power. Nevertheless, let me share it with you.

2 Kings 6:4-6 says, "So he (Elisha) went with them. And when they came

5

to Jordan, they cut down wood. But as one was felling a beam, the axe head fell into the water: and he cried, and said, Alas, master! For it was borrowed. And the man of God said, Where fell it? And he showed him the place. And he cut down a stick, and cast it in thither; and the iron did swim." The King James Version of the Bible says that the iron did swim. However, some of the new translations say the iron floated. Well this observation is not whether the iron swam or floated. However, I would be remiss if I did not caution the Church about how the words of God are being changed through some of these new translations. Nevertheless, in summary, the scriptures say that God gave Elisha supernatural powers. Like Elisha, I discovered that God has given me some supernatural power.

I have discovered that everything I touch with my hands becomes subject to this power when I praise God. My hands act as magnets and draw everything they touch. I can raise my hand, books, pens, iron pots, glass, plastic items, bricks, and wood they all become suspended in the air against my hand. I do not have to grip these items, I can raise my hands in a vertical position and these objects will defy the law of gravity. I have found that instead of a magnet drawing me, I draw the magnet. This is supernatural power.

Others have the same power. I discovered this power while I was praising God. I held a book, "America, America - A Check Up For The Body Of Christ" in my hands lifting it up to God. The book became magnetized to my hand. Now allow me to share several other testimonies.

In January 1998, I was traveling from Jackson, Tennessee en-route back to Los Angeles, California, when I had an experience that I will never forget. It was about 2:00 A.M. I was driving west on Interstate 40. I exited off the Interstate highway just west of Oklahoma City, Oklahoma. While I was refueling my car, a man approached me and told me to be careful on the highway because the weather was going to turn bad. I looked at the bank thermometer. It read 32 degrees. After seeing this reading, I thought that this was not a big deal. Little did I know

6

what was in store for me farther up the road. As I continued my trip, I encountered a powerful thunderstorm. It was thundering, lightning, raining, hailing, sleeting, and snowing. Ice had formed on the road.

I slowed my car down to about 45 miles per hour. It appeared as if I was the only driver on the Interstate. For over five minutes I did not see any cars. No one came pass me and there was no on coming traffic. The storm became very severe. Ice formed on the pavement and the car started to lose traction.

Then there was a bolt of lightning that appeared to hit my car. Thunder followed immediately after. The lightning was so intense. It appeared that the panel lights inside my car flickered. When this happened, I said a simple prayer, "Lord, take your servant safely through this." **Immediately,** after this prayer, the rain stopped, the hail stopped, the lightning flashed from afar. It happened so fast it took my breath away. I said thank you Jesus. I had no other problems on the trip from Okalahoma City to Los Angeles. God is good.

Before I end these personal testimonies, allow me to share this one. This happened many years ago in the early 1970's while I was in Tampa, Florida. I recalled leaving the public library in downtown Tampa. While walking to my car I had to cross a busy one-way street. I decided to cross the street in the middle of the block. At my right, I observed cars approaching at high speed, but the Holy Spirit told me to step out in front of those cars. All of those cars stopped to allow me to cross. Then I looked to my left, and around the bend of the one-way street was a car coming, going the wrong way. The driver was allowed to make a u-turn by the other drivers. I went back onto the sidewalk and waved all cars safely through as I thought about how God used me to ensure the safety of that driver. God is good.

On September 10, 2001, God revealed to me the destruction of the World Trade Center and the United States of America preparing for war. However, before I give a detailed account of that revelation, let us review the foundation for seeking the righteousness of God.

Chapter Two

Laying The Foundation For Seeking The Righteousness Of God

There have been many great nations that have come and gone over the years. The United States of America, as great as it is today, can also fall if we do not fear God and if we fail to hearken to the commandments of God regarding His righteousness. We must understand as it is recorded in Romans 15:4, "For whatsoever things were written aforetime were written for our learning, that we through patience and comfort of the scriptures might have hope."

The Book of Isaiah, 51:5 states, "My righteousness is near; my salvation is gone forth and mine arms shall judge the people; the isles shall wait upon me, and on mine arm shall they trust." Isaiah 51:7 states, "…but my righteousness shall be forever, and my salvation from generation to generation." Every Christian, Jew, and individual who truly loves God must clearly understand these two statements in respect to righteousness and salvation. However, many Christians cannot recall ever hearing these two statements.

But, most Christians can recall the word as recorded in Matthew 6:33, "Seek ye first the Kingdom of God, and His Righteousness; and all these things shall be added unto you." Thus, today many Christians are familiar with these words; however, they do not fully understand how to apply these words of God in their life experiences. On the other hand, most of the children of Israel (Jews) rejected Christ and failed to understand the righteousness of God. Nevertheless, today we find most Christians, like the Jews, do not understand nor seek the righteousness of God. We must confront these problems now. In this Chapter, we will examine the scriptures that lay the foundation for seeking the

9

righteousness of God and set in order steps for seeking the righteousness of God.

The Book of Romans, 10:9 - 10, states, "That if thou shalt confess with thy mouth the Lord Jesus, and shalt believe in thine heart that God hath raised him from the dead, thou shalt be saved. (10) For with the heart man believeth unto righteousness; and with the mouth confession is made unto salvation." Please note, with the heart, man believeth unto righteousness. 1 John 2:3-4 says, "And hereby we do know that we know him, if we keep his commandments. He that saith, I know him, and keepeth not his commandments, is a liar, and the truth is not in him." Meditate on this truth.

God called me to preach His word. Why did he call me? How do I know that he called me? What is my specific purpose? I knew God called me to preach His word, but I did not know exactly what His specific reasons were for calling me. In the book of Romans 10:14 - 15, it reads, "How then shall they call on him in whom they have not believed? And how shall they believe in him of whom they have not heard? And how shall they hear without a preacher? (15) And how shall they preach, except they be sent? ..." Jesus wants His lambs, His sheep, and His sheep to be properly fed. And I have been called to play a role in ensuring that this occurs.

This became very clear to me while preparing a sermon, "Yes I love Jesus, Try Me Lord." While preparing that sermon, I read John 21:15 - 17. Whereby, Jesus asked Peter three times - do you love me? And then gave him specific commands after each time. The commandments were to (1) Feed my lambs (2) Feed my sheep and (3) Feed my sheep. Peter was saddened after Jesus asked him the third time. However, Jesus did not do this to make Peter sad. He did it for Peter to search himself because Jesus had taught Peter well about what was required of him, if he loved Him.

Jesus commanded Peter to feed His lambs because Jesus knew that His lambs were meek, and easily led. He knew about the false teachers. In Matthew

10

24:3-5, Jesus warned his disciples what shall be the sign of his coming and of the end of the world. Jesus told them, "Take heed that no man deceive you. For many shall come in my name, saying I am Christ; and shall deceive many." Jesus knew that Satan is always waiting to destroy.

The second command given was to feed my sheep. Jesus knew that His sheep are meek and easily led, just as the lambs. However, Jesus knew they had to be properly fed to know and understand the word of God.

The third command given was to feed my sheep. Jesus knew that His sheep, which include His under-shepherds, must be continually fed. Jesus knew as it is recorded in 2 Timothy 4:3 - "For the time will come when they will not endure sound doctrine; but after their own lusts shall they heap to themselves teachers, having itching ears; and they shall turn away their ears from the truth, and shall be turned unto fables."

Therefore, Jesus knew that His sheep must be properly fed at all times. Jesus knew that in order for His sheep to love him - they must learn about him and they too must understand the requirements of following His commandments. Many Christians have been deceived and have never been taught this truth, "He that saith, I know him and keepeth not his commandments, is a liar, and the truth is not in him." (1 John 2:4) Jesus knew that when His sheep learned of these things and followed his commandments, that His joy would remain in each of His sheep, and that His sheep's joy might be full.

Today, I clearly understand why He called me. I am one of God's prophets. I must warn His people of the destruction to come to the United States if we fail to hearken to the commandments of God. Moreover, the second coming of our Lord and Savior Jesus Christ is near. Jesus wants His Church ready to receive him without spot, wrinkle, or blemish, or any such thing. Prior to being called to the ministry, for over thirty years my job had been to fight for justice, looking for root causes of injustice and working to end corruption. For the world,

I have worked diligently to that end. Today, however, my job is to help the Church get ready to meet the bridegroom and to provide counsel for the leaders of this nation on the righteousness of God.

"Mercy and truth are met together; righteousness and peace have kissed each other. Truth shall spring out of the earth; and righteousness shall look down from heaven. Yea, the Lord shall give that which is good; and our land shall yield her increase. Righteousness shall go before him; and shall set us in the way of his steps." (Psalm 85:10-13) According to Matthew 21:32, John came unto the Jews in the way of righteousness and they believed him not. Today, however, truth is springing out of the earth and righteousness is looking down from heaven. To that end God has given me dreams and visions on how to provide good counsel to the people who love the Lord.

Chapter Three
The Righteousness of God

Before addressing the problems of the nation, each Christian must examine himself or herself. I pray that you will have patience; this is spiritual food. This food was not written for the world; the world cannot receive it. Listen carefully, "For the mystery of iniquity doth already work: only he who now letteth will let, until he be taken out of the way. And then shall the wicked be revealed, whom the Lord shall consume with the spirit of his mouth, and shall destroy with the brightness of this coming. Even him, whose coming is after the working of Satan with all power and signs and lying wonders, and with all deceivableness of unrighteousness in them that perish; because they received not the love of the truth, that they might be saved. And for this cause God shall send them strong delusion, that they should believe a lie: that they all might be damned who believed not the truth, but had pleasure in unrighteousness." (2 Thessalonians 2:7-12) **I pray that you have love for the truth.**

Brothers and Sisters in Christ, to receive this message you must have love for the truth because many have deceived many. However, they too say that Jesus is the Christ. Although Jesus is Christ, many will go forth and some have gone forth and deceived many. Consequently, if you do not have love for the truth, God will send you strong delusion, so you will believe a lie. Because you have love not for the truth you will be damned.

Some Christians quote part of the scripture from Romans 8:1 which says, "There is therefore now no condemnation to them which are in Christ Jesus, ..." I have heard Christians quote this portion of this verse. However, I admonish them to continue to read the verse, "... who walk not after the flesh, but after the Spirit." We must seek the righteousness of God, by faith in the spirit.

13

In the book of Isaiah, like the prophecy regarding the birth of our Lord and Savior, Jesus Christ, whereby we receive salvation, the book gives the prophecy regarding God's righteousness. We must bring understanding to the prophecy of Isaiah regarding the righteousness of God. God has established standards regarding his righteousness. We must understand these standards and seek the counsel of God. Consequently, if the United States of America fails to seek counsel of God, this nation will fall under the declared and published standards for Babylon and the images of Babylon.

Today, we must clearly understand how the prophecy of Isaiah pertains to us. Like God gave his word to Isaiah for Judah and Israel, today, God has given me the same message for His people, in the United States of America.

In Isaiah 48:16 - 18, it is recorded, "Come ye near unto me, hear ye this: I have not spoken in secret from the beginning; from the time that it was, there am I: and now the Lord God, and His spirit, hath sent me. (17) Thus saith the Lord, thy Redeemer, the Holy One of Israel, I am the Lord Thy God which teacheth thee to profit, which leadeth thee by the way that thou shouldest go. (18) O that thou hadst hearkened to my commandments then had thy peace been as a river, and thy righteousness as the waves of the sea."

Have you experienced peace as a river? Do you believe that your righteousness is as the waves of the sea? Now look at the United States and ask the same questions. Is the United States of America experiencing peace as a river? Does the United States of America have righteousness as the waves of the sea? If you carefully evaluate the facts, your answers for both of these questions regarding the United States would be "NO." If we hearken to the commandments of God, we would be His children, we would be established in righteousness; we would be far from oppression; we would not have fear and terror would not come near us, and God would show us how to profit. What is wrong? Is there something wrong with the word of God or is there something wrong with us?

14

We know that God's word is true. However, before we examine the United States' actions, first let us look at Christians, especially in the United States. In Romans Chapter 11, it explains how the Gentiles were ingrafted branches into the tree of life. We must examine these scriptures carefully. Starting with verse 11:15, "For if the casting away of them be the reconciling of the world, what shall the receiving of them be, but life from the dead?" This verse shows that when the Jews rejected God, God offered salvation to the rest of the world. Today, the ones who believe are alive through Christ Jesus.

(16) "For if the first fruit be holy, lump is also holy: and if the root be holy, so are the branches." Here the first fruit refers to Abraham and the other patriarchs. They were holy, therefore their children were also holy.

(17) "And if some of the branches be broken off, and thou, being a wild olive tree, wert grafted in among them, and with them partakest of the root and the fatness of the olive tree;" Some of the branches from Abraham's tree, were the Jews that were broken off. The Gentiles are referred to as wild olive trees.

(18) "Boast not against the branches. But if thou boast, thou bearest not the root, but the root thee." Here the Gentiles are told be careful not to brag about being grafted in to replace the Jews that were broken off.

(19) "Thou wilt say then, The branches were broken off, that I might be grafted in."

(20) "Well; because of unbelief they were broken off, and thou standest by faith. Be not high-minded, but fear:" Here the Gentiles are reminded that the Jews were broken off because they did not believe God. And the Gentiles were grafted in because they believed. However they were told not to think too highly of themselves but fear what could happen.

(21) "For if God spared not the natural branches, take heed lest he also spared not thee."

(22) "Behold therefore the goodness and severity of God: on them which fell, severity; but toward thee, goodness, "if thou continue in his goodness: otherwise thou also shalt be cut off."

(23) "And they also, if they abide not still in unbelief, shall be grafted in: for God is able to graft them in again."

(24) "For if thou wert cut out of the olive tree which is wild by nature, and wert grafted contrary to nature into a good olive tree: how much more shall these, which be the natural branches, be grafted into their own olive tree?

Christians must understand that they too can be broken off. And the children of Israel must understand that they can be grafted back in. However, believers must seek first the Kingdom of God, and His righteousness; and all these things shall be added unto them. Isaiah 54:14-15 says, "In righteousness shalt thou be established: thou shalt be far from oppression; for thou shalt not fear: and from terror; for it shall not come near thee. Behold, they surely gather together, but not by me: whosoever shall gather together against thee shall fall for thy sake." As Paul prayed in Romans 10:1, "Brethren, My heart's desire and prayer to God for Israel is, that they might be saved." This is also my prayer and I pray that all Christians would pray that the Jews would be saved.

However, today besides praying for the Jews, Christians that truly know who Jesus is must pray for other Christians who really do not know Jesus because they have been deceived. The First Epistle of John 2:4-5 says, "He that saith, I know him and keepeth not his commandments, is a liar, and the truth is not in him. But whoso keepeth his word, in him verily is the love of God perfected: hereby know we that we are in him. He that saith he abideth in him ought himself also so walk, even as he walked.

Why were the children of Israel broken off? Answer: Because they did not believe that Jesus was the only begotten Son of God. In other words, they did not know who Jesus was. Today, we have many that say they are Christians,

16

however, they do not know who Jesus is because they do not do what Jesus commanded them to do.

Due to deception, many do not understand that in Jesus dwelleth all the fullness of the Godhead bodily. Christians are complete in Jesus, which is head of all principality and power. (Colossians 2:9-10) In the work, "Edifying the Body of Christ: Unbinding the Strong Man," God has allowed me to fully reveal the mystery of Godliness through this work. Praise the Lord.

The word of God in Mathew 6:33 says, "Seek ye first the Kingdom of God, and His Righteousness; and all these things shall be added unto you." Every Christian must know how to seek the kingdom of God and God's righteousness. Isaiah 51:5 say, My righteousness is near; my salvation is gone forth. Most Christians know that we receive salvation through our Lord and Savior Jesus Christ. However in respect to His righteousness, many do not have a clue. Some would even refer back to Isaiah 64:6, and refer to their righteousness as filthy rags.

When we receive Jesus as the Lord and Savior of our lives, Jesus Christ does not want us to view ourselves as filthy rags because we have been redeemed. John 1:12 says, "… As many as received Him, to them gave He power to become the sons of God, even to them that believe on his name…" If we follow His commandments, our peace will be like the river and our righteousness will be as the waves of the sea. Our goal here is to help you experience this level of peace and righteousness. However, without Jesus as Lord of our lives, surely, our righteousness is as filthy rags. Remember, Jesus must be Lord of our lives for us to be the love of our Heavenly Father and to become children of God.

Sometimes scriptures are misunderstood because we fail to understand to whom they were written to. For example, the book of Ephesians, this book was written to the saints that were at Ephesus and to the faithful in Christ Jesus. Today, if you are not faithful in Christ Jesus, the blessings contained therein are

17

not for you. Some teach that you do not have to do anything; they say when you say that you believe, that is all you have to do. This teaching is in error.

Listen. Today the faithful in Christ Jesus are the ones who have all spiritual blessings in heavenly places in Christ. It is the faithful in Christ Jesus that were chosen before the foundation of the world, that they should be holy and without blame before Him in love. Today, it is the faithful in Christ Jesus that were predestinated unto the adoption of children by Jesus Christ to himself, according to the good pleasure of his will, to the praise of the glory of his grace, wherein He hath made us accepted in the beloved.

Isaiah 51:5 states, "My righteousness is near; my salvation is gone forth, and mine arm shall judge the people; the isles shall wait upon me, and on mine arm shall they trust." It is very important that we understand this statement. We must understand that God is our Savior and He sent our Lord and Savior Jesus Christ to redeem all that would believe in Him, God's only begotten son. We must understand when Jesus saved us, He redeemed us and we were in the right standing with God. Remember, we seek the kingdom of God and His righteousness. For with the heart man believeth unto righteousness. Therefore, our heart must be right before God. Hebrews 3.12 warns us to take heed, how an evil heart of unbelief can cause us to depart from the Living God.

If our hearts are not right, we can be broken off, like the children of Israel. To keep this from happening to us, we must remember that as many as received Jesus, to them gave he power to become sons and daughters of God. Therefore, we must have faith and seek after God's righteousness by hearkening to God's commandments.

The United States is a power nation. We put our trust in our military and esteem it as the most powerful military in the world. Many believe that with the strength of our military we could overthrow Iraq and any other nation that comes up against us or if we desire to over take them even if there is no provocation.

Although we have a powerful military, we must learn to fear God. "The fear of the Lord is the beginning or wisdom: a good understanding have all they that do his commandments: his praise endureth for ever." (Psalm 111:10)

Before we go any further, we first must visit Isaiah 54:14. It says, "In righteousness shalt thou be established: thou shalt be far from oppression; for thou shalt not fear; and from terror; for it shall not come near thee." Again, the word of God is true. Why did terror visit America on September 11, 2001? Isaiah 54:17 says, "No weapon that is formed against thee shall prosper; and every tongue that shall rise against thee in judgment thou shalt condemn. This is the heritage of the servants of the Lord and their righteousness is of me, saith the Lord." Here we could make a mistake if we fail to study God's word.

We must note this is the heritage of the servants of the Lord, whereby God says their righteousness was of Him. Who are servants of God? They are ones who follow His commandments. Let's pray for our leaders, for each one of them to understand that it is not through our military might, but only by seeking the righteousness of God that this land will continue to prosper and be free from terrorism. **We must fear God!**

Isaiah 51: 7 gives clarity here. It says, "Hearken unto me, ye that know righteousness, the people in whose heart is my law; fear ye not the reproach of men, neither be ye afraid of their revilings. (8) For the moth shall eat them up like a garment, and the worm shall eat them like wool: but my righteousness shall be forever, and my salvation from generation to generation." Every Christian should know and understand this foundational statement regarding God's righteousness and God's salvation. Again, God's righteousness is forever - God's salvation is from generation to generation.

In Appendix Two, "Sermon - A Check Up For The Body of Christ, The Church" you will find the inspired word of God that gives new converts and every believer the much needed information to help them see clearly how they can serve

19

the Lord in a more perfect way.

Appendix Two covers the following areas.

(1) Who is Christ?

(2) Our Relationship with Christ

(3) Who are we?

(4) What are our benefits?

(5) What powers do we have?

(6) What should we do to get along with one another and why is that important?

(7) What should we do to experience the full joy of God's love?

Note: If you have a special need to learn more about salvation, I encourage you to read Appendix Two and then read Chapter Four. Let us turn our attention back to the righteousness of God and learn from Israel's mistakes.

Chapter Four

Learning From Israel's Mistakes

We must serve the Lord in a more perfect way. Over the years the Christians and the Jews have made some serious errors. One of the most severe mistakes of the Christians was to not focus on the righteousness of God. Primarily, most churches have been focusing on salvation and not spending enough time on seeking the righteousness of God. We must understand God's word regarding both, salvation and His righteousness. The children of Israel made a mistake because of their unbelief. Nor did they accept Christ as their Savior; therefore, they were not able to enter into God's rest.

Hebrews 3:7-19 explains God's rest. (7) "Wherefore (as the Holy Ghost saith, today if ye will hear his voice, (8) Harden not your hearts, as in the provocation, in the day of temptation in the wilderness: (9) When your fathers tempted me, proved me, and saw my works forty years. (10) Wherefore I was grieved with that generation, and said, They do always err in their heart; and they have not known my ways. (11) So I sware in my wrath, They shall not enter into my rest.) (12) Take heed, brethren, lest there be in any of you an evil heart of unbelief, in departing from the living God. (13) But exhort one another daily, while it is called Today; lest any of you be hardened through the deceitfulness of sin. (14) For we are made partakers of Christ, if we hold the beginning of our confidence stedfast unto the end; (15) While it is said, Today if ye will hear his voice, harden not your hearts, as in the provocation." Hebrews 3:19 says, "So we see that they could not enter in because of unbelief."

In Hebrews, Chapter 4, Paul explains the promise that was left for us to enter into God's rest. Hebrews 4:9 - 12 says, (9) There remaineth therefore a rest to the people of God. (10) For he that is entered into his rest, he also hath ceased from his own works, as God did from his. (11) Let us labour therefore to enter into that rest, lest any man fall after the same example of unbelief. (12) For the word of God is quick, and powerful, and sharper than any two edged sword, piercing even to the dividing asunder of soul and spirit, and of the joints and marrow, and is a discerner of the thoughts and intents of the heart.

God's people have not been properly fed and today they find themselves trying to be righteous under their own power and not of the Spirit of God, the Holy Spirit. Thousands of hours are being spent preaching to people on how they should act toward one another, instead of placing emphasis on the word of God. Only through the word of God can we ensure that people learn about the Holy Spirit and are given every opportunity to receive power from the Holy Spirit. The scriptures say hearing the word of God increases faith and the fear of the Lord is the beginning of knowledge. We must learn to fear God.

However, often the word of God is not preached, but man's knowledge and ideas. This is one of the reasons why people can go to church and hear a sermon, and then leave and continue to engage in their same ungodly conduct, as if they never heard the sermon by the preacher. When the word of God is not preached, there is no opportunity to receive the Holy Spirit; therefore their faith cannot increase, and people do not learn to fear God. Without faith, believers cannot please God.

However, in the case of Israel, they heard the word of God, but they did not believe. Romans 10:16-19 states, (16) "But they have not all obeyed the gospel. For Esaias saith, Lord, who hath believed our report? (17) So then faith cometh by hearing, and hearing by the word of God. (18) But I say, Have they not heard? Yes verily, their sound went into all the earth, and their words unto the ends of the world. (19) But I say, Did not Israel know?"

Most of the children of Israel worshiped false gods and rejected Christ; they thought that they could please God by following the Law. They could not

22

please God; first God cast the kingdom of Israel out of His sight, then God cast out the Kingdom of Judah. Nevertheless, according to the scriptures, God reserved to himself seven thousand men who had not bowed the knee to the image of Baal. And today, there is a remnant according to the election of grace. (Romans 11:4-5) The children of Israel are God's chosen people. God ensured that they knew His word, but who believed His report?

Christians should have learned from the mistakes of Jews. Like God cast the children of Israel out of His sight, God will cast His people in the United States of America out of His sight if we fail to hearken to His commandment and defile His holy name. However, today, we find both Jews and Christians trying to live righteous lives on their own accord. Today, some have heard the report and have not believed and some have not heard the report because it has not been preached to them. Isaiah 56:8 - 12 and Isaiah 57:1 explains what happened and why some Christians are without power and in a state of unbelief, like the Jews who rejected Christ.

Isaiah 56: 8 - 12 states, "The Lord God which gathereth the outcasts of Israel saith, Yet will I gather others to him, besides those that are gathered unto him. (9) All ye beasts of the field, come to devour, yea all ye beasts in the forest. (10) His watchmen are blind: they are all ignorant, they are all dumb dogs, they cannot bark; sleeping, lying down, loving to slumber. (11) Yea, they are greedy dogs which can never have enough, and they are shepherds that cannot understand; they all look to their own way, every one for his gain, from his quarter. (12) Come ye, say they, I will fetch wine, and we will fill ourselves with strong drink; and tomorrow shall be as this day and much more abundant."

Isaiah 57:1 says, "The Righteous perisheth, and no man layeth it to heart: and merciful men are taken away, none considering that the righteous is taken away from the evil to come."

Some say they believe. However, they do not know who Jesus is

23

because they do not do what Jesus has commanded them to do. Consequently, they have not surrendered themselves to the Spirit of God, and made Jesus Lord of their lives. To please God, we must have faith and submit ourselves to the Holy Spirit. As we study the history of the Jews through the word of God, we will find that we cannot please the Lord on our own accord. We must allow His Spirit to lead us; this is key to seeking the righteousness of God.

In Romans, Chapter one, Paul writes beginning with the 17th verse, "For therein is the righteousness of God revealed from faith to faith: as it is written, the just shall live by faith. (18) For the wrath of God is revealed from heaven against all ungodliness and unrighteousness of men, who hold the truth in unrighteousness; (19) Because that which may be known of God is manifest in them; for God hath shown it unto them. (20) For the invisible things of him from the creation of the world are clearly seen, being understood by the things that are made, even His eternal power and Godhead; so that they are without excuse: (21) because they knew God, they glorified him not as God, neither were thankful; but became vain in their imaginations, and their foolish heart was darkened."

Jesus warned us about the signs of his coming and of the end of the world. Jesus said, "Take heed that no man deceive you. For many shall come in my name, saying, I am Christ; and shall deceive many." Today in America, many of **our leaders** have been deceived **and they do not know who Jesus is**. They **do not fear God**, and they do not believe that God has prophets today. Consequently, this nation continues to add sin to sin. The kingdom of Israel and the kingdom of Judah was cast out of the sight of God because of the errors of their kings, and the kings caused the people to sin.

God is a just God. God has sent me to warn this nation to repent or the wrath of God is sure to come. Today many in this nation worship the works of their hands… devils, idols of gold, silver, brass, stone, and of wood. Moreover, we have misused our military to murder hundreds of thousands, sorceries for evil, we continue to take from the poor, oppress the hireling in wages within the United States and through out sourcing of jobs around the world, engage in false swearing (lying), and fornication is throughout the land. (Malachi 3:5) God wants us to repent from these things.

Chapter Five

Leaders Cause God's People to Err

Most of the kings of the Kingdom of Israel and the Kingdom of Judah did not fear God and they caused God's people to err. We must learn from their mistakes and fear God because God is faithful to all of his promises to include His blessing and His cursing. We have included an appendix to this work that reviews the history of the kings of Israel and Judah. This work is very important to understand why it is essential for us to fear God. However, in this chapter we focus on how our leaders have caused God's people in this nation to err. Note, the basic content of this chapter was first written in 2001 in the book titled, "America! America!: A Checkup for the Body of Christ, The Church."

Isaiah, Chapter 10, beginning with verse one states, "Woe unto them that decree unrighteous decrees, and that write grievousness which they have prescribed; (2) To turn aside the needy from judgment, and to take away the right from the poor of my people, that widows may be their prey, and they may rob the fatherless!"

Isaiah, Chapter 9, beginning with verse 16 states, "For the leaders of His people cause them to err; and they (His people) that are led of them are destroyed. (17) Therefore the Lord shall have no joy in their young men, neither shall have mercy on their fatherless and widows: for every one is an hypocrite and an evildoer, and every mouth speaketh folly. For all this His anger is not turned away, but His hand is stretched out still. (18) For the wickedness burneth as the fire: it shall devour the briers and the thorns, and shall kindle in the tickets of the forest, and they shall mount up like the lifting up of smoke."

Isaiah 3:15 states, "What mean ye that ye beat my people to pieces, and grid the faces of the poor? Said the Lord of hosts." Isaiah 5:20 states, "God has an answer, "Woe unto them that call evil good, and good evil; and put darkness for light and light for darkness, that put bitter for sweet and sweet for bitter!" Isaiah 5:21 - 23 states, "Woe unto them that are wise in their own eyes, and prudent in their own sight!" Take a moment and think about this thought. Reflect on the various laws in this country. Are they written in the best interest of God's people or are they designed to oppress the poor and to destroy? Look at the corruption of the police around the country, the shedding of innocent blood through warfare, and corruption in the criminal justice system in the United States.

On September 11, 2001, there were about three-thousand innocent people killed in the United States of America by terrorists. Why did terror come near us? Most of these people were killed in New York City, the same city where ten years earlier we celebrated a war where we kill thousands of innocent people. Most of the people killed in Iraq in the Gulf war were innocent people. Did the United States shed innocent blood through warfare? Are there any consequences for killing innocent people? We must search ourselves and see if we are out of the counsel of God. Let us look at the last 50 years of history of the United States' involvement in various wars. Below is a summation of some of our actions.

Rush to Shed Blood

- ➢ 1963 - 1975 American military killed 4 million people in Southeast Asia
- ➢ 1977 U. S. backs military rulers of El Salvador – Seventy-Thousand Salvadorans and 4 American nuns killed
- ➢ 1980 U. S. trains, Osama bin Laden and fellow terrorists to kill Soviets. CIA gave them three billion dollars
- ➢ 1981 Reagan's administration trained and funded "contras" -

30,000 Nicaraguans died.

- ➢ 1982 U. S. provides billions in aid to Saddam Hussein for weapons to kill Iranians
- ➢ 1983 White House secretly gives Iran weapons to kill Iraqis
- ➢ 1989 - CIA Agent Manuel Noriega (also serving as President of Panama) disobeys orders from Washington - U. S. invades, removes Noriega, 3,000 civilians killed.
- ➢ 1990 Iraq invades Kuwait with weapons from U. S.
- ➢ 1991 U. S. enters Iraq - President Bush reinstates dictator of Kuwait.
- ➢ 1998 U. S. bombs "weapon factory" in Sudan - factory turns out to be making aspirin.
- ➢ 2000 - 2001 - U. S. gives Taliban ruled Afghanistan $245 million in aid - September 11, 2001, Osama bin Laden used his expert CIA training to murder 3, 000 people in the United States.
- ➢ 2001 - U. S. invades Afghanistan
- ➢ 2003 - U. S. invades Iraq without provocations

We must learn from lessons of the past. God's righteousness is forever. The same standards apply today as they did 2500 years ago. America must learn, America must learn.

Isaiah 13:11 states, "And I will punish the world for their evil, and the wicked for their iniquity, and I will cause the arrogancy of the proud to cease, and will lay low the haughtiness of the terrible." Do we have the same God today? Does God change? Answers: There is only one God, the same yesterday, today, and forever, and He changes not.

Isaiah 13:12 states, "I will make a man more precious than fine gold; even a man than the golden wedge of Ophir." In God's sight all men and women are precious. They are made in His image. God wants us to see each other as precious. Therefore, we must value life. How much value do we place on the lives of people who live outside of the United States? Is oil more valuable than the life of a man? Is the life of a man more valuable than our national interests within the border of the United States? Is the life of a man more valuable than our national interests six thousand miles away?

Before we close this segment, let us take a closer look at the prophecy that was given to Isaiah that shows how Israel rebelled against the Lord. In Chapter 30, he writes, "Woe to the rebellious children, saith the Lord, that take counsel, but not of me; and that cover with a covering, but not of my spirit, that they may add sin to sin; (2) That walk to go down into Egypt, and have not asked at my mouth; to strengthen themselves in the strength of Pharaoh, and to trust in the shadow of Egypt! (3) Therefore shall the strength of Pharaoh be your shame, and the trust in the shadow of Egypt your confusion." Do we seek counsel from God?

In Isaiah, Chapter 30, the Word of God continues to warn His people of their destruction to come. God told Isaiah to write it before them in a table, and note it in a book, that it may be for the time to come for ever and ever: Continuing at verse 9, "That this a rebellious people, lying people, children that will not hear the law of the Lord: (10) Which say to the seers, See not; and to the prophets, Prophesy not unto us right things, speak unto us smooth things, prophesy deceits: (11) Get you out of the way, turn aside out of the path, cause the Holy One of Israel to cease from before us. (12) Wherefore thus saith the Holy One of Israel, because ye despise this word, and trust in oppression and perverseness and stay thereon:

(13) Therefore this iniquity shall be to you as a breach ready to fall, swelling out in a high wall, whose breaking cometh suddenly at an instant."

Take a moment and meditate on these precious words of God. Are they applicable to what happened at the World Trade Center on September 11, 2001? Did we take counsel of God when we developed our international trade agreements? Did we take counsel of God when we outlined our policies on global economy? Did we take counsel of God when we expanded our labor pool to the uttermost parts of the earth to include China, and then failed to ensure that our trading partners paid these workers living wages? Do our trading agreements foster oppression of the poor, child labor, sweatshops, and perverseness? The word of God says, leaders of His people cause them to err, and they (His people) that are led of them are destroyed. Consequently, God's people are destroyed on their jobs and in warfare because of leaders who cause God's people to err.

Isaiah 30:13 describes what happened on September 11, 2001 in New York at the World Trade Center. God wants you to know that these scriptures give an account of a rebellious Judah and they also apply to us today. Remember the word of God says, "God's righteousness is forever." Isaiah 30:8 says, "Now go, write it before them in a table, and note it in a book, that it may be for time to come forever and forever:" Today, God wants His people to know it was written in a book not just to make record of the event. However, it was also written for His rebellious people today to learn the consequence of their actions, when they continue to trust in oppression and perverseness.

God does not want the leaders of the United States or any leaders of any other nation to fail to seek His counsel. God has richly blessed America. In 2001, nations around the world held America in high esteem. Many nations see the leaders in America as their Pharaoh and they trust in the shadow of the United States. Nevertheless, since 9/11 (September 11, 2001) America's leaders have not consulted God and have made plans contrary to His will. **Pray for the leaders of the United States to trust not in oppression and perverseness, but in God. Pray that nations put their trust in God and not in the shadow of the United**

31

States. Pray. Pray that we repent, learn to fear God, and trust in the only true and Living God, in the name of JESUS.

God knows the hearts of leaders; the ones who will receive this report. Therefore, Isaiah writes in Chapter 30:9-12 what describes their frame of mind of leaders who will receive this report. Lets review God's word. (9) "That this is a rebellious people, lying children, children that will not hear the law of the Lord. (10) Which say to the seers, See not; and to the prophets, Prophesy not unto us right things, speak unto us smooth things, prophesy deceits: (11) Get you out of the way, turn aside out of the path, cause the Holy One of Israel to cease from before us. (12) Wherefore, thus saith the Holy One of Israel, Because ye despise this word, and trust in oppression and perverseness and stay thereon:"

One may have an opinion that these scriptures do not pertain to us today. Oh how we err here. We must learn from the prophets. Consequently, God has given me this spirit and the task of warning this nation, as God gave the task to Isaiah to warn Judah and Israel. Isaiah 58:1 says, "Cry aloud, spare not, lift up thy voice like a trumpet, and show my people their transgression, and the house of Jacob their sins." I started blowing this trumpet on October 6, 2001, however like Isaiah, I have not been received. Today, however God is warning you to listen to my testimonies and His word, repent, pray, and help sound this trumpet to wake up our brothers and sisters in Christ and to warn our leaders.

We must sound this trumpet because our leaders continue to err. Isaiah, Chapter 9, beginning with verse 16 states, "For the leaders of His people cause them to err; and they that are led of them are destroyed." Isaiah, Chapter 30, says, "Woe to the rebellious children, saith the Lord, that take counsel, but not of me;" Today, America is at war not because of the massive destruction in New York, Washington D.C., and the loss of lives in Pennsylvania, but because of errors of our leaders. Here, God must be our counsel, if we are to be truly victorious. If we do not seek the righteousness of God, in the long run, we will lose. To win this war, we must work to change people's hearts, to include our own hearts. The Church must come forth and speak the word of God.

The Church must stand on God's word; there is no compromise. Men and women of God, this is the most important test you will experience in your lifetime to stand for God or to yield to leaders who desire that you prophesy not unto them right things, but speak unto them smooth things, and to prophesy deceits.

Here is a simple prayer that each man and woman of God should pray. Psalm 139:23-24, "Search me, O God, and know my heart: try me, and know my thoughts: And see if there be any wicked way in me, and lead me in the way everlasting."

The next chapter reflects on a Rod out of the Stem of Jesse; this chapter contains information that is essential to understanding the righteousness of God. God has commanded me as it is recorded in Isaiah 58:1 "Cry aloud, spare not, lift up thy voice like a trumpet, and show my people their transgression, and the house of Jacob their sins." We must learn from our mistakes.

Chapter Six

A Rod Out of the Stem of Jesse

Isaiah 11:1 says, (1) "And there shall come forth a rod out of the stem of Jesse, a branch shall grow out of his roots. (2) And the spirit of the Lord shall rest upon him, the spirit of wisdom and understanding, the spirit of counsel and might, the spirit of knowledge and of the fear of the Lord. (3) And shall make him of quick understanding in the fear of the Lord: and he shall not judge after the sight of his eyes, neither reprove after the hearing of his ears: **(4) But with righteousness shall he judge the poor, and reprove with equity for the meek of the earth: and he shall smite the earth with the rod of his mouth, and with the breath of his lips shall he slay the wicked."**

In 1994, while I was writing my book titled, "The Power Pack: 101 Points To Social And Economic Justice", God allowed me to lay horizontally, and look down on the earth. I saw people devouring one another. After that experience, I searched the scriptures and discovered how Paul reminded the Christians in Galatians, Chapter 5:13-15. (13) "For, brethren, ye have been called unto liberty; only use not liberty for an occasion to the flesh, but by love serve one another. (14) For all the law is fulfilled in one word, even in this, Thou shalt love thy neighbour as thy self. (15) But if ye bite and devour one another, take heed that ye be not consumed one of another."

Today, I find myself looking down from the position of a horizontal view. Later in this text you will be given an opportunity to do the same.

God is using me to let the church know that our hearts must change. The leaders of America must seek Him. If leaders of America shall fail to seek Him, Chapter ten of Isaiah, pertains to each of them, in verse one and two: "(1) Woe unto them that decree unrighteous decrees, and that write grievousness which they

35

have prescribed; (2) to turn aside the needy from judgment, and to take away the right from the poor of my people, that widows may be their prey, and that they may rob the fatherless!"

Now let me call your attention to some very shocking word of God. Isaiah 10:3 - 6. says "And what will ye do in the day of visitation, and in the desolation which shall come from far? To whom will ye flee for help? And where will ye leave your glory? (4) Without me they shall bow down under the prisoners, and they shall fall under the slain. For all this anger is not turned away, but his hand is stretched out still. (5) O Assyrian, the rod of mine anger, and the staff in their hand is mine indignation. (6) I will send him against an hypocritical nation, and against the people of my wrath will I give him a charge, to take the spoil, and to take the prey, and to tread them down like the mire of the streets. (7) Howbeit he meaneth not so, neither doth his heart think so, but it is in his heart to destroy and cut off nations not a few. (Note: This prophecy is unfolding today before your eyes. Open your eyes and see.)

Is this passage of scriptures applicable to America? Is America a hypocritical nation? Here is the real test of judgment. God wants the leaders and His people in America to take a real look at ourselves by asking and answering probing questions. We must look deep and open up our hearts. We must take a look at how we treat people in America... the poor, and minorities and people around the world. We must ask questions, i.e.

> Why are there so many African Americans in prisons?
> Is our criminal justice system working?
> Can we still justify denying food and medicine to dying babies in Iraq? Were we justified in the way we bombed Iraq?
> Did we celebrate after the bombing that included the killing of thousands of innocent people in 1991?
> How much suffering did we cause in 1991 to the people in Iraq

and continue to cause?

- Are they Saddam Hussein's people or are they not God's people?
- Do we see these innocent people, the hundred of thousands lives that were lost, to include innocent children, who have been denied food and medicine, as God's people?
- How do we look at the lives of people other than Americans? Do we value their lives?
- Are the more than three thousand Americans lives lost on September 11, 2001 in the terrorist attack more important than 100,000 innocent people in Afghanistan?
- Are we a nation that has been willing to shed innocent blood?
- What is the purpose of the global economy trading policies?
- Do our trading policies take advantage of poor nations by expanding our labor force to produce goods without ensuring the laborers are paid living wages?
- Is this a form of modern day slavery?
- Do you agree that this is a more cost effective way than owning personal slaves?
- Are our goals to help these developing nations? Or is our real goal to line the pockets of a few wealthy men? Is this perverseness?
- By what means does less than 1 percent of the world's population control most of the wealth? Was this done through oppression and perverseness?
- Why are some people angry at America?
- What can we do to reduce the anger?
- Are we a just nation?
- Do we really try to treat people fair within our borders?

- Are our public defenders effective in defending the poor?
- Do juveniles have fair representation in our juvenile court system?
- In 1998, did we allow law enforcement officials in Hawthorne, California to shoot a white business man 106 times and not hold anyone accountable?
- Have we turned our prisons into large industrial complexes? Do we use these prisoners as slaves?
- Do we ensure that all suspects have fair trials?
- The people who view America as evil, if their perception is wrong, would bombing and killing more innocent people change that perception?
- What is the United States doing to change the perception about America, if this perception is based on false or misleading information?
- Have we adequately addressed the race problem in this country?
- Have we adequately addressed the problem of the poor in this country?
- Did America rush to shed innocent blood in Iraq in 1991?
- Did America rush to shed innocent blood in Iraq in 2003?

The opening of this Chapter referred to a Rod out of the stem of Jesse working in the best interest of the poor and with the breath of his mouth, and the breath of his lips slaying the wicked. Reference Isaiah 11:4 "But with righteousness shall He judge the poor, and reprove with equity for the meek of the earth: and He shall smite the earth with the rod of His mouth, and with the breath of His lips shall He slay the wicked."

I am only doing what the Holy Spirit is leading me to do. Thus, today as you note, you see the prophecy of Isaiah unfolding before you. I pray that you have spiritual eyes to ask God to open your eyes so you can see. Pray for me that

I will remain focused and do only what God commands me to do. Pray for our leaders that they will listen to the counsel of God.

God commanded me to include Isaiah 11:5-16 for all to read and understand this prophecy is at hand.

(5) "And righteousness shall be the girdle of his loins, and faithfulness the girdle of his reins.

(6) The wolf also shall dwell with lamb, and the leopard shall lie down with the kid; and the calf and the young lion and the fatling together; and a little child shall lead them.

(7) And the cow and the bear shall feed; their young ones shall lie down together: and the lion shall eat straw like the ox.

(8) And the sucking child shall play on the hole of the asp, and the weaned child shall put his hand on the cockatrice's den.

(9) They shall not hurt nor destroy in all my holy mountain: for the earth shall be full of the knowledge of the Lord, as the waters cover the sea.

(10) And in that day there shall be a root of Jesse, which shall stand for an ensign of the people; to it shall the Gentiles seek: and his rest shall be glorious.

(11) And it shall come to pass in that day, that the Lord shall set his hand again the second time to recover the remnant of his people, which shall be left, from Assyria, and from Egypt, and from Pathros, and from Cush, and from Elam, and from Shinar, and from Hamath, and from the islands of the sea.

(12) And he shall set up an ensign for the nations, and shall assemble the outcasts of Israel, and gather together the dispersed of Judah from the four corners of the earth.

(13) The envy also of Ephraim shall depart, and the adversaries of Judah shall be cut off: Ephraim shall not envy Judah, and Judah shall not vex Ephraim.

(14) But they shall fly upon the shoulders of the Philistines toward the west; they shall spoil them of the east together: they shall lay their hand upon

39

Edom and Moab; and the children of Ammon shall obey them.

(15) And the Lord shall utterly destroy the tongue of the Egyptian sea; and with his mighty wind shall he shake his hand over the river, and shall smite it in the seven streams, and make men go over dryshod.

(16) And there shall be an highway for the remnant of his people, which shall be left, from Assyria; like as it was to Israel in the day that he came up out of the land of Egypt.

A Servant of God Pleads to Christians Today

Isaiah 28:9-13, says (9) "Whom shall he teach knowledge? And whom shall he make to understand doctrine? Them that are weaned from the milk, and drawn from the breasts."

(10) For precept must be upon precept, precept upon precept; line upon line, line upon line; here a little, and there a little.

(11) For with stammering lips and another tongue will he speak to this people.

(12) To whom he said, this is the rest wherewith ye may cause the weary to rest; and this is the refreshing: yet they would not hear.

(13) But the word of the Lord was unto them precept upon precept, precept upon precept; line upon line, line upon line; here a little, and there a little; that they might go, and fall backward, and be broken, and snared, and taken.

(14) Wherefore hear the word of the Lord, ye scornful men that rule this people, which is in Jerusalem.

(15) Because ye have said, We have made a covenant with death, and with hell are we at agreement; when the overflowing scourge shall pass through, it shall not come unto us: for we have made lies our refuge, and under falsehood

have we hid ourselves:

(16) Therefore thus saith the Lord God, Behold, I lay in Zion for a foundation, a stone, a tried stone, a precious cornerstone, a sure foundation: he that believeth shall not make haste.

(17) Judgment also will lay to the line, and righteousness to the plummet; and the hail shall sweep away the refuge of lies, and the waters shall overflow the hiding place.

(18) And your covenant with death shall be disannulled, and your agreement with hell shall not stand; when the overflowing scourge shall pass through, then ye shall be trodden down by it.

(19) From the time that it goeth forth it shall take you: for morning by morning shall it pass over, by day and by night: and it shall be a vexation only to understand the report.

(20) For the bed is shorter than that a man can stretch himself on it: and the covering narrower than that he can wrap himself in it.

People of God, stand up and fear God. God is Real.

Note: I admonish you to observe very closely various translations of the Holy Bible. Some of the translators have changed the meaning and the intent of the word of God.

Chapter Seven

Vision About America Preparing For War

And

Ending Terrorism and Healing the Land

Amos 3:6 states, "Shall a trumpet be blown in the city, and the people not be afraid? Shall there be evil in a city, and the Lord had not done it?" Amos 3:7 states, "Surely the Lord God will do nothing, but he revealeth his secret unto his servants the prophets."

On September 10, 2001, God revealed to me the destruction of the World Trade Center and the United States of America preparing for war. While asleep on September 10, 2001 about 5:00 A.M. Pacific Daylight Savings Time, God revealed to me the United States preparing for war. First, I saw people running and there was fire on a tall building. Immediately after, I saw United States military planes, waves and waves, flying overhead. I recall asking a woman, "Have we declared war?" The woman responded, "We are responding to what they did." I woke up immediately, and turned the television on to hear the latest news. Of course there was no news report about this incident. I was quite disturbed because I knew that God had revealed this to me. Moreover, I was concerned because when God reveals things to me they always come to fruition.

The thought that we are going to war kept ringing in my head. I normally went to the gym every day at Los Angeles Air Force Base. So I followed my routine schedule on this day. However, this thought of war was still with me. I then shared my dream with a friend of mine, Willie Mays. Willie is a retired military man (navy) about 70 years old. I also shared the dream with Chuck Howell, a retired Master Sergeant. I do not know Chuck personally, but I see he

43

and his wife quite often in the gym. I told Chuck, "Man this dream was so real." Chuck laughed and then told me a story about one of his dreams.

Chuck stated that he'd had a dream also that seemed so real. He stated that he was fighting a lion and the lion was on top of him. He then woke up, only to discover that he had kicked his wife out of the bed. I assured Chuck that the dream I had was not like that. Later, I shared the dream with a dear friend of mine, Janice Carter. The three witnesses live in the Los Angeles area and will verify this account.

Throughout the day I thought about the national intelligence network. I thought they knew something they were not sharing with the public. Now I know according to the word of God, God reveals His secrets. In the book of Amos, Chapter 3, verse 7 states, "Surely the Lord God will do nothing, but He revealeth His secret unto His servants the prophets." Amos 3:6 states, "Shall a trumpet be blown in the city, and the people not be afraid? Shall there be evil in a city, and the Lord hath not done it?"

Yes, God revealed this to me, but who will believe my report. Well in this case there are at least three witnesses who I told about the revelations regarding the United States preparing for war on September 10, 2001. Besides revealing this information to me, the Holy Spirit gave me instructions 30 days prior on how to address this problem. God wants me to, "Cry aloud, spare not, lift up my voice like a trumpet, and show His people their transgression, and the United States government their sins." God wants me to share the knowledge about His righteousness to churches around the world because it is only through God's righteousness that we can obtain a true victory.

The events on September 11 regarding the World Trade Center and the Pentagon go beyond the physical realm. It is spiritual, because it was revealed to me, a servant, one of God's Prophets. I have never referred to myself as one of God's Prophets. However, God wants you to know who I am, and therefore I will

44

refer to myself as Elmore Richmond Jr., a Prophet of God, in the name of Jesus Christ.

I first wrote President Bush on October 6, 2001 and shared with him what God had revealed to me; why terror came to America and what we must do to end terrorism within our borders. Twenty days later, I wrote President Bush another letter. Here is a quote from the letter of October 26, 2001.

"I wrote you twenty day ago as God directed me. However, you have failed to adhere to the word of God. God has commanded me to write you again. Mr. President, you continue to add sin onto sin. God knows every one of them, even the ones that you classify as Top Secret and God has revealed some of those secrets to me. Mr. President, if you do not change this destructive path, terror will continue to visit America. Moreover, America will experience a plague of national disasters at a level that this nation has not experienced in its short 200 year history. Many lives will be lost and fear will continue within the borders of the United States. However, if you should hearken to the word of God, terror will not come near this nation, and America's peace will be as a river, and nation's righteousness will be as the waves of the sea."

Now it is 2005, as I prepare this work for publication. It has been truly amazing watching the storms, the tornados, hurricanes, wild fires, floods, hail stones, damaging winds, accidents, chemical leaks, shooting, oil spills, all forms of national disasters at a level this nation has not experienced in its short 200 year history. As one of God's prophet, I can share with confidence that God has not repented from His plan to bring about other calamities. We will experience calamity after calamity until we repent and turn to God.

God continues to reveal His secrets to me after I received these

45

revelations; the Holy Spirit guides me in taking the appropriate action. I have shared most of them with the President of the United States and other leaders. God showed me the wild fires and the floods of 2002, the apartment explosion in California, the destruction of the bridge in Oklahoma, the large crowd protesting that President Bush confronted overseas in 2002. The tornados of 2003, the destructive wind of 2004 and 2005, the plane crashing into a building, the bus running off the interstate hitting a parked truck, then separating from its frame, the tourists stranded in Mexico during hurricane Wilma. The revelations keep coming. Until we turn to God we will face calamity after calamity here in the United States. Jesus said, "Whatsoever ye shall bind on earth shall be bound in heaven: and whatsoever ye shall loose on earth shall be loosed in heaven." (Matthew 18:18)

In January 2003, President Bush proclaimed that he was losing his patience with Saddam Hussein. At the same time, when the President made this declaration, God had revealed to me his final warning for President Bush. I had written the President eight times to no avail. The final message was to repent from your rush to shed innocent blood and your trust in oppression and perverseness, and turn to God. This final warning was the same as God's first message. However, now God revealed to me that the U. S. battlements were no longer His and that the United States would face calamity after calamity until His people repented and turned from their wicked ways. Below is a quote from a letter I wrote to President Bush, dated January 14, 2003.

> "On January 3, 2003, God revealed to me in a vision that I was on a military base; it was as if I was performing a commander's walk-through inspection of a barrack. I observed the conditions of the barrack; the barrack was in need of many repairs including painting. After the walk-through of the barrack, I stepped outside the barrack's door and I was met with a mass of

flies, they were all over the place, then I woke up. During the same night, God gave me another vision, again I was on a military base and I observed a structure on fire, the fire moved to another structure. Then I awoke from the vision, I asked the Holy Spirit to give me the interpretation of these visions. Here is the interpretation. Our nation will suffer financially and consequently, our military will suffer in maintaining its quality of life and will experience much destruction by fire."

After I mailed this letter, I received even more clarification about the flies in the vision. The flies symbolized enemies. Dr. C. Rice, the National Security Advisor to the President affirmed in 2004, that President Bush did in fact refer to these enemies as flies. The fires; we have lost many lives by fires in this war with Iraq. Have we suffered financially because of this war?

On November 17, 2005, United States Representative John Murtha, Defense Appropriations Subcommittee, Ranking Member called a news conference and gave a status report on the impact of the war with Iraq on the nation. He reported the following:

- ✓ The main reason for going to war has been discredited
- ✓ The military is suffering and the future of our country is at risk
- ✓ It was no longer in the best interest of the military and the nation to continue the war
- ✓ Deficit is growing out of control
- ✓ There is a cut in the defense budget
- ✓ Defense personnel costs are sky rocketing, especially health care
- ✓ Most of the ground equipment is worn out
- ✓ There is a huge short fall on bases at home
- ✓ Money will not be available for new weaponry
- ✓ In 2004 the State Department announced an increase in global

terrorism
- ✓ The military and the Administration agree that Iraq cannot be won militarily
- ✓ Deaths and Injuries are increasing
- ✓ Deaths - 2079 American Troops
- ✓ Serious Injuries 15,500 – half have returned back to duty
- ✓ Estimated 50,000 troops will suffer from battle fatigue
- ✓ Representative Murtha recommended the redeployment of the military from Iraq over the next six months.

No official challenged the accuracy of the information that Representative Murtha reported. However, the President and Vice President of the United States disagreed with his recommendation of the redeployment of the troops from Iraq within the next six months. The content of Representative Murtha's report summaries the affects of the war on the military and the nation; in effect it serves as an official report that validates the prophecy that God had given me has come to past.

The first book that gave accounts of these revelations was written in 2001. It was published on October 6, 2001. The title of the book is "America, America: A Checkup For The Body of Christ, The Church." God has revealed so much to me regarding this war; I was lead to write a second book to cover this subject so we can learn from this failure to adhere to God's word.

God revealed to me that the U. S. Battlements were no longer His. This means that God has removed his protective covering from around our military. Our iniquities, our rush to shed innocent blood and our trust in oppression and perverseness are before God. To understand this we must look at the last 50 years of the history of the United States' involvement in various wars. Below is a summation of our actions.

Rush to Shed Blood

- 1963 - 1975 American military killed 4 million people in Southeast Asia
- 1977 U. S. backs military rulers of El Salvador - 70,000 Salvadorans and 4 American nuns killed
- 1980 U. S. trains Osama bin Laden and fellow terrorists to kill Soviets. CIA gave them $3 billion
- 1981 Reagan's administration trained and funded "contras" - 30,000 Nicaraguans died.
- 1982 U. S. provides billions in aid to Saddam Hussein for weapons to kill Iranians
- 1983 White House secretly gave Iran weapons to kill Iraqis
- 1989 - CIA Agent Manuel Noriega (also serving as President of Panama) disobeys orders from Washington - U. S. invades, removes Noriega; 3,000 civilians killed.
- 1990 Iraq invades Kuwait with weapons from U. S.
- 1991 U. S. enters Iraq - President Bush reinstates dictator of Kuwait.
- 1998 U. S. bombs "weapon factory" in Sudan - factory turns out to be making aspirin.
- 2000 - 2001 - U. S. gives Taliban ruled Afghanistan $245 million in aid - September 11, 2001, Osama bin Laden used his expert CIA training to murder 3, 000 people in the United States.
- 2001 - U. S. invades Afghanistan
- 2003 - U. S. invades Iraq without provocations

We must learn from lessons of the past. God's righteousness is forever. The same standards apply today as they did 2500 years ago. America must learn.

America must learn.

In November 2002, I wrote the Secretary of State to no avail. In January 2003, I wrote members of the Senate and House of Representatives. After writing these letters, President Bush's father spoke out about his son, expressing that he was upset because people believed his son was rushing to shed innocent blood. At that point, I knew somehow the message had gotten to President Bush.

In February 2003, God commanded me to write to the Secretary General of the United Nations. In this communication, I was commanded to express to Secretary General Kofin Annan, the importance of working for peace. Below is a quote from the letter.

"I am writing you to let you know that the United States is not walking in the counsel of God; this error puts nations around the world on the path of destruction. Today, the United States is like ancient Egypt, a very powerful nation. Consequently, many nations strengthen themselves in the strength of President Bush and trust in the shadow of the United States. Like God warned nations in Isaiah Chapter 30:3, the strength of Pharaoh would be these nations' shame, and the trust in the shadow of Egypt their confusion. God wants you to take action that helps guide nations around the world to turn to Him, and stop going to the President of the United States for their strength, trusting in the Shadow of the United States."

Daily I would pray for peace and ask God to move on the hearts of people and leaders around the world. The Spirit of God moved, and millions of people began to protest around the world. Nevertheless, President Bush's heart was hardened and he continued in his quest to shed the blood of the innocent.

On February 20, 2003, I prayed and asked God to use me as his vessel, and the Holy Spirit moved upon me. While praying in an unknown tongue, I cried out as tears ran down my face until my eyes were sore. The affect was overwhelming. After I was still I asked God why did I weep bitterly? The Holy

Spirit directed me to the Book of Jeremiah, chapter 13.

Immediately, I turned to Jeremiah, chapter 13. As I read through the verses, it became clear to me what the Lord was saying. When I got to verse 17, I knew why I was crying. Below is a quote from the text beginning with verse 14.

"And I will dash them one against another, even the fathers and the sons together, said the Lord: I will not pity, nor spare, nor have mercy, but destroy them. Hear ye, and give ear; be not proud: for the Lord hath spoken. Give glory to the Lord your God, before your feet stumble upon the dark mountains, and while ye look for light, he turns it into the shadow of death, and makes it gross darkness. **But if ye will not hear it, my soul shall weep in secret places for your pride; and mine eye shall weep sore, and run down with tears, because the Lord's flock is carried away captive."** As I continued to read the scriptures, once again I wept because I knew it was the pride of the United States that would cause this nation to fall. However, if we would repent and turn from our wicked ways, pray, and seek the face of God, God would heal our land.

This is not a popular message. However, this message is from God. Like God told Isaiah to warn Judah before the doom of Jerusalem, God has told me to warn His people in the United States. "Now go, write it before them in a table, and note it in a book, that it may be for ever: time to come for ever and ever: This is a rebellious people, lying children, children that will not hear the law of the Lord: Which say to the seers, See not; and to the prophets, Prophesy not unto us right things, speak unto us smooth things, prophesy deceits: Get you out of the way, turn aside out of the path, cause the Holy One of Israel to cease from before us. Wherefore, thus saith the Holy One of Israel, "Because ye despise this word, and trust in oppression and perverseness, and stay thereon: Therefore this iniquity shall be to you as a breach ready to fall, swelling out in a high wall, whose breaking cometh suddenly at an instant." (Isaiah 30:8-13)

I know who I am; I am a servant of God, one of His prophets. God wants each one of His children to know who they are. Jesus wants His sheep to receive the gift of the Holy Spirit and then receive gifts from the Holy Spirit. Then God wants us to use those gifts, in the office ordained by Him, for the edifying and perfecting of the Body of Christ. I pray in the name of Jesus that we all come in the unity of the faith, and of the knowledge of Jesus Christ, the Son of God, unto a perfect man, and unto the measure of the stature of the fullness of Christ. Amen.

As God gave His word to Isaiah, God has given His word to me. Over the next several pages you will find a reprint of part of the first work that was recorded in the first book, "America, America: A Checkup for The Body of Christ, The Church" in 2001.

Thus said the Lord, "**Woe unto you rebellious leaders. If you fail to adhere to the word of God, there will be no place for you to run and hide. God's people will be destroyed because of the rebellious leaders and you will cause them to err. This is not a war on terrorism. The destruction at the World Trade Center is about My righteousness. It had to come down to end the very system that feeds it.**" Thus said the Lord.

Before I continue and receive attacks by the leaders of the country that I love, allow me to share a similar event in history that now confronts this nation. It is recorded in 2 Chronicles, Chapter 18. This is the account of Ahab King of Israel, Jehoshaphat king of Judah, and Micaiah, a prophet of God. Let's take a moment to review this history.

Let's read 2 Chronicles, Chapter 18: 3 - 27. (This translation was taken from the Holy Bible, New Living Translation, by Tyndale.) We will start with verse 3.

(3) "Will you join me in fighting against Ramoth-Gilead?" Ahab asked. And Jehoshaphat replied, "Why, of course! You and I are brothers, and my troops are yours to command. We will certainly join you in battle."

(4) Then Jehoshaphat added, "But first let's find out what the LORD

says."

(5) So King Ahab summoned his prophets, four hundred of them, and asked them, "Should we go to war against Ramoth-Gilead or not?" They replied, Go ahead, for God will give you a great victory!"

(6) But Jehoshaphat asked, "Isn't there a prophet of the LORD around, too? I would like to ask him the same question."

(7) King Ahab replied, "There is still one prophet of the LORD, but I hate him. He never prophesies anything but bad news for me! His name is Micaiah son of Imlah." "You shouldn't talk like that," Jehoshaphat said. "Let's hear what he has to say."

(8) So the king of Israel called one of his officials and said, "Quick! Go and get Micaiah son of Imlah."

(9) King Ahab of Israel and King Jehoshaphat of Judah, dressed in their royal robes, were sitting on thrones at the threshing floor near the gate of Samaria. All of Ahab's prophets were prophesying there in front of them. (10) One of them, Zedekiah son of Kenaanah, made some iron horns and proclaimed, "This is what the LORD says: With these horns you will gore the Arameans to death!"

(11) All the other prophets agreed. "Yes," they said, "go up to Ramoth-Gilead and be victorious. The LORD will give you a glorious victory!"

(12) Meanwhile, the messenger who went to get Micaiah said to him, "Look, all the prophets are promising victory for the king. Be sure that you agree with them and promise success."

(13) But Micaiah replied, "As surely as the LORD lives, I will say only what my God tells me to say."

(14) When Micaiah arrived before the king, Ahab asked him, "Micaiah, should we go to war against Ramoth-Gilead or not?" And Micaiah replied, "Go right ahead! It will be a glorious victory!"

(15) But the king replied sharply, "How many times must I demand that

53

you speak only the truth when you speak for the LORD?"

(16) So Micaiah told him, "In a vision I saw all Israel scattered on the mountains, like sheep without a shepherd. And the LORD said, "Their master has been killed. Send them home in peace."

(17) "Didn't I tell you?" the king of Israel said to Jehoshaphat. "He does it every time. He never prophesies anything but bad news for me."

(18) Then Micaiah continued, "Listen to what the LORD says! I saw the LORD sitting on this throne with all the armies of heaven on his right and on his left. And the LORD said, "Who can entice King Ahab of Israel to go into battle against Ramoth-Gilead so that he can be killed there? There were many suggestions,

(20) Until finally a spirit approached the LORD and said, "I can do it!" "How will you do this? the LORD asked.

(21) And the spirit replied, "I will go out and inspire all Ahab's prophets to speak lies." "You will succeed,' said the LORD. 'Go ahead and do it.'

(22) "So you see, the LORD has put a lying spirit in the mouths of your prophets. For the LORD has determined disaster for you."

(23) Then Zedekiah son of Kenaanah walked up to Micaiah and slapped him across the face. ""When did the Spirit of the LORD leave me to speak to you?" he demanded.

(24) And Micaiah replied, "You will find out soon enough, when you find yourself hiding in some secret room!"

(25) King Ahab of Israel then ordered, "Arrest Micaiah and take him back to Amon, the governor of the city, and to my Joah.

(26) Give them this order from the king: 'Put this man in prison, and feed him nothing but bread and water until I return safely from the battle!"

(27) But Micaiah replied, "If you return safely, the LORD has not spoken through me!" Then he added to those standing around, "Take note of what I have said."

King Ahab was killed in battle.

In 2004, we were able to see how God also allowed a lying spirit to be sent to the Executive Branch of the Government of the United States to affect their decision to go to war with Iraq. We must learn from this. Let us continue to review the message that God gave in 2001.

The leaders of the United States must change their current direction and take counsel of God. If not there will be no hiding place for them. Thus said the LORD.

Thus said the LORD, **"I was with the founding fathers of America and I blessed the land. They expressed My righteousness in the nation's Declaration of Independence. I was with them when they wrote these precious words, "We hold these truths to be self-evident, that all men are created equal, that they are endowed by their Creator with certain unalienable rights, that among these are life, liberty and the pursuit of happiness." They took My counsel and fought a civil war. Thousands of My people were killed in that civil war. You fought because it was justified and you were seeking My righteousness. I blessed your land.**

You have turned from seeking My righteousness and have put your trust in oppression and perverseness. Your failure to seek My counsel has piled sin on sin. Consequently, today America is oppressing people not only within the borders of the United States, but around the world. Thus said the LORD.

Today, the United States' global economy polices work to oppress millions and have a more far-reaching affect on the world, than the South's cruel

55

slavery. A slavery that ultimately the United States fought a civil war to end. All nations that are participating in these oppressive policies and practices are not working toward the righteousness of God.

Why America Experienced Terrorism

Today, the leaders of the United States of America continue to seek counsel from those other than God. They have written unjust laws that make prisoners out of the innocent. The United States justice system has fail, police, prosecutors, defense, and judges. Consequently, the United States prisons are now slave plantations and industrial complexes. Thus, there is slavery within the United States' borders. Leaders add sin on sin. They break their treaties, and now they have broken the founding father's covenant they made with God.

Thus said the LORD, **"Now, you want to kill the innocent for your wickedness. My people were destroyed within your border because of your wickedness. You are a proud and arrogant people. You are a sinful nation, a people laden with iniquity, a seed of evildoers, children that are corrupters; you have forsaken the Lord. Now you are studying war. The whole head is sick, and the whole heart is faint. You have declared a war against terrorism. The terrorism that you are experiencing is the fruit of your trust in oppression and perverseness."** Thus said the LORD.

The statement, **"The terrorism that you are experiencing is the fruit of your trust in oppression and perverseness"** is a hard pill to swallow; however this is the word God gave me in September 2001. But I did not see it in the Bible until September 2004 when I was finalizing this work. God had me to study the book of Hosea. As God told Israel and Judah in Hosea 10:13, the same holds true for us today in the United States, "Ye have plowed wickedness, ye have reaped iniquity; ye have eaten the fruit of lies; because thou didst trust in thy way, in the multitude of thy mighty men." People who love God must understand this in order to end terrorism. Let us continue to review God's message that was conveyed to the President of the United States and others in 2001.

Therefore, the leaders in the United States must put down your arms and start warring within yourselves. The people who were involved in the attack on New York and Washington are dead now. The leaders in the United States helped create them. There are others that are still alive that leaders in the United States help created. Some are Americans within the United States' borders and some are not Americans, and they are around the world. Taking action to round all of them up and killing them all will not end terrorism.

This action does not end terrorism; it only gathers bad fruit that has ripened. There is some bad fruit within the borders and outside the borders of the United States that have not ripened. If the leaders of the United States continue to trust in oppression and perverseness and fail to take this counsel of God, they will plant more seeds, which will produce more bad fruit. To end terrorism, leaders in the United States must change their wicked ways and seek the counsel of God. (This message in this paragraph was first conveyed to the President of the United States and other in October 2001.)

How to End Terrorism

The United States Government and other governments must take a look at all of their ways. In the United States, we must do the following. God has given instructions to the United States government as recorded in Hosea 10:12, **"Sow to yourselves in righteousness, reap in mercy; break up your fallow ground: for it is time to seek the Lord till he come and rain righteousness upon you."** God wants the leaders in the United States to hearken to His commandments and be established in righteousness. Like God told Israel in Isaiah 48:17-18, the same applies to us today, "Thus saith the Lord, thy Redeemer, the Holy One of Israel, I am the Lord Thy God which teacheth thee to profit, which leadeth thee by the way that thou shouldest go. O that thou hadst hearkened to my commandments then had thy peace been as a river, and thy righteousness as the waves of the sea." Isaiah 54:14 says, "In righteousness shall thou be established: thou shalt be far from oppression; for thou shalt not fear; and from terror; for it shall not come near thee."

Now God wants us to break up our fallow ground and sow to ourselves righteousness. To effect this we must identify the fallow grounds. Fallow grounds are plowed grounds that have been left unseeded for one or more growing seasons. In our search for fallow grounds we find the nations of Cuba, Iran, and North Korea. It is time that we sow righteousness in our dealing with these nations and work to end all unjustified sanctions and then receive **God's mercy.**

Moreover, we must ask probing questions about present actions compared to those tenets of the Declaration of Independence, the Constitution, and the Bill of Rights. Examine laws, treaties, and agreements and see the corruption. Work to end this deceit. Then we can truly work to end terrorism from within the United States' borders and outside the United States' borders. This should be the action taken to end terrorism.

The United States cannot win with military might because the nation is warring against God's righteousness.

"Woe unto the leaders of the United States, if they continue in their wickedness and fail to adhere to the word that I have given My prophet." Thus said the LORD.

"Recall your planes, ships, and My people. Remove all unjust sanctions against countries around the world. Rewrite your trade agreements to ensure that they are fair to the workers. End your eagerness

to shed innocent blood. Seek out the bad fruit that has now ripened. Apply just laws to all suspects that are still alive, that were involved in the planning and operation of the terrorist attack on America. Do not prosecute the innocent. Bad fruits that have not ripened, treat them with care, love, and understanding, because you helped create them. Change your hearts and take on a new resolve to end oppression and perverseness. Thus, you will end the terrorism in America if you turn to Me. My righteousness is forever.

Shall there be evil in a city and I have not done it? If I shut up heaven that there be no rain, or if I command the locusts to devour the land, or if I send pestilence among my people; If my people, which are called by my name, shall humble themselves, and pray, and seek my face, and turn from their wicked ways; then will I hear from heaven, and will forgive their sin, and will heal their land. Now mine eyes shall be open, and mine ears attent unto the prayer that is made in this place. Thus said the LORD.

As I close the writing of this book and prepare it for publication, it is now November 20, 2005. Except for the information that came from the book of Hosea, what you just read was first written in 2001. The above message was recorded in the book America! America!: A Checkup For The Body of Christ, The Church. Besides that, writing more than thirteen letters have been written to President Bush as the Lord has directed me; now everything has come to fruition. The report from Representative John Murtha serves a twofold purpose; first to inform the people and to validate the fact that what God has given me to convey to the President and the leaders of this nation has come to fruition. We all have witnessed the plague of national disasters, to include natural, accidents, and man made. Now it is time for the people of this nation to wake up and take concise action and repent and turn to God.

In the spring of 2005, God showed me military vehicles traveling along the road. The vehicles were moving very slow, stopping along the way because all along the road there was what appeared to be children toys. As far as I could see up the road there were these toys. These toys represented the improvised explosive devices that are being planted along the way. As long as we are going in the direction that we are going in Iraq we will face these devices. There is no end. They appeared to be toys of children because as long as there is life in Iraq and our military continues to travel this road, even the children of those killed will continue to plant these deadly improvised explosive devices.

In Chapter Six - A Rod Out of The Stem of Jesse, we listed probing questions. We have provided that list of questions again because we know that some of you did not bother to read that section. However, Chapter Six is very important for you to read because it is prophecy unfolding before you as was prophesied by Isaiah; these same standards apply to us today.

Answer these probing questions. (These questions were prepared in September 2001, before we went to war with Iraq in 2003.)

- ➢ Why are there so many African Americans in prisons?
- ➢ Is our criminal justice system working?
- ➢ Can we still justify denying food and medicine to dying babies in Iraq? Were we justified in the way we bombed Iraq?
- ➢ Did we celebrate after the bombing that included the killing of thousands of innocent people?
- ➢ How much suffering did we cause in 1991 to the people in Iraq and continue to cause?
- ➢ Are they Saddam Hussein's people or are they not God's people?
- ➢ Do we see these innocent people, the hundreds of thousands of lives that were lost, to include innocent children, who have been denied food and medicine, as God's people?
- ➢ How do we look at the lives of people other than America? Do

we value their lives?

- Are the more than three thousand Americans lives lost on September 11, 2001 in the terrorist attack more important than 100,000 innocent people in Afghanistan?
- Are we a nation that has been willing to shed innocent blood?
- What is the purpose of the global economy trading policies?
- Do our trading policies take advantage of poor nations by expanding our labor force to produce goods without ensuring the laborers are paid living wages?
- Is this a form of modern day slavery?
- Do you agree that this is a more cost effective way than owning personal slaves?
- Are our goals to help these developing nations? Or is our real goal to line the pockets of a few wealthy men? Is this perverseness?
- By what means does less than 1 percent of the world's population control most of the wealth? Was this done through oppression and perverseness?
- Why are some people angry at America?
- What can we do to reduce the anger?
- Are we a just nation?
- Do we really try to treat people fairly within our borders?
- Are our public defenders effective in defending the poor?
- Do juveniles have fair representation in our juvenile court system?
- In 1998, did we allow law enforcement officials in Hawthorne, California to shoot a white business man 106 times and not hold anyone accountable?
- Have we turned our prisons into large industrial complexes? Do

we use these prisoners as slaves?

> Do we ensure that all suspects have fair trials?

> The people who view America as evil, if their perception is wrong, would bombing and killing more innocent people change that perception?

> What is the United States doing to change the perception about America, if this perception is based on false or misleading information?

> Have we adequately addressed the race problem in this country?

> Have we adequately addressed the problem of the poor in this country?

A Prophet of God

Jesus says, "Verily I say unto you, **No prophet is accepted in his own country**." (Luke 4:24) God had me to prepare this list of questions before 9/11. However, the questions regarding Afghanistan were added after 9/11. Many cannot relate to the experiences of a prophet of God; however, this does not mean that they are not true. Some pastors make their mistakes because they have not had similar experiences. 1 Corinthians 14:32 says, "And the spirits of the prophets are subject to the prophets." God has given prophets these spirits that are only subjected to the prophets. Remember, God designed it that way.

Nevertheless, there are some who still do not believe that God has prophets today, although Ephesians 4:11, Amos 3:7, and Acts 2:18 clearly state that God has prophets. Para-phasing what Jesus said, why should you believe me if you do not believe what is written in the scriptures. Nevertheless, there is a provision in Deuteronomy 18:21-22 that provides a test to determine if a prophet speaks for God. The scriptures say, "And if thou say in thine heart, How shall we know the word which the Lord hath not spoken? When a prophet speaketh in the name of the Lord, if the thing follow not, nor come to pass, that is the thing which the Lord hath not spoken, but the prophet hath spoken it presumptuously: thou shalt not be afraid of him."

I have included copies of letters that were sent to President Bush and others; the revelations contained therein have come to fruition.

In 2003, a pastor at a local church in Jackson, Tennessee performed the test. Below is an account of what took place.

On April 6, 2003, I shared with Straight Way Church in Jackson, Tennessee various revelations that God had revealed to me. After I shared these revelations, Pastor Richard Rodgers asked me to share with him the next revelation that God reveals to me because he wanted to watch for it. On April 7, 2003, I sent Pastor Rodgers a copy of the communications that I had sent you. In those communications there were two letters to President Bush that warned of destructive winds and calamity after calamity. (December 2, 2002 and December 20, 2002) Then on April 9, 2003, God revealed to me the following revelation. (I shared it with Pastor Rodgers on April 9, 2003)

God showed me people with very little cash in their pockets and youth and adults were competing for the same few jobs. Then a lady in a crowd warned me that the store's owners should secure their goods. I asked her why? She replied look around you. I was in a black community; I saw hundreds of black people standing around looking for something to do. I immediately woke up; it was about 6:00 A.M."

On April 15, 2003, I wrote Pastor Rodgers another letter and expounded on the vision that God had shown me. Here is a quote from that letter.

"... Now allow me to expound on the vision that I shared with you on April 9, 2003. I discovered that I must pay close attention to details. When God shares visions with me a lot of information is shared over a short period of time. On April 9, 2003, the first thing He showed me was a situation where a team that was playing a game of baseball refused to continue to play. The team that refused to play was smaller and weaker than the other team. I did not understand this vision so I did not share it with you. Then I saw the vision regarding the unemployment situation. Pastor, as I was looking at these people, first I saw many brown faces. Then it was as if there was a zoom lens on the black faces. I saw many of our black brothers in America. Therefore, I am confident that this vision was also pertaining to a future event that will happen in America. Pastor Rodgers, this will come to pass unless there is increased effort to change these conditions; my job is to send out the warning.

On May 4, 2003, twenty-five days after God gave me the revelation, Pastor Rodgers was able to witness this vision come to pass in Jackson, Tennessee. Two tornadoes hit Jackson and a black neighborhood was impacted. Store owners had to secure their goods, and looting did take place. It was a clear sign to me that this was the vision God gave to me. On the morning of May 4, 2003, after the Tornadoes hit Jackson, Tennessee, I was in Detroit, Michigan, watching the report on CNN. The camera zoomed in on these three black faces. These were the same three black faces that God had revealed to me 25 days prior in a vision.

Moreover, I first warned President Bush on October 26, 2001 that this nation would face a plague of national disasters at a level that had not been experienced in its short 200 year history. I also wrote President Bush after God showed me destructive winds and floods that impacted the nation in the fall of 2002. On December 2, 2002, I explained to the President that these acts of nature we were experiencing are only examples of what we will experience if we continue to place our trust in oppression and perverseness and continue to study war.

Let us review some tornado facts. The average number of tornadoes that we experience in the month of November is 30. However, over one weekend in

November 2002, we experienced 77. Moreover, the average number of tornadoes we experienced in the month of May is 180. But, in the first seven days in May 2003, we experienced 395. These calamities are a measured response from God. (Jeremiah 30:11, Isaiah 27:8)

The above information was written in 2003. However, in 2004 and 2005, the destructive winds that won the nation's attention were hurricanes. The season of 2005 broke all records for this nation. God has showed me a plague of national disasters. That means these disasters will not be limited to those caused by nature. And since it is a plague, they will become progressively worst.

Before we close this discussion, it is very important to understand the complete message that God gave me on April 9, 2003. God took me to Iraq in the spirit and I was able to see many brown faces in distress. Then God brought me to my hometown Jackson, Tennessee. I was able to see black faces with destruction around, and people being warned to secure their businesses. Listen carefully; like we bring destruction upon Iraq, God will bring destruction upon us, here in the United States. Today as we hear reports of the destruction in the United States, some compare the destruction with places that have been bombed.

June 9, 2003, I wrote President Bush and shared this information with him. Below is a quote from that letter.

"Mr. President, listen carefully and learn from these scriptures. "Woe to the crown of pride, to the drunkards of Ephraim, whose glorious beauty is a fading flower, which are on the head of the fat valleys of them that are overcome with wine! Behold, the Lord hath a mighty and strong one, which as a tempest of hail and a destroying storm, as a flood of mighty waters overflowing shall cast down to the earth with the hand. The crown of pride, the drunkards of Ephraim, shall be trodden under feet:" (Isaiah 28:1-3) God's mighty and strong one controls the destroying storms.

God Revealed War In Iraq as a Baseball Game

Here is another quote from the letter I sent to Pastor Rodgers on April 9, 2003. "I did not understand the vision about the baseball game until I heard a comment from Mohammed Aldouri, the Ambassador of Iraq, when he made the statement that the game is over. Pastor Rodgers, since God revealed to me the war with Iraq as a game of baseball, this means there will be other opponents and more competitions (wars). Who is next? Pastor we are headed for destruction."

In 2005, we could clearly see why God showed me the war as a game of baseball. At that time in 2003 there were about **150** American soldiers that had been killed in the war in Iraq. God removed his protective covering. In May 2007, about 3350 American soldiers had died in Iraq and more than 24,000 American soldiers have been wounded. In January 2006, CBS News reported that over 500,000 U. S. military members have served in Afghanistan or Iraq since 9/11; more than 100,000 of those that have served have filed for some form of disability. These lists will continue growing until we repent. **There have been many other opponents and much destruction as prophesied.**

Jackson, Tennessee - A Hub City for God

The Vision of the Lord's Strong and Mighty One:
"The Tornado on the Ground in Jackson, Tennessee"

May 31, 2003 - In a dream I received a report that a tornado was headed for Jackson, Tennessee. I woke up immediately. However, after I awoke, I noticed that the television was still on, so I questioned the creditability of the dream.
June 1, 2003 - after studying the word of God and prior to retiring for the night, I

66

asked God to make it clear to me regarding the dream about the tornadoes' warning for Jackson. While asleep, God revealed to me in a vision, tornadoes approaching. The site that I saw the tornadoes approaching reminded me of Muse Park here in Jackson. I recalled watching a large tornado, on the ground; a baseball diamond was between the tornado and my location as I watched the storms. Besides the tornado on the ground, there was another funnel cloud that had not hit the ground. Next, while I was still in a vision, I recalled that I tried to determine the exact location of the storm. As I surveyed the area, I remember seeing a structure made of sheet metal. Then I woke up immediately. This was more than a dream; it was as if I was actually there. This will come to pass shortly I believe it will happen here in Jackson, Tennessee within thirty days. After this happens, the people in Jackson, Tennessee will be more willing to hear from God and to make Jackson a "Hub City for God." However, the thought kept coming to me that God was looking for a place that would hearken to His word. I knew that the message God wanted me to convey was for people to repent, and seek his face, then he would heal their land. Moreover, I knew these storms were all related to God's judgment in the land so the people would learn His righteousness.

On June 2, 2003, I went to Muse Park in Jackson. I have confidence that Muse Park was the sight in the vision where I saw the tornado on the ground and the funnel cloud. Moreover, I believe that the sheet metal structure I saw in the vision is a church, Jackson Family Worship Center that is near the park on Parkway. I pray that the Lord will have mercy on this place."

Pastor Treece was the pastor of Jackson Family Worship Center. On Sunday June 8, 2003, God led me to attend the service. I attended the service. As I entered the doors, and before I could take a seat, the guest speaker said, "You just cannot reveal everything that God reveals to you to just anybody, because some people will look at you like you are crazy." I enjoyed the guest speaker

67

who emphasized moving and doing the will of God. After the service I shared the vision with Pastor Treece and gave him two copies of the book, "Check-up For The Body of Christ." Pastor Treece was not too receptive or he was very guarded. He explained that he did not know me. I then told him that I would come to one of the revival services later on during the week and give him a complete package.

On June 10, 2003, I attended a revival service at the church. The guest speaker was talking about sound doctrines, stirring up the gifts and mobilizing the people to share the word of God throughout the community. I enjoyed the service, and the message was powerful and effective. As the speaker was giving his message, often he would make a gesture with one of his hands a whirling motion. After the service was over, I shared with him briefly about the vision I had and told him the gesture he made reminded me of a tornado. In fact, I thought about the word of God as it is recorded in Isaiah 28:2, "Behold, the Lord hath a mighty and strong one, which as a tempest of hail and a destroying storm, as a flood of mighty waters overflowing, shall cast down to the earth with the hand." After sharing with the guest speaker, I shared with Pastor Treece the communications I had shared with President Bush in the past.

I was led by the Holy Spirit to prepare a communication for the Mayor of Jackson, Tennessee and the pastors of Jackson. On the morning of June 17, 2003, I asked God to make it very clear to me regarding the tornadoes approaching Jackson, Tennessee. I asked God to show me destruction, if these tornadoes are designed to bring destruction. In a vision, I found myself in the home of people I did not know. People were sharing with one another. It appeared to be in the evening. Then there was an eruption of water coming down through the ceiling, and then the house began to shake. The people started to shout, "It's a tornado." We were moving through the house seeking cover. I woke up from the vision and sat up in my bed.

Later on that day, I hand-carried a letter to Mayor Charles Farmer's office. I shared a file with The Jackson's Sun (a local news paper) and the local television station. On June 18, 2003, I sent letters to about 100 pastors in Jackson giving them the warning. Below is a quote from the letter I wrote to the pastors.

"Jackson is known as the Hub City. God is looking for a Hub City for Himself. Are you willing to help make Jackson a Hub City for God? If so you may start today and respond to this warning of destruction like the people did in the great city of Nineveh, after they had received the warning from Jonah (Jonah, Chapter 3). Or you may wait until after the destruction."

According to Jonah, 3:4-10, the people of Nineveh believed God, proclaimed a fast, put on sackcloth, from the greatest to the least of them. The King rose from his throne, removed his robe, covered himself in sackcloth, and sat in ashes. Moreover, the king of Nineveh proclaimed and published a decree saying, "Let neither man nor beast, herb nor flock, taste any thing: let them not feed, nor drink water: But let man and beast be covered with sackcloth, and cry mightily unto God: yea, let them turn every one from his evil way, and from the violence that is in their hands." God saw their works. They turned from their evil ways and God repented of the evil he had said he would do unto them; and he did it not. Therefore, I was led to take this message to the mayor and the pastors of Jackson, Tennessee

On Sunday, June 22, 2003, I had planned to go to worship at Straight Way Church. However, I asked God to order my footsteps. The Holy Spirit led me to go by Jackson Family Worship Center. When I arrived there I realized the service was almost over. Nevertheless, I was able to witness two baptisms in the name of Jesus Christ. I rejoiced to see these two souls give their lives to Christ. Now I was pleased and I knew that God was pleased that they were using sound doctrines and had not forgotten the name of the Lord, Jesus Christ.

After the service was over, with patience I waited until Pastor Treece finished talking with several of his members. After he finished, I approached him. He rebuked me immediately, and stated that he had read every one of the letters and he does not receive it. He then told me I made my mistake when I passed my books out to some of his members without his permission. (I gave two books to his members as I walked back to my car after a brief conversation with them.) Moreover, Pastor Treece exclaimed that he was going to cancel out everything that I was doing here in Jackson, so I would not have any influence in the city. He clarified his statement that this would be done in the spirit. I attempted to explain to him that I only delivered to him a message I had received from God. He said he did not have time to talk to me not even for ten minutes. I looked at him and said, "Pastor, you will be hearing from God later on this week; and you need to pray for this place." He stated that he hears from God all the time.

I attempted to shake his hand; he withdrew his hand. I looked at him and spoke very softly and said, "Pastor". (I was praying that the Holy Spirit touched the pastor with His Love.) Pastor Treece reluctant shook my hand as several of his members looked on. As I was walking away, he began to share with some of his members.

I prayed for Pastor Treece because I knew that he was not able to receive the truth because our common enemy works deep in the dark to hide God's counsel from His people. Moreover, I realized that God had poured out the spirit of deep sleep and all the people in the United States had been covered to include Pastor Treece. Like God poured out spirit of deep sleep on Judah before the doom of Jerusalem, God has poured out the spirit of deep sleep on the people in the United States.

Let us review the scriptures and see what happened before the doom of Jerusalem.

Isaiah 29:10-15 states, "For the Lord hath poured out upon you the spirit of deep sleep, and hath closed your eyes: the prophets and your rulers, the seers hath he covered. (11) And the vision of all is become unto you as the words of a book that is sealed. Which men deliver to one that is learned, saying, Read this, I pray thee: and he saith, I cannot; for it is sealed: (12) And the book is delivered to him that is not learned, saying, Read this, I pray thee: and he saith, I am not learned. (13) Wherefore the Lord said, Forasmuch as this people draw near me with their mouth, and with their lips do honour me, but have removed their heart far from me, and their fear toward me is taught by the precept of men: (14) Therefore, behold, I will proceed to do a marvelous work among this people, even a marvelous work and a wonder: for the wisdom of their wise men shall perish, and the understanding of their prudent men shall be hid. (15) Woe unto them that seek deep to hide their counsel from the Lord, and their works are in the dark, and they say, Who seeth us? And who knoweth us?"

I realized the same thing that happened to Judah before the doom of Jerusalem was happening in the United States. All had been covered with the spirit of deep sleep and people were working deep in the dark to hide the counsel of God for His people. I knew that in order for Pastor Treece to wake up from this spirit of deep sleep, he must be provided with data.

Therefore as it is recorded in Psalm 85:11, "Truth shall spring out of the earth; and righteousness shall look down from heaven." I knew that God would allow this to take place. However, my immediate concern was that it was imperative that Pastor Treece and the congregation at Jackson Family Worship would pray for mercy.

On Monday, June 23, 2003, I attended a prayer meeting with several ministers and individuals. Prior to attending this meeting I had listened to the weather station regarding this cold air mass that had brought snow to the state of Wyoming, hail stones in Nebraska the size of volley balls, (six and one half inches in diameter) and several tornadoes. During the meeting, as the Holy Ghost fell on me I cried out for mercy for the land. The Holy Spirit fell on all who were present. I did not realize at the time the affects of this action. By faith I knew that God had heard and answered our prayers.

During the evening of June 24, 2003, there were 54 tornadoes impacting several states and the storm was headed southeastward. I prayed again for mercy on the land. On June 25, 2003, as I was listening to the weather report, the meteorologist stated on Thursday (June 26), the storms should be in West Tennessee. This is where Jackson, Tennessee is located. He said, "West Tennessee should prepare themselves for this one." **This was the fulfilling of the dream I had on May 31, 2003, when I received the warning.** In the past, I have experienced a 25-day cycle regarding the revelations I received from God. The 25-day cycle includes the vision and when the vision comes to fruition. This 25-day cycle held true in this case. I prayed even more for mercy on the land.

However, on June 25, there were 82 reports of severe wind damage and 25 reports of large hail to hit in neighboring states. On the morning of Thursday, June 26, I went to Muse Park to do my daily walk/run. I normally walk about 4 miles. (This is five times around the paved perimeter on the side where the baseball diamonds are located.) However, I decided I would walk seven times around the perimeter and prayed to God to have mercy on the land. I completed my objective.

Later on that day the front passed through Jackson, and brought only showers. Moreover, there was not one tornado anywhere as result of the storm front, nor was there any report of damaging wind or hail from this storm front. (However, there were three reports of wind damage and hail damage in Texas, North Dakota and Ohio.) The front quickly moved through the area. Now I was very happy because I knew that the Lord had heard and answered my prayers and the prayers of many others. The storms that were headed for West Tennessee just dissipated.

72

The next three pages contain information from the National Weather Service, Storm Prediction Center for June 24, 2003 through June 26, 2003. You will witness the storm system as it approaches West Tennessee, where Jackson is located. However, on June 26, 2003, the storm system just dissipates. This is the result of the power of prayer.

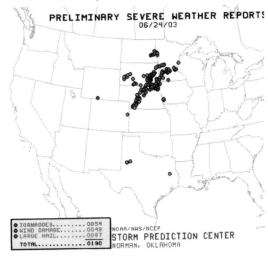

20030624's Storm Reports

PRELIMINARY SEVERE WEATHER REPORTS
06/24/03

Search SPC
SPC search Go

SPC Products
  All SPC Forecasts
  Current Watches
  Meso. Discussions
  Conv. Outlooks
  Fire Wx Forecasts

Research
  Exper. Products
  Forecast Tools
  Svr. Tstm. Events
  SPC Publications

Weather Information
  Watch/Warning Map
  Storm Reports
  Current Radar
  Product Archive
  SPC FAQ
  Live SPC Weather

Education & Outreach
  About the SPC
  About Tornadoes
  Cool Images
  Our History
  Public Affairs

Misc.
  Staff
  What's New
  Links

Contact Us
  SPC Feedback

```
● TORNADOES........ 0054
● WIND DAMAGE...... 0049      NOAA/NWS/NCEP
● LARGE HAIL....... 0087      STORM PREDICTION CENTER
  TOTAL............ 0190      NORMAN, OKLAHOMA
```

Note: All data are considered preliminary

Tornado Reports

Time	F-Scale	Location	County	State	Lat	Lon	
2110	UNK	PONCA	DIXON	NE	4256	9670	REI STO (FS
2130	UNK	WOONSOCKET	SANBORN	SD	4404	9826	REI RAI (FS
2200	UNK	7 W MITCHELL	DAVISON	SD	4371	9817	REI STO (FS
2214	UNK	7 W MITCHELL	DAVISON	SD	4371	9817	REI STO

National Weather Service
www.nws.noaa.gov

Storm Prediction Center

Site Map   News   Organization   Search [Enter Search Here] [Go]

Search SPC
[SPC search] [Go]

SPC Products
All SPC Forecasts
Current Watches
Meso. Discussions
Conv. Outlooks
Fire Wx Forecasts

Research
Exper. Products
Forecast Tools
Svr. Tstm. Events
SPC Publications

Weather Information
Watch/Warning Map
Storm Reports
Current Radar
Product Archive
SPC FAQ
Live SPC Weather

Education & Outreach
About the SPC
About Tornadoes
Cool Images
Our History
Public Affairs

Misc.
Staff
What's New
Links

Contact Us
SPC Feedback

20030625's Storm Reports

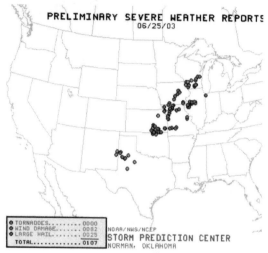

PRELIMINARY SEVERE WEATHER REPORTS
06/25/03

TORNADOES.........0000
WIND DAMAGE.......0082
LARGE HAIL........0025
TOTAL.............0107

NOAA/NWS/NCEP
STORM PREDICTION CENTER
NORMAN, OKLAHOMA

Note: All data are considered preliminary

Tornado Reports
No reports received

Hail Reports

Time	Size	Location	County	State	Lat	Lon	
1724	75	GAYS MILLS	CRAWFORD	WI	4345	9073	REF HIG DEF
1800	100	WAUZEKA	CRAWFORD	WI	4308	9088	REF PUE
1800	75	GILLINGHAM	RICHLAND	WI	4343	9045	REF PUE
1815	88	WAMEGO	POTTAWATOMIE	KS	3919	9631	PUE NICI (TOI

20030626's Storm Reports

Search SPC
SPC search Go

SPC Products
  All SPC Forecasts
  Current Watches
  Meso. Discussions
  Conv. Outlooks
  Fire Wx Forecasts

Research
  Exper. Products
  Forecast Tools
  Svr. Tstm. Events
  SPC Publications

Weather Information
  Watch/Warning Map
  Storm Reports
  Current Radar
  Product Archive
  SPC FAQ
  Live SPC Weather

Education & Outreach
  About the SPC
  About Tornadoes
  Cool Images
  Our History
  Public Affairs

Misc.
  Staff
  What's New
  Links

Contact Us
  SPC Feedback

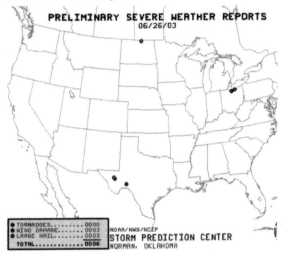

Note: All data are considered preliminary

Tornado Reports

No reports received

Hail Reports

Time	Size	Location	County	State	Lat	Lon	Comme
1900	75	2 SW SARAGOSA	REEVES	TX	3099	10367	REPORTED ALO INTERSTATE 10 PUBLIC. EVENT DURATION 15 M (MAF)
2035	75	31 N FORT DAVIS	JEFF DAVIS	TX	3109	10388	REPORTED BY COOPERATIVE OBSERVER. (MA
2055	75	5 W BELCOURT	ROLETTE	ND	4883	9985	PENNY SIZE HAI COVERED (BIS)

Now let us take a closer look at the vision and what actually took placed.

May 31, 2003 - In a dream I received a report that a tornado was headed for Jackson, Tennessee. I woke up immediately. However, after I awoke, I noticed that the television was still on, so I questioned the creditability of the dream. **Warning received on May 31, 2003 and realized on June 25, 2003, when the Weather Channel issued the warning**.

June 1, 2003 - after studying the word of God and prior to retiring for the night, I asked God to make it clear to me regarding the dream about the tornadoes' warning for Jackson. While asleep, God revealed to me in a vision, tornadoes approaching. The site that I saw the tornadoes approaching reminded me of Muse Park here in Jackson. I recalled watching a large tornado, on the ground; a baseball diamond was between the tornado and my location as I watched the storms. Besides, the tornado on the ground I saw a **funnel cloud that had not hit the ground.**

Next while I was still in the vision, I recalled that I tried to determine the exact location of the storm. As I surveyed the area, I remember seeing a structure made of sheet metal. Then I woke up immediately. On June 2, 2003, I went to Muse Park in Jackson; I have confidence that Muse Park was the sight in the vision where I saw the tornado on the ground and the funnel cloud. Moreover, I believe that the sheet metal structure that I saw in the vision is a church, Jackson Family Worship Center.

This vision had **two dimensions**, a spiritual dimension and a natural dimension. The **large tornado on the ground** was the Lord's **mighty and strong one**, who controls and directs the tempest of hail and destroying storm and overflowing waters, as if it is done by hand. (Isaiah 28:2) The Lord's mighty and strong one was located in the location where the Jackson Family Worship Center is located. Surely, this was the Lord's mighty and strong one, I have never seen

77

anything like it; all examples that I have seen on television come short of describing the fury of the Lord's mighty and strong one. It was in one location, whirling, and pulsating upward and downward. The Lord's mighty and strong one was seen prior to the appearance of the **funnel cloud that did not hit the ground.** The **funnel cloud** that did not hit the ground was the **natural dimension** of the vision. Surely these storms were headed for Jackson, Tennessee, however they did not start in Jackson, but hundreds of miles away. I was warned and saw them coming. Moreover, I saw the mighty and strong stay the storms.

Some believed and prayed as I prayed for mercy. God has shown us favor and we can rebuild Jackson, Tennessee with the assurance that God has blessed this place. The appearance of the Lord's mighty and strong one was not just for the one storm, but it will control and prevent many storms to come. Like the storms that passed through Carroll, Henderson, and McNairy Counties on July 21, 2003 and the storms that passed through Shelby and Fayette Counties on July 22, 2003. The people of Jackson, Tennessee should count these as blessings. Many do not realize what had occurred. However in time they will learn how they were blessed and how God kept these destructive storms from hitting Jackson twice in one year. I pray that the people of Jackson, Tennessee will work together and share in love and truly reach out and edify the body of Christ.

Why did God reveal His mighty and strong one over Jackson Family Worship Center? Their doctrines are sound. In the revival in June, each member was charged to go out and use their gifts, mobilize throughout the community, sharing the word of God to make the city of Jackson a community for God. In other words, they were charged to make Jackson, Tennessee a Hub City for God. Moreover, they are still holding fast to His name, the name of Jesus Christ. God has taken special note of this.

I wrote the mayor and some of the pastors and gave them the update as written above. Here is a quote from the letter I wrote to the pastors. "I beseech each of you to continue to seek the face of God, ensure that the doctrines you teach and the traditions you follow line up with the words of God. Today, unfortunately many worship the Lord in vain because they teach for doctrines the commandments of men. (Mark 7:7.)" Here is a quote from the letter of July 23, 2003, to Mayor Farmer. "These storms are part of God's judgment on this nation. However, God has found a remnant of His people here in Jackson, Tennessee who will hearken to His word. Mayor Farmer, as you rebuild, work to make Jackson a Hub City for God."

Prior to retiring for the night, I reflected on scriptures. I thought maybe God has now repented of the wicked thing that He had planned like He did for the city of Nineveh as outlined in Jonah Chapter Three. I asked the Holy Spirit to lead me and order my footsteps. I retired for the night. Then I had a dream; I was sitting at the table with others without any pants on with only my under wear. Then I woke up. I asked God to reveal to me what did this mean. I knew my thoughts were incomplete about God repenting, since on a daily basis, I ask God to order my footsteps and God always answers each prayer request. The Holy Spirit directed me to Jeremiah Chapter Nine. **It was clear to me that God had not repented as He had done for the city of Nineveh.** Here is a quote from Jeremiah Chapter Nine.

God Weeps In Secret Places

"Oh That my head were waters, and mine eyes a fountain of tears, that I might weep day and night for the slain of the daughter of my people." (According to Jeremiah 13:17, God says, "But if ye will not hear it, my soul shall weep in secret places for your pride; and mine eye shall weep sore, and run down with tears, because the Lord's flock is carried away captive.") Let us continue to read Jeremiah Chapter 9.

79

"Oh that I had in the wilderness a lodging place of wayfaring men; that I might leave my people, and go from them! For they be all adulterers, an assembly of treacherous men. And they <u>bend their tongues</u> like <u>their bow for lies</u>: but <u>they are not valiant for the truth</u> upon the earth; for <u>they proceed from evil to evil</u>, and <u>they know not me</u>, saith the Lord... And <u>they will deceive every one his neighbour,</u> and **will not speak the truth**: they have taught **their tongue to speak lies,** and weary themselves to commit iniquity. **Thine habitation is in the midst of deceit; through deceit they refuse to know me, saith the Lord**. ... <u>Shall I not visit them for these things</u>? Saith the Lord: **<u>shall not my soul be avenged for such a nation as this?</u>"** (Jeremiah 9:1-9)

As I continue to read it became clear to me that God had not repented. However, God is a merciful God and He had mercy because I had asked for mercy. But had I really learned from this experience? I soon discovered there was more learning for me. A very quick lesson.

Learning A Lesson From God The Hard Way

During the weekend, the weather services reported a tropical storm; they named the storm Bill. Again, I found myself praying for mercy on the land. On Sunday night, June 29, 2003, I asked God to order my footsteps before I retired for the night. I had this dream. I was busy helping people. There was a lot of work to do. People were depending on me to do a variety of tasks. I was wearing a military jacket but I had Senior Master Sergeant stripes on one shoulder board and captain bars on the other shoulder board. Then I went to my office. I saw on my desk certificates I had received from many years ago. They included one from the student council when I was in high school and a number of blue military awards and decoration jackets. Then someone came in and requested advice. I began to assist him. Then I woke up. I wanted to know the meaning of this dream.

On morning about 7:00 a. m., I went to Muse Park for my daily walk/run. As I was walking around the park, I asked God to reveal to me the meaning of this dream. The Holy Spirit began to teach me as I walked. Here is a summation of the teaching.

"You have been chosen as a prophet of God. You must love Me more than anything. You have cried out for mercy after I have given you my message to deliver to the people. Your actions are not of one that loves me more than his sister, brothers, and things of this world. **I have warned you. Think not about the destruction the storms will bring, but think about what happens when a soul has not been saved.** I want to promote you. However, you are holding on to too many things in the past. If you should continue, then you have seen your rewards. However, to continue to be one of my servants, one of my prophets, you must change your heart. When you speak in my name you speak for me. People must learn to fear me from the messages that I give you to speak. I am bringing forth judgments to the land so the people will learn righteousness."

"Up until this task you have done well. After, I give you an assignment, your role is to carry out the assignment. Deliver My word. Do not cry out to me for mercy after you have delivered my word. I am a merciful God; I continue to show mercy. As many as I love, I rebuke and chasten: be zealous therefore, and repent. Share this experience with others so they too can learn."

Yes, I did learn from that experience. In 1989 when I retired from the United States Air Force I was a Senior Master Sergeant. The Lord of Hosts was telling me that He wanted to promote me to captain in His army. Since that time, God has shown me that I have received that promotion. We all must learn from this experience.

The tornado did not hit Jackson, Tennessee because of God's mercy and the prayers of the saints. Many people in Jackson, Tennessee prayed for mercy.

God heard our prayers. Nevertheless, while some were praying for mercy some were praying against me to cancel out my influence in the area. Isaiah, Ezekiel, Jeremiah, and Amos, they all went through the same thing because they had very little influence on the people to turn from their wicked ways. Today, we look at these men as great prophets. However, we have not learned from all the lessons that have gone forth. Jesus said, "A prophet is not without honour, but in his own country, and among his own kin, and in his own house." (Mark 6:4) In Luke 4:24, Jesus said, "Verily I say unto you, No prophet is accepted in his own country." I pray that we will learn. However, the book has been already written.

Warning Of a Plague of National Disasters

In June 2004 as I was reviewing the communications I sent to President Bush I reread a letter dated October 26, 2001. Here is a quote from that letter. "Mr. President, if you do not change this destructive path, terror will continue to visit America. Moreover, America will experience a plague of national disasters at a level that this nation has not experienced in it short 200 year history." Now I clearly understand why God told me to stop crying out for mercy after He gives me His messages to declare to His people. God wants people to fear Him and repent of their wicked ways.

Moreover, as I look back, it is apparent on April 9, 2003, in the spirit, I was in Iraq, then God took me from Iraq in the spirit to Jackson, Tennessee. As we release our destructive forces on Iraq, the heavens released its destructive forces upon the United States. Destruction was all around the country. We have truly experienced a plague of national disasters since October 26, 2001.

People around the country have compared the destruction we have experienced as bombs being dropped on us. As hundreds of thousands of people in Iraq were without power, hundreds of thousands of people in America were without power. God has shown me there is a direct relation to our actions on earth with God's actions in the heaven. Listen carefully to the word of God "...and whatsoever thou shalt bind on earth shall be bound in heaven: and whatsoever thou shalt loose on earth shall be loosed in heaven." (Matthew 16:19)

The United States is out of the counsel of God and all of these revelations have come to past. As I write in June 2004, I am preparing this book for publication. However, as I look back to last year it is very clear why God did not repent from the destruction to come to the United States. Today, many can clearly see the lies and deceptions of some of our leaders. But, some refuse to receive truth. They have not receive this truth because they do not have love for truth. According to the word of God, for them who do not have love for truth, Satan has all power, and signs and lying wonders. Many will perish because of their love not for the truth and taking pleasure in unrighteousness. They will be in a state of deceivableness of unrighteousness. In other words, they will be in a state of mind whereby they are most gullible to be deceived. The word of God says, "for this cause God shall send them strong delusion, that they should believe a lie: that they all might be damned who believed not the truth, but had pleasure in unrighteousness." (2 Thessalonians 2:8-12)

During the summer of 2004, the question for many was what do we do now since our troops are already in Iraq. We must win this war on terrorism many have exclaimed. In the fall of 2005, many are having the same discussion; but more are beginning to realize we cannot win with our military might and we must do something different. I wrote the President Bush on October 6, 2001. God had given me the answer before 9/11 and the reasons for the destruction. Before we sent our first ship or soldier, God had given the word to recall. God has showed me the destruction our military would face and how this nation would suffer financially, and the destruction through fires, storm, and floods.

The second time that I wrote President Bush regarding this crisis was on

October 26, 2001. Here is a quote from that letter.

"**I am a Prophet of God**. I wrote you twenty days ago as God directed me. However, you have failed to adhere to the word of God. God has commanded me to write you again . Mr. President, you continue to add sin onto sin. God knows every one of them, even the ones you classify as Top Secret and God has revealed some of those secrets to me. Mr. President, if you do not change this destructive path, terror will continue to visit America. Moreover, America will experience a plague of national disasters at a level this nation has not experienced in its short 200 year history. Many lives will be lost and fear will continue within the borders of the United States. However, if you should hearken to the word of God, terror will not come near this nation, and America's peace will be as a river, and nation's righteousness will be as the waves of the sea."

This all has come to pass. This all has come to pass and we will continue to experience a plague of national disasters; God wants us to know that He controls all of these natural disasters and will allow other national disasters to happen if this nation continues to fail to hearken to the commandments of God. We will continue to experience a plague of national disasters and we will not be able to end terrorism if we do not change our course.

In 2004 as I was working to finalize this book, many were wresting with the question what do we do now since we are already engaged in warfare? Now, as I prepare to publish this work, it is 2005. Many are still wresting with the same question. The answer to this question is simple. Repent and hearken to the commandments of God. If God said recall our troops in 2001 before we sent them, what would God tell us today? Would God tell us to keep them there to make things right? God has not given me the message that our troops should

84

remain in Iraq. Nor has God shown me that He is pleased with the actions of our leaders in the United States. God knows their hearts. Our actions have deceived many people, and the leaders of this land have caused God's people to sin, just like King Jeroboam of Israel and King Manasseh of Judah who caused the children of Israel to sin. People have been deceived, but they can never deceive God. **God wants us to withdraw our troops now.**

God's Words Have Not Changed - The U. S. Has Plowed Wickedness

God's words have not changed. The terrorism that the United States is experiencing is the fruit of our trust in oppression and perverseness. Therefore, as long as this nation trusts in oppression and perverseness we will experience terrorism. To end terrorism, we must understand why it happened, repent, and then adhere to the word of God. Let us examine again why we are experiencing terrorism.

As God told Israel in Hosea 10:13, God is saying the same to us today, "Ye have plowed wickedness, ye have reaped iniquity; ye have eaten the fruit of lies: because thou didst trust in thy way, in the multitude of thy mighty men." Moreover as God told Judah in Isaiah 30:12-13, "Wherefore thus saith the Holy One of Israel, Because ye despised this word, and trust in oppression and perverseness, and stay thereon: Therefore this iniquity shall be to you as a breach ready to fall, swelling out in a high wall, whose breaking cometh suddenly at an instant."

This wickedness was plowed before to 9/11. However, the United States has added sin to sin by waging the war on Iraq. God showed me in September 2002, that this war was without provocation; I shared with President Bush on September 3, 2002. I have shared with President Bush since October 6, 2001 to no avail.

85

Does this government admit that we have made some errors? Or do we continue to justify our actions so we can appear as this strong and mighty nation? If we continue in this warfare, there will be other wars; our pride and failing to adhere to the commandments of God will cause the fall of this nation. We must not just carry on as if we have not done anything wrong. We must acknowledge our errors, repent, and learn from them before we proceed. It is a grave mistake for the leaders of this nation to believe that we are justified to attack any nation without provocation.

Many lives have already been lost because of our pride and the deception of our leaders. Consequently, America has lost its status of the greatest super power in the world. Our military might is not enough. Today, this nation lacks integrity in the eyes of the world. Moreover, the nation is out of the counsel of God. Until we repent and hearken to the commandments of God, we will continue to experience terrorism, wars, and national disasters and eventually this nation will be destroyed.

Now, what do we do as a nation to regain our status in the world? Leaders are trying to come up with the best approach to this problem. However, in their efforts to come up with the solution some are still playing politics. This game of politics will only place a bandage on a very deep and deadly wound.

There is only one way to resolve the problem and regain our status and end terrorism. We must ask the right questions. How did we lose our status and why did the terrorists attack us? Answer: We failed to hearken to the commandments of God. What commandments? Trust not in oppression and perverseness but seek the counsel of God. Do not add sin to sin. Do not rush to shed the blood of the innocent. The list goes on. We must examine ourselves and use the Word of God as the gauge and not political polls.

How to Read God's Gauge Regarding His Righteousness

Let us use the gauge of God in Proverbs 6:16-19. These six things doth the Lord hate: yea, seven are an abomination unto him: A proud look, a lying tongue, and hands that shed innocent blood, An heart that deviseth wicked imaginations, feet that be swift in running to mischief, A false witness that speaketh lies, and he that soweth discord among brethren.

People who love God must carefully examine what the word of God says. What does God's gauge reads? If you love truth, you will agree that the leaders in the United States Executive Branch of Government are at 100% in respect to doing the things that God hates.

(1) A proud look

(2) A lying tongue

(3) Hands that shed innocent blood

(4) A heart that deviseth wicked imaginations

(5) Feet that are swift in running to mischief

(6) A false witness that speaketh lies

(7) He that soweth discord among brethren.

According to truth, the United States leaders are guilty of doing all of these things. Therefore, we must repent and turn from our **wicked ways** pray and seek the face of God, and God will see us repenting and God will heal our land. The end result, terror will not come near us. We will be established in righteousness. We will experience peace as the river and righteousness as the waves of the sea and God, the creator of the heavens and the earth, will show us how to profit.

But some will cry out, "But what must we do?" When we repent and seek the counsel of God, then God will order our footsteps. God has equipped this nation with everything we need to profit. However, we have failed to trust God,

87

so our leaders have lied and operated in deception. God has given us one of the richest lands in the world. Some claim that we have only three percent of the world's oil supply. We have placed our trust in that information. However, only God really knows. Nevertheless, we do not mine all of these fields because we do not want to use our oil supply up and have become dependent on other supply channels. We do not trust God that He will show us another alternative to oil, so we kill, deceive, rob from the poor nation, displace people, and support big oil companies agendas. This must change; we must put our trust in God.

During the summer and fall of 2004, President Bush's camp and John Kerry's camp, worked to convince America that they have the best approach to end this crisis. If we want peace in this nation, this nation must first admit that we were wrong to invade Iraq without provocation. We have done the same thing that we have accused Saddam Hussein of doing when he invaded Kuwait. **Saddam invaded Kuwait without provocation in the eyes of the world.** Today, in Iraq, America is seen as the enemy, the occupiers of the land by many. Therefore, Americans and the supporters of America's policies are the target of the violence. God knows the hearts and minds of our leaders. I pray that we will repent and end our deception and this game of politics.

However, many are puzzled what will happen if we remove our troops from Iraq today. It is not that simple some exclaim. That is true because we must not only withdraw our troops, we must repent of our other actions and compensate the people for the injury and damages we have caused that nation. Moreover, we must repent of all of our oppressive and perverse ways and God must see us repenting.

Now some will say we must be rational here. We are now in Iraq and we have started this military action. Our troops are there and now we have to complete it. We must ensure that democracy has a chance to work in Iraq. This will be a free society. This sounds good; however, if any group does not agree with our approach to this we will see them as terrorists and insurgents and we will destroy them. Consequently, Bush's administration fails to see that we are the invaders imposing our values on these people in Iraq, values that we have not mastered throughout North America and Central America.

What is the advantage of having a free society? Is Kuwait a free society? Answer: No, America helped to reinstate the dictator. What is a "free society?" Is Haiti a free society? Do we want Iraq to become another "free society" like Haiti? Is Panama a "free society?" Record shows that we invaded this nation and killed three thousand and arrested their President and put him in prison in the United States. Is Nickerson Garden in Los Angeles a "free society?" This is part of the United States of America. However, in this community people fear for their lives daily and then lock themselves behind bars in their homes.

Besides worrying about security, there are places in America where people need to be liberated. Here is an example.

The Black Man from Slidell

In the process of preparing me to see the difficult task that is before us on December 1, 2005, about 12:30 P. M., after running several errands, I returned home in Jackson, Tennessee and drove my car onto the driveway. After I exited my car, a man approached me and asked me if I was a minister. I told him yes. He told me he was from Slidell, Louisiana. He showed me his pictured I.D. that appeared to be a driver's license from Louisiana. (Slidell is about thirty miles from New Orleans.) He told me he had paid a woman in advance for a place to stay; he had paid the woman $200.00 in cash. He told me where the woman said she was employed; I told him I would take him there. While en-route, he explained that he had just given two guys a one-hundred dollar bill, out of the hundred dollars he had planned to give them $20.00. However, they took the one-hundred dollar bill and did not take him where he wanted to go. I expressed

89

my concerns; but the man told me it was all right because they did not take the money from him, he gave them the money.

The man asked me how old was I; I told him that I was fifty-five years old. Then I asked him how old he was; he told me that he was "four" "two". Then he stated that he did not know how old he was because he could not read, but he said he thought he was "four" "two". He said that he lived on a farm in Slidell and he is paid forty dollars a week. The owner of the farm takes care of everything and pays him forty dollars. I said to him so you live on a plantation; he corrected me and said he lives on a farm. We continued our discussion.

The man from Slidell then told me that his father died and left him some money. The owner of the farm gave him seventy-five thousand dollars. The man said the owner of the farm went into the bank and came back and gave him seventy-five thousand dollars in cash money. The man explained to me that the owner of the farm told him he could not take him in the bank to open a savings account because it takes two white men to take a black man into the bank to open a savings account. I explained to him that this was not true; it did not take two white men to go with you to open a savings account. When I parked the car in the parking lot of the store, the man from Slidell gave me a letter to read to him from the insurance company. I read the letter to him.

In summary, the letter said the man was the sole beneficiary of an insurance policy. His father had a seventy-five thousand dollar insurance policy with double indemnity in case of accidental death. The death was ruled as accidental; the total amount that was due him at that time was one hundred and eighty-five thousand dollars. After reading this letter aloud, I explained it to the man and told him again that it does not take two white men to go to the bank with him to open a savings account. The man became adamant, as if what I was telling him was not the true.

Then a black man came out of the store and as he approached my car, I motioned him over. The man from Slidell asked him if he knew how to get to the place that was on the card the woman had given him. The man said that he was not familiar with the address and the woman did not work in the store. (He identified himself as an employee at the store.)

Then I explained to the store's employee that this man is from Slidell, Louisiana and he has been told that it takes two white men to go with him to the bank to open a savings account. The store employee assured the man that this was not the case. Then the man from Slidell became even more adamant and said, it takes two white men to go with him into the bank to open a savings account. Then he took out of a black plastic bag, a roll of one hundred dollar bills about the size of a brick. Immediately, the store employee and I told him to put the money away and not show it to anyone else, like that. Then we told him with urgency to take the money to the bank and we would go in with him to set up a savings account. We were not able to convince the man. The man from Slidell left our presence saying, I need to get from around you guys. It takes two white men. If black men go into the bank, they would call the police and beat them and take them to jail. We brought truth to the man from Slidell, but, he was from the wilderness, and he believed his master. I have informed the FBI of this incident.

God sent this man to me. One of the reason he sent him to bring truth forth out of the earth. We must end this form of slavery in America. We must work to end this form of racism in America. We must liberate Americans. Slidell, this is no longer a secret; this racism must end. America, America, wake up from the spirit of deep sleep. God is revealing the secrets of people hearts in this report.

God continues to reveal His secrets to me after I receive these revelations The Holy Spirit guides me in taking the appropriate action. God showed me the wild fires and the floods of 2002, the apartment explosion in California, the destruction of the bridge in Oklahoma, the large crowd protesting that President

91

Bush confronted overseas in 2002. The revelations keep coming.

God revealed to me at the outset of the war in Iraq I saw the missile as it hit the barrack and three individuals running from it after it hit, our troops standing in the long chow lines, and troops without sleeping quarters. In addition, God revealed the destruction by fires, the abuse of the prisoners, the sexual perverted acts, the chemical leak in Oak Ridge, Tennessee in 2004, the lack of trust within the ranks, and the loss of the unity of command in 2004. Until we turn to God we will face calamity after calamity here in the United States. Jesus said, "Whatsoever ye shall bind on earth shall be bound in heaven: and whatsoever ye shall loose on earth shall be loosed in heaven." (Matthew 18:18)

I know who I am; I am a servant of God, one of His prophets. God wants each one of His children to know who they are. Jesus wants His sheep to receive the Gift of the Holy Spirit and be refined as gold and as silver. Then receive gifts from the Holy Spirit and offer God an offering in righteousness. (Malachi 3:3) Then God wants us to use those gifts, in the office ordained by Him, for the edifying and perfecting of the Body of Christ. I pray in the name of Jesus that we all come in the unity of the faith, and of the knowledge of Jesus Christ, the Son of God, unto a perfect man, and unto the measure of the stature of the fullness of Christ. Amen.

The Problem of Being Politically Correct with the World

The church is not part of the world, although we are in the world. We are not of the world. Jesus prayed to the Father that we may have His joy fulfilled in us. Jesus prayed that we would not be taken out of the world but that we be kept from evil. We are not of the world; we must always remember that. In Luke 12:51 - 53 Jesus says, "Suppose ye that I am come to give peace on earth? I tell you, Nay; but rather division: (52) For from henceforth there shall be five in one house divided, three against two, and two against three. (53) The father shall be divided against the son, and the son against the father; the mother; against the daughter, and the daughter against the mother; the mother-in-law against her daughter-in-law, and the daughter-in-law against her mother-in-law. We must decide today, as Christians, if we are going to serve God or are we going to remain asleep and continue to do the things that God hates.

I pray that Christians would wake up from the spirit of deep sleep and have love for truth and take actions that would be pleasing in God's sight and then give the leaders of the United States of America a mandate to not do the things that God hates.

(1) A proud look

(2) A lying tongue

(3) Hands that shed innocent blood

(4) A heart that deviseth wicked imaginations

(5) Feet that are swift in running to mischief

(6) A false witness that speaketh lies

(7) He that soweth discord among brethren.

I first wrote President George W. Bush on October 6, 2001. It was very unpopular to say anything about our activities to end terrorism. Nevertheless, I did what God commanded me to do. On October 9, 2001, I wrote religious leaders around the country and shared copies of the book, "America, America: A Checkup For the Body of Christ, The Church." Shortly after I sent the book out, the Holy Spirit showed me a large lion watching me and I was throwing rocks at him to keep him at bay. I then knew that the government was watching me and sending out these books was keeping the government from taking physical actions against me. I had planned to send members of Congress copies of the book, however, we had the anthrax threat. After the anthrax threat, I thwarted sending out information to Congress at that time.

God's Final Warning To President Bush - God Removes Covering From The U. S. Military

In January 2003, President Bush proclaimed that he was losing his patience with Saddam Hussein. At the same time, President Bush made this declaration God revealed to me his final warning for President Bush. I had written the President eight times to no avail. The final message was to repent from your rush to shed innocent blood and your trust and oppression and perverseness and to turn to God. This last message was the same as God's first message. However, now God revealed to me that the U. S. Battlements was no longer His and that the United States would face calamity after calamity until His people repented and turned from their wicked ways.

We must learn from lessons learned of the past. God righteousness is forever. The same standards apply today as they did 2500 years ago. America must learn. America must learn to fear God.

In November 2002, I wrote the Secretary of State to no avail. In January 2003 I wrote members of the Senate and House of Representatives. After writing these letters, President Bush's father spoke out about his son expressing that he was upset because people believed his son was rushing to shed innocent blood. At that point, I knew that somehow the message had gotten to President Bush.

God's Warning to the Senators And the House of Representatives

On January 21, 2003, I wrote Senator Edward Kennedy and nine other Senators and Representatives and shared all of the communications that I had sent to President. Here is a quote from the letter I sent to Senator Kennedy.

"Senator Kennedy, God has given me this message to deliver to the Leaders here in the United States, "Woe unto the leaders of the United States, if they continue in their wickedness and fail to adhere to the word that I have given My Prophet. Recall your planes, ships, and My people. Remove all unjust sanctions against countries around the world. Rewrite your trade agreements to ensure they are fair to the workers. End your eagerness to shed innocent blood. Seek out the bad fruit that have now ripened. Apply just laws to all suspects that are still alive, that were involved in the planning and operation of the terrorism attack on America. Do not prosecute the innocent. Bad fruits that have not ripened, treat them with care, love, and understanding, because you helped create them. Change your hearts and take on a new resolve to end oppression and perverseness. Thus, you will end the terrorism in America if you turn to Me. My righteousness is forever." Thus said the Lord. God gave me this message in October 2001 before we sent out any of our troops, planes, or ships. In God's final warning, He showed me how America will suffer financially and our strong military will be reduced to a military that cannot sustain its basic quality of life that we have grown accustomed to."

In March 2003, I sent e-mails to everyone I could that was listed in the TBN address book. I received two replies. One of the replies cursed me and the other one blessed me.

On March 17, 2003, I sent e-mails to 99 of our 100 United States Senators. I was not able to e-mail one of the Senators. I urged them to call an emergency Session of Congress to Prevent the War on Iraq. I have included a copy of the letter in this book. After I e-mailed these letters, my internet program with America On Line crashed; I was not able to bring it on line again even with technical support.

On April 8, 2003, I received a reply from Senator George Allen from Virginia. It was very clear that Senator Allen was convinced that the President, CIA, Department of Defense and the State Department had prevented clear and convincing evidence that posed a credible threat and had weapons of mass destruction. (A copy of Senator Allen's Letter is included in this book.)

God's Message to the Secretary General of the United Nations

In February 2003, God commanded me to write to the Secretary General of the United Nations. In this communication, I was commanded to express to Secretary General Kofin Annan, the importance of working for peace. Below is a quote from the letter.

"I am writing you to let you know that the United States is not walking in the counsel of God; this error puts nations around the world on the path of destruction. Today, the United States is like ancient Egypt, a very powerful nation. Consequently, many nations strengthen themselves in the strength of President Bush and trust in the shadow of the United States. Like God warned nations in Isaiah Chapter 30:3, the strength of Pharaoh would be these nations' shame, and the trust in the shadow of Egypt their confusion. God wants you to take action that help guide nations around the world to turn to Him and to stop going to the President of the United States for their strength and trusting in the Shadow of the United States."

On March 12, 2003, I received a reply from the United Nations. A copy of the reply is included in this book.

Daily I would pray for peace and ask God to move on the hearts of people and leaders around the world. The Spirit of God moved and millions of people began to protest around the world. Nevertheless, President Bush's heart was hardened and continues in his quest to shed the blood of the innocent.

On February 20, 2003, I prayed and asked God to use me as his vessel and the Holy Spirit moved upon me. While praying in an unknown tongue, I cried out as tears ran down my face until my eyes were sore, the affect was overwhelming. After I was still I asked God for an answer as to why I wept bitterly? The Holy Spirit directed me to the Book of Jeremiah, chapter 13.

Immediately, I turned to Jeremiah, chapter 13. As I read through the verses, it became clear to me what the Lord was saying. When I got to verse 17, then I knew why I was crying. Below is a quote from the text beginning with verse 14.

"And I will dash them one against another, even the fathers and the sons together, said the Lord: I will not pity, nor spare, nor have mercy, but destroy them. Hear ye, and give ear; be not proud: for the Lord hath spoken. Give glory to the Lord your God, before your feet stumble upon the dark mountains, and while ye look for light, he turns it into the shadow of death, and makes it gross darkness. **But if ye will not hear it, my soul shall weep in secret places for your pride; and mine eye shall weep sore, and run down with tears, because the Lord's flock is carried away captive."** As I continue to read the scriptures, once again I wept, because I knew that it was the pride of the United States that would cause this nation to fall.

In John 15:18 - 19, Jesus says, "If the world hate you, ye know that it hated me before it hated you. (19) If ye were of the world, the world would love his own: but because ye are not of the world, but I have chosen you out of the world, therefore the world hateth you." When we look at some countries in the world we find every sin legal in some countries. Moreover, some things that are abominations unto God are politically correct in some nations. Christians must stop being politically correct in the sight of the world to things that are not right in the sight of God. Let us ponder on this for a few minutes.

God's Warning to the Church: The Bride of Christ Falls Onto Broken Scattered Glass

In July 2004, I monitored programs on Trinity Broadcasting Network, WORD Network, and DAYSTAR that were focusing on the current state of America. After seeing a broadcast July 22, 2004, I asked God what he wanted me to do because God has given me a different message for the Church? Before I retired for the evening, I prayed and asked God to order my footsteps in this matter. God showed me the Bride of Christ as she was falling onto broken scattered glass. After she fell, I helped the Bride onto her feet; she had cuts and bruises on her backside from the fall. She needs to be healed. God wants me to turn on the water and then control the water-valve so His Bride could be hosed off. However, God wants me to be careful that the water is not too hot because God wants healing to take place. This dream was very clear to me. I knew that the water God wanted to apply is His word, "living water" and the control-valve had to be tempered with His love.

Let us take a close look at what this all means. The Bride of Christ fell onto broken scattered glass. Now she has cuts and bruises on her backside. God wants his Bride healed without spot, wrinkle, blemish or any such thing. I clearly understood the vision.

The water: The water represented the word of God, His living water.

The water control valve: The device was used to temper the Word of God, with His Love. I carefully used this device throughout this work.

98

Why did the Bride Fall? She fell as a confused person because individuals at all levels have allowed their feelings and emotions to affect their messages; these individuals failed to be sober and have gotten caught up in a debate which is a delusion sent from God. As you know when programs are aired on TBN the entire Body of Christ is impacted; surely this is the reason the Bride of Christ fell as a confused person onto broken scattered glass.

The Broken Scattered Glass: The broken scattered glass represents the doctrines that are taught that consist of philosophy, vain deceit, after the traditions of men, after the rudiments of the world and not after Christ. Please note, the glass was not part of the foundation. However, the broken scattered glass was lying on top of the foundation.

What does God want me to do? God wants me to deliver the message He gave me in 2001 to His People in the United States, and to deliver this most recent message to his apostles, prophets/prophetess, evangelists, pastors, and teachers.

What the Church must do? The Church must repent and do the first work. Effect the edification process as outlined in Ephesians 4:11-16. Then we can work to ensure that the Bride of Christ is healed. The Bride is not ready for warfare because we, the called, chosen and faithful, have failed to use all of our gifts in love to effect the edification process. We must repent and return to the first work; we must preach the **everlasting gospel** of Jesus Christ to all creatures throughout the world and ensure that His lambs, His sheep, and His sheep (pastors and teachers) are properly fed the **everlasting gospel** of our Lord and Saviour Jesus Christ.

The Called, the Chosen and the Faithful: The called, the chosen, and the faithful must work together in love and remove the broken glass. Therefore, the called, the chosen, and the faithful, must work together and get rid of all commandments of men and traditions that are contrary to the word of God that are taught to the body of Christ for doctrines. It is imperative that we work to this end because we are connected unto one another; there is only one Body of Christ.

This is a complex problem. The leadership of the United States of America is not within the counsel of God. The mystery of iniquity is at work and Satan has used all power and signs and lying wonders for the ones who do not have love the truth. Some use for doctrines, the commandments of men, instead of the word of God. Moreover, God has sent and is sending strong delusions to the ones who do not have love for the truth, but take pleasure in unrighteousness so they would be damned. Feelings and emotions are controlling many of God's leaders. Consequently, the Bride of Christ is wounded.

The complexity of the problem is compounded because we have created destruction in Iraq and God has released destruction onto this land. God has removed the protective covering from our military; our battlements are no longer His. Consequently, as of May 2007, over twenty-four thousand of our troops have been wounded; over 3,350 killed and these lists keep growing. There are military shortfalls on bases at home; we lack adequate fund to address destruction throughout the nation and the growing list of factors that affect this nation's stability. Moreover, our leaders lack the wisdom to resolve the problems at home and in Iraq. Some of the leaders have lied to the people; and their pride keeps these leaders from repenting. Some elected officials are more concern about their political careers than what is in the best interest of the country. We need mercy from God; however, we continue to play political games. However, God is not interested in our games.

Now, it is imperative that the people of God wake up from the spirit of deep sleep and understand that we must be sober in all things and have love for the truth. God has clearly shown me that the United States is in serious trouble and the leaders of His people are in error because many have fail to receive the truth.

Remember we are the light, like Jesus. We must let our light shine. If we should let our light shine we would give light to the ones in the dark and they can come out. However, when we dim our light, by turning our heads, looking the other way, we are in error and are being led by the wicked one. Sometimes for a Christian to be politically correct with the world, the Christian's light must be completely turned off. **Listen, this will happen to MYSTERY BABYLON THE GREAT!** When this occurs, the light of a candle will shine no more at in thee; and the voice of the bridegroom and of the bride shall be heard no more at all in thee. (Revelation 18:23)

The candle is the church. (Revelation 1:20) Remember the story about the ten virgins. (Matthew chapter 25) The five wise virgins were ready for the marriage, they had oil in their lamps, the light shined from their lamps and they were taken away. On the other hand, the five foolish virgins were left behind because their lamps had gone out. We must understand when the cry is made, "the bridegroom cometh" half of the Church will be left behind because they will be found "playing church" and there is no light shining from their lamps. Only half of saints of God will be wise, and letting their light shine. The foolish saints of God will be left behind.

This explains why the scriptures says, "the light of a candle will shine no more at all in thee; and the voice of the bridegroom and of the bride shall be heard no more at all in thee. It is imperative that Christians in the United States of America pay close attention to this message. God **will not remove** the candle stick from Mystery Babylon before the fall. However, the five wise virgins, (half of the church), the true bride of Christ, with oil in their lamps and vessels, with their light shining will be taken away because they have made themselves ready for the marriage of the Lamb. The five foolish virgins will be left behind. This represents fifty percent of the church, people who believe that they are saved, they will not be ready. Jesus will say to them, "I know you not." (Matthew 25:12)

God has given me a task similar to what He gave to Isaiah, to warn Judah before the doom of Jerusalem. Moreover, God has done the same things to the United States as He did to Judah up to this point. Below are some of the factors we are experiencing here in America as Judah experienced.

(1) God has poured out the spirit of deep sleep and closed the eyes of the prophets, rulers, and the seers (Isaiah 29:10-15)

(2) People drew near God with their mouth and honor God with their lips; however, their hearts were far from Him. They were taught to fear God from the precepts of men.

(3) People worked deep in the dark to hide the counsel of God from His people.

Judah was not within the counsel of God. Therefore, they added sin to sin. Moreover, Judah put their trust in oppression and perverseness and Judah did not want to hear the word of God. Judah only wanted to hear smooth things. The United States of America has done the same things that Judah did. Consequently, like God told Judah through his prophet Isaiah, God has given me the same message to give to the United States of America. "Because ye despise this word, and trust in oppression and perverseness and stay thereon: Therefore this iniquity shall be to you as a breach ready to fall, swelling out of a high wall, whose breaking cometh suddenly and at an instant." (Isaiah 30:13)

The terrorism the United States is experiencing is the fruit of our leaders trust in oppression and perverseness; we must understand this. We cannot win this war with our military might. Moreover, God has removed His covering from

102

around our military. Our battlement is no longer His. (Reference my letter to President Bush dated January 14, 2003.) God showed me that the United States would experience a plague of national disasters until we repent. (Reference my letter to President Bush dated October 26, 2001.)

In Isaiah chapter 28, God warned Ephraim about the crown of pride. God has sent the same warning to the leaders in the United States. Like Ephraim, the leaders in the United States have made lies their refuge and have elected to hide under falsehood. (Isaiah 28:15) Isaiah 26:9 says, "...For when thy judgments are in the earth, the inhabitants of the world will learn righteousness." Judgment is in the land. Isaiah 28:17 says, God will lay judgment to the line, and righteousness to the plummet: and the hail shall sweep away the refuge of lies, and the water shall overflow the hiding place.

Moreover, as it is recorded in Psalm 85:11, "Truth shall spring out of the earth, and righteousness shall look down from heaven. Surely truth has sprung out of the earth. The films like "Fahrenheit 9/11", "Iraq and the West," "The Hidden Wars of Desert Storm," "Good Kurds/Bad Kurds," "Palestine is Still The Issue," and "Profit of Doom," and the most recent news reports are some of the ways truth is springing out of the earth. However, the people of God must have love for the truth.

II Thessalonians 2:7-12 explains the mystery of iniquity and how God would send strong delusion to them that do not love the truth so they would believe a lie and be damned. God is faithful to all of His promises. Consequently, in 2004 God has sent strong delusion regarding amending the Constitution of the United States to protect the Union of Marriage. Man's law cannot protect the Union of Marriage. The Union of Marriage can only be protected by the fear of God and people hearkening to the commandments of God. Everything else comes short. The Church has failed to teach people the word of God precept on precept, precept on precept, line upon line, line upon line, here a little and there a little. The debate regarding amending the Constitution of the United States to protect the Union of Marriage is a delusion sent from God.

In 2004, before the presidential election, many allowed their feelings and emotions to control them because they were involved in the debate. This was understandable because people who love God know that the institution of marriage is an honorable institution established by God between a man and a woman. We also know according to the scriptures, when man lies with man, it is an abomination unto God. Moreover, the scriptures explain how women would engage in conduct against nature and consequently, God gave these individuals up to uncleanness through the lusts of their own hearts, to dishonor their bodies between themselves. We must understand God's principles. God has given them up unto vile affections and reprobate minds to do those things, which are not convenient, like God gave others who are filled with all unrighteousness. We must understand God's principles as outlined in Roman Chapter one and two and work to lead these people to repentance as we do for the fornicators, backbiters, and others.

We must be sober in all things; if we are not sober, we will allow these debates to become the center of our actions. We must remember that this sin is caused by the **lusts of their own hearts and they dishonor their own bodies between themselves.** (Romans 1:24) Therefore, if individuals' personal conduct between themselves becomes the center of our actions, we will fail to understand the charge that God has given us. Now some think we must protect the institution of marriage with an amendment to the Constitution of the United States. Personally, I would like to see man's law, reflect God's law. However, in some instances, this is not a reality. Again, an amendment to the Constitution of the United States will not protect the troubled institution of marriage; people must fear God and hearken to His commandments.

They must learn to fear God from the precepts of God; marriage counseling is not enough. We must teach them when they are young and reinforce the teaching by examples.

Let us reason together. America is a democratic federal republic. As a republic and representative democracy, the people chose directly or indirectly who will represent them. There are primarily two parties. However there are not two Gods, one for the Democrats and one for the Republicans. God forbid. America is not the kingdom of God; moreover, America is no longer a nation under God. Today, **America is a nation of the world**. Listen. **Christians are not of the world.** Jesus prayed to the Father for Christians not to be taken out of the world, however to keep them from evil. (John 17:14-15)

Christians must reach and teach more people to observe all things that Jesus commanded us; this is our first work. Therefore, when the people of God are strengthened, the Spirit of Truth will guide them and then God's people will elect leaders that are willing to hearken to the word of God. God gave us the charge to teach all nations to observe all things that Jesus commanded us and God has given us a gauge regarding the things he hates.

"Nevertheless the foundation of God standeth sure, having this seal, the Lord knoweth them that are His. And let every one that nameth the name of Christ depart from iniquity. But in a great house there are not only vessels of gold and of silver, but also of wood and of earth; and some to honor, and some to dishonor." (2 Timothy 2:19-20)

God is merciful and God does not want us to be consumed. Therefore, God has sent His Holy Spirit as a fuller soap and a refiner fire to purify and purge us as gold and silver (Malachi 3:3) 2 Timothy 2:21 says, "If a man therefore purge himself from these, he shall be a vessel unto honour, sanctified, and meet for the master's use, and prepared unto every good work."

I pray that the Holy Spirit will give the ones who love truth, wisdom, knowledge and self-control and I pray they will use the gauge that God has given us. The gauge of God is in Proverbs 6:16-19. These six things doth the Lord hate: yea, seven are an abomination unto him: A proud look, a lying tongue, and hands that shed innocent blood, An heart that deviseth wicked imaginations, feet that be swift in running to mischief, A false witness that speaketh lies, and he that soweth discord among brethren.

United States Executive Branch of Government Does the Things that God Hates

People who love God must carefully examine what the word of God says. What does God's gauge reads? God has brought truth out of the earth for us. If we truly love God, we would take time out and discover truth and not lean unto our own misunderstanding, and then provide good counsel to God's people. I love truth; the Spirit of Truth has clearly shown that the leaders in the United States Executive Branch of Government are at 100% in respect to doing the things that God hates.

(1) A proud look

(2) A lying tongue

(3) Hands that shed innocent blood

(4) An heart that deviseth wicked imaginations

(5) Feet that be swift in running to mischief

(6) A false witness that speaketh lies

(7) He that soweth discord among brethren.

According to truth, these leaders of the United States are guilty of doing all of these things. In Jeremiah chapter nine, Jeremiah can be described as a broken hearted prophet because he clearly understood the state of the nation and the impending retribution. Today, I share the same concerns about God's people in the United States of America. Ponder these thoughts. "Oh that I had in the wilderness a lodging place of wayfaring men; that I might leave my people, and go from them! For they be all adulterers, an assembly of treacherous men. And they <u>bend their tongues</u> like <u>their bow for lies</u>: but <u>they are not valiant for the truth</u> upon the earth; for <u>they proceed from evil to evil</u>, and <u>they know not me</u>, saith the Lord... And <u>they will deceive every one his neighbour,</u> and **will not speak the truth**: they have taught **their tongue to speak lies,** and weary themselves to commit iniquity. **Thine habitation is in the midst of deceit; through deceit they refuse to know me, saith the Lord**. ... <u>Shall I not visit them for these things</u>? Saith the Lord: **<u>shall not my soul be avenged for such a nation as this?</u>"** (Jeremiah 9:1-9)

Let us continue to read God's gauge. There are different levels of sin. Here are three: (1) when individuals dishonor their bodies between themselves (2) when man transgresses against others and (3) Blasphemes against the Holy Ghost. However, Satan has been quite effective in diverting the attention of many from the transgression of man against others; the things that **GOD hates.** We must not be deceived and get caught up in feelings and emotions concerning man's laws or the absent thereof.

Moreover, feelings and emotions can blind us and then we fall into Satan's trap and overlook man's transgressions against other men, i.e. rush to shed innocent blood, discrimination, and a false witness. This blindness causes people to focus more on individuals dishonoring their bodies between themselves and not seeing the other things that God hates. We must remember man's law cannot change God's law. Same sex unions do not qualify for God's institution of marriage, for it is not "what man joins together," it is what God joins together, let not man put asunder. Preach the word. **Let us heed to this counsel from God and do the first work.**

Judgment is in the land. Truth has sprung up out of the earth, and righteousness is looking down from heaven. Now many leaders are faced with the crown of pride. Some of those leaders are God's people; some hold the

107

current administration of the government of United States in high esteem. Some will not repent, but they will hold onto what they first believed. They will refuse to discover the truth and will not use the gauge that God has given us. In their hearts they know that they are holding on to lies; nevertheless, because of their pride they will continue to mislead God's people. Woe unto the crown of pride.

Consequently, the Bride of Christ has fallen and she has received bruises on her backsides. God wants His Bride healed, without wrinkle, spot, blemish or any such thing. This is the water of God's words; moreover, the word of God has been tempered with the love of God. I pray that the leaders of God's people will wake up from the spirit of deep sleep and receive the Spirit of Truth. Then embrace truth, repent, and go forth to strengthen God's people.

The Bride of Christ was impacted by these feelings and emotions at all levels, from their local pastors to men and women of God on programs aired on TBN, Daystar, TCC, WORD, BYU, and other cable channels. Feelings and emotions cause conflicting messages and this creates confusion. The program that aired on July 22, 2004 reached millions of people throughout the United States and around the world. After this program was aired, God showed me that the Bride of Christ was knocked down off of her feet and she has been wounded.

I am a prophet of God; the Holy Spirit showed me this. The Bride of Christ was knocked off her feet because of some of God's ministers have erred and allowed their feelings and emotions to affect their messages. Moreover, they have failed to discover the truth regarding things that God hates, lend to their own misunderstanding, failed to allow the Holy Spirit to teach them and to order their footsteps. Consequently, the Bride of Christ was in a state of confusion and she fell onto the ground like a confused person. "A house divided cannot stand."

This is a complex problem. The leadership of the United States of America is not within the counsel of God. The mystery of iniquity is at work; Satan has all power and signs and lying wonders for the ones who do not have

108

love for the truth. Some use for doctrines the commandments of men instead of the word of God. Moreover, God has sent strong delusions. Feelings and emotions are controlling many of God's leaders; consequently, the Bride of Christ is wounded.

I conveyed this message to several principle players that have an impact in reaching Christians throughout the United States. But, they elected not to use the gauge that God has given us. However, they focused on the issue of same sex marriage and abortion. In respect to abortion, they have failed to address the "base sin," sex between a male and a female who are not married to one another. Consequently, these religious leaders became scribes and Pharisees of 2004, in effect declaring the Republican Party, the Christian's Party of Choice.

Moreover, the **doctrine of men** has removed the two top echelons that Christ gave us to effect the edification process of the Body of Christ, the Apostles and Prophets. These two echelons were removed by the philosophy of men and not by the word of God. **God forbid.**

Nevertheless, we have a merciful God. God is looking down on us as He did when He looked down at the people in the great City of Nineveh. First we must repent, then do the first work, effect the edification process as outlined in Ephesians 4:11-16. Then we can work to ensure that the Bride of Christ is healed and ready for the marriage. The Bride of Christ is not ready for warfare because we, the called, the chosen, and the faithful, have failed to use all of our gifts in love to effect the edification process. Therefore, we must repent and return to the first work. We must preach the gospel of Jesus Christ to all creatures throughout the world and ensure that His lambs, His sheep, and his sheep (pastors and teachers) are properly fed the gospel of our Lord and Saviour Jesus Christ.

We must work to remove the broken glass. Therefore, the called, the chosen, and the faithful must work together and get rid of all commandments of men, traditions that are contrary to the word of God that are being taught to the body of Christ for doctrines. It is imperative that we work to this end because we are connected unto one another; there is only one body of Christ. Therefore, we must repent and turn from our wicked ways and pray and seek the face of God and God will see us repenting and God will heal our land.

II Chronicles 2:14 says, "If my people, which are called by my name, shall humble themselves, and pray, and seek my face, and turn from their wicked ways; then will I hear from heaven, and will forgive their sin, and will heal their land."

In Malachi chapter three, God explains to Christian, that he wants us to be refined as gold and as silver and offer him an offering in righteousness. He promises to come near to us in judgment and he would be a swift witness against the following:

(1) Sorcerers

(2) The adulterers

(3) The false swears

(4) Those that oppress the hireling in his wages (This includes the hireling within the United States and the ones employed through out sourcing.)

(5) Those that oppress the widow and the fatherless

(6) Those that turn aside the stranger from his right

(7) Those that do not fear God

God wants to heal America. However, we must learn to fear God from his precepts and not from the precepts of men. Therefore, the people who love God in America must love truth more than they love the things in the world. We must demand of our leaders who we elect to always operate in the truth. The end result, we will be established in righteousness. Then terror will not come near us, we will experience peace as the river and our righteousness will be as the waves of the sea, and God, the creator of the heavens and the earth, will show us how to profit.

110

Chapter Eight
Records of Communications
Revealing the Revelations from God
To President Bush and Others

This chapter contains copies of communications that were sent to or received from individuals regarding the warnings that God has given me. Several of these letters were changed to correct grammatical errors, however the messages are have not been altered in any way. I am one of God's prophets. God has given me this calling. God has given me the responsibility to deliver His message to His people. I cannot make people change their mind. However, I pray that the wicked would repent of their wickedness so they can be saved.

In October 2001, after I sent out copies of the book, "America! America! A Checkup For The Body of Christ, The Church" to the President of the United States and leaders around the nation, through the Holy Spirit, God showed me a lion watching me. In a dream, I was throwing rocks to keep the lion at bay. The lion looked very healthy at that time. The interpretation is as follows. The lion was the government of the United States and the rocks were the books that I was sending out that contained the message from God.

Besides seeing the lion in October 2001, on or about January 23, 2005, I had another dream about this lion. However, the lion was not watching me, I was watching the lion. I watched the lion as he watched over people as if he was performing sentinel duty. The lion did not appear healthy and looked as if it was suffering from battle fatigue. I had this dream during the week of an election in Iraq. The interpretation is as follows. The United States government (military) was suffering from battle fatigue as they monitored the election process in Iraq. God continues to reveal some of His secrets to me, I pray that the people who want to do what is right in the sight of God will ensure that this message go forth and adhere to this warning.

Some of these communications in this chapter appear to be very critical of the actions of the Government of the United States. The reason they are critical is because this government is out of the counsel of God. These communications were not politically inspired. These communications are the inspired word of the Holy Spirit. I do not have anything personal to gain from these communications. I love America, but I love God more. Therefore, I must do what God wants me to do. God loves the people in America too; God does not want to destroy this land. But God will destroy this land if we do not repent and hearken to His commandments.

Before people hearken to the commandments of God, they first must learn to fear Him. To this end, Chapter 10 of this book, "Learning to Fear God," is a must reading. Besides Chapter 10, we have included an appendix to this book, "Review of the History of the Kings of Israel and Judah: Learning to Fear God." This review is very important. "For whatsoever things were written aforetime, that we through patience and comfort of the scriptures might have hope. (Romans 15:4) It is very important for Christians to understand that God cast his chosen people from his sight because of their sin; God changes not. If we continue in sin, God will use a declared and published standard to bring destruction to this land. God established a standard for Babylon and her images. Jeremiah chapters 50 and 51 explain this standard. This standard also applies for the Daughter of Babylon that is mention in Isaiah chapter 47 and MYSTERY, BABYLON THE GREAT, THE MOTHER OF HAROLOTS AND ABOMINATIONS OF THE EARTH. (Revelation chapter 17) <u>You are encouraged to read Chapter 10 and Appendix 1 to this book carefully.</u>

112

ELMORE RICHMOND JR.

A PROPHET OF GOD
3856 W. MARTIN LUTHER KING JR., BLVD. SUITE 102
LOS ANGELES, CALIFORNIA 90008
(323) 239-4564, FAX (323) 294-7368, EMAIL pwrpack@pacbell.net

October 6, 2001

President George W. Bush
The White House
Washington, D. C. 20500

Dear Mr. President:

I am a Prophet of God. The prayers of God's people have been answered. We have asked for answers and a peaceful solution to this crisis. God has given me His word to give to you, other leaders, and His people around the world. Isaiah, Chapter 11 explains the role that God has given me in this crisis. I pray that you will receive this message because the consequences are too grave, if you should rush to shed innocence blood.

Mr. President, God revealed to me this destruction and the United States preparing for war on September 10, 2001. Moreover, 30 days prior, God gave me an assignment to prepare the attached work. I told three people about this revelation on September 10, 2001. They included two military retirees (one of the retirees was a colonel) and I also told my bride to be. Several people can verify my work on the Righteousness of God, 30 days prior to the destruction of the World Trade Center.

The message that God wants me to give you is not smooth to your ears; however, it is the word of God. The terrorism that we are experiencing in America is the fruit of the leaders of the United States trust in oppression and perverseness. Isaiah 30:12-13 explains why the World Trade Center was destroyed. "(12) Wherefore thus saith the Holy one of Israel, because ye despise this word, and trust in oppression and perverseness and stay thereon: (13) Therefore this iniquity shall be to you as a breach ready to fall, swelling out in a high wall, whose breaking cometh suddenly at an instant." This was first written for Judah; however, God's righteousness is forever. Therefore, the same standard applies to America today for trusting in oppression and perverseness. Isaiah 9:16 states, "For the leaders of His people cause them to err; and they that led of them are destroyed." The leaders of America are also responsible for the death of these

113

people who were killed on September 11, 2001. It is imperative that we understand the part we have played in this destruction and take action to ensure that it never happens again.

We cannot win this war with our military might, because we created the bad fruit. Some have ripened, some have not ripened. And the more military might we employ, the more bad seeds we will plant. Page 40 of the attached book outlines specific commands that you must follow to secure this land and to help bring about peace to the world. Below is a quote from the word of God that God gave to me.

FOR PRESIDENT BUSH EYES ONLY

"Recall your planes, ships, and My people. Remove all unjust sanctions against countries around the world. Rewrite your trade agreements to ensure that they are fair to the workers. End your eagerness to shed innocent blood. Seek out the bad fruit that has now ripened. Apply just laws to all suspects that are still alive, that were involved in the planning and operation of the terrorist attack on America. Do not prosecute the innocent. Bad fruits that have not ripened treat them with care, love, and understanding, because you helped create them. Change your hearts and take on a new resolve to end oppression and perverseness. Thus, you will end the terrorism in America if you turn to me. … If my people, which are called by my name, shall humble themselves, and pray, and seek my face, and turn from their wicked ways; then will I hear from heaven, and will forgive their sin, and will heal their land."

These are not my words, but this is the word of God. Nevertheless, I understand His reasons for giving you each of these commands. Let's discuss the reason he gave the command "Recall your planes, ships, and My people." Millions of God's people in Afghanistan are being terrorized by the threats of war by the United States. Thousands will die if the United States maintains this act of terrorism. Mr. President, we are only adding sin to sin. God looks at the 300 millions dollar efforts, your form of righteousness, as filthy rags. Turn to God. The United States cannot win this war with military might. We must understand that we have created this bad fruit by our trust in oppression and perverseness instead of taking counsel from God. **Mr. President, you do not understand - you are battling with God.**

Mr. President, we cannot win this war by supporting the northern forces in Afghanistan as they fight Taliban and the other measures that you have outlined. We have created far too much bad fruit around the world to resolve this problem using this strategy. It will only make matters worse and more bad seeds will be planted. However, if we humble ourselves, turn to God, and change our wicked ways, we will cutoff the nutriment that gives life to terrorism.

Mr. President, now hear this! "Come ye near unto me, hear ye this: I have not spoken in secret from the beginning; from the time that it was, there am I: and now the Lord God, and His Spirit, hath sent me. Thus saith the Lord, thy Redeemer, the Holy One of Israel, I am the Lord Thy God which teacheth thee to profit, which leadeth thee by the way that thou shouldest go. O that thou hadst hearkened to my commandments then had thy peace been as a river, and thy righteousness as the waves of the sea." (Isaiah 48:16-18) "In righteousness shalt thou be established: thou shalt be far from oppression; for thou shalt not fear; and from terror; for it shall not come near thee. (Isaiah 54:14) Mr. President, turn to God, seek his counsel, and these promises will become a reality in America.

I pray that you do not take this communication lightly. I have shared a copy of this work with the following Servants of God: (1) Dr. Billy Graham (2) Dr. Paul Crouch (3) Dr. Oral Roberts (4) Pastor Charles Blake, Dr. Robert Schuller, and Elder Robert Richmond. Mr. President, if you fail to take counsel of God, there will be nowhere for you and other leaders to run. I pray that you will make the correct decision.

Mr. President, I have a divine intelligence-gathering network with God. God has been revealing His secrets with me for years, however, until now I had not accepted the call as one of His Prophets. God is using me as His mouthpiece to smite the earth with the rod of my mouth, and with the breath of my lips to slay the wicked. (See Isaiah Chapter 11.)

FOR PRESIDENT BUSH'S EYES ONLY

President Bush, the United States is not walking within the counsel of God. Isaiah Chapter 30 says, " (1) Woe to the rebellious children, saith the Lord, that take counsel, but not of me; and that cover with a covering, but not of my spirit, that they may add sin to sin, (2) That walk to go down into Egypt, and have not asked at my mouth; to strengthen themselves in the strength of Pharaoh, and to trust in the shadow of Egypt! (3) Therefore shall the strength of Pharaoh be your shame, and the trust in the shadow of Egypt your confusion." Today may nations get their strength from the Government of the United States and they trust in the shadow of the United States. Consequently, today the world is in a state of confusion. We are leading the world in the path of destruction.

Mr. President if your goal is to bring an end to terrorism, take counsel of God and follow His instructions. If you should adhere to the word of God, you will be able to bring an end to terrorism, and then stimulate economic growth. Moreover, your example of strong leadership in the sight of God will return safety back to our schools in America. Besides, these positive factors, nations at war around the world will seek peace. Truly, God will heal this land.

Mr. President, I am an American. I will continue to fight for the flag for which it stands, one nation, under God... God has chosen me to be his mouthpiece. I pray that America will continue to prosper. However, I realize for this to occur, we must change and seek counsel of God. There are some painful words contained in this letter. Nevertheless, they are from God. I am not an enemy of America for I am an American, an American fighting man. However, I know how to best serve God, my country and people around the world. Therefore, I must obey the commands of God.

Praying that America's Leaders would turn to God,

Elmore Richmond Jr.
A Prophet of God

Enclosure: Manuscript "America! America! - A Checkup For The Body of Christ The Church"

Elmore Richmond Jr.
A Prophet of God in the Name of Jesus Christ
3856 W. Martin Luther King Jr. Blvd., Suite 102
Los Angeles, California 90008
(323) 294-4564, FAX (323) 294-7368, E-mail pwrpack@pacbell.net

AMERICA'S LEADERS NEED TO SEEK THE COUNSEL OF GOD

October 8, 2001

Dear Servant of God:

I am a Servant of God and one of God's Prophets. God has given me His word to give to you, other leaders, and His people around the world. Isaiah, Chapter 11 explains the role that God has given me in this crisis. God revealed to me this destruction and the United States preparing for war on September 10, 2001. Moreover, 30 days prior, God gave me an assignment to prepare the attached work. I told three people about this revelation on September 10, 2001. They included two military retirees (one of the retirees was a colonel) and I also told my bride to be. Several people can verify my work on the Righteousness of God, 30 days prior to the destruction of the World Trade Center.

After you read the word of God contained herein, you will make the most important decision in your life as a Servant of God. You will decide if you are going to serve the Lord or are you going to yield to the desires of men. Men who are leaders of this nation, a nation that we all love. However, their desires are for you to speak smooth things, not the right things, and to prophesy deceits.

The message that God wants me to give you is not smooth to your ears; however, it is the word of God. The United States is currently out of step with the righteousness of God. We have made a serious mistake. We have been focusing on salvation and not giving enough attention to the righteousness of God. The following scriptures best describe the reasons for our failure to have a greater Christian influence on the leaders and our society. Isaiah 56: 10 - 12 states, " (10) His watchmen are blind: they are all ignorant, they are all dumb dogs, they cannot bark; sleeping, lying down, loving to slumber. (11) Yea, they are greedy dogs which can never have enough, and they are shepherds that cannot understand; they all look to their own way, every one for his gain, from his quarter. (12) Come ye, say they, I will fetch wine, and we will fill ourselves with

117

strong drink; and tomorrow shall be as this day and much more abundant." Isaiah 57:1 says, the righteous perisheth, and no man layeth it to heart: and merciful men are taken away, none considering that the righteous is taken away from the evil to come.

The terrorism that we are experiencing in America is the fruit of the leaders of the United States trust in oppression and perverseness. Isaiah 30:12-13 explains why the World Trade Center was destroyed. "(12) Wherefore thus saith the Holy one of Israel, because ye despise this word, and trust in oppression and perverseness and stay thereon: (13) Therefore this iniquity shall be to you as a breach ready to fall, swelling out in a high wall, whose breaking cometh suddenly at an instant." This was first written for Judah; however, God's righteousness is forever. Therefore, the same standard applies to America today for trusting in oppression and perverseness. Isaiah 9:16 states, "For the leaders of His people cause them to err; and they that led of them are destroyed." The leaders of America are also responsible for the death of these people who were killed on September 11, 2001. It is imperative that we understand the part we have played in this destruction and take action to ensure that it never happens again.

We cannot win this war with our military might, because we created the bad fruit. Some have ripened, some have not ripened, and the more military might we employ, the more bad seeds we will plant. Page 40 of the attached book outlines specific commands that we must follow to secure this land and to help bring about peace to the world. Below is a quote from the word of God that God gave to me.

"Recall your planes, ships, and My people. Remove all unjust sanctions against countries around the world. Rewrite your trade agreements to ensure that they are fair to the workers. End your eagerness to shed innocent blood. Seek out the bad fruit that has now ripened. Apply just laws to all suspects that are still alive, that were involved in the planning and operation of the terrorists attack on America. Do not prosecute the innocent. Bad fruit that has not ripened treat with care, love, and understanding, because you helped create them. Change your hearts and take on a new resolve to end oppression and perverseness. Thus, you will end the terrorism in America if you turn to me. ... If my people, which are called by my name, shall humble themselves, and pray, and seek my face, and turn from their wicked ways; then will I hear from heaven, and will forgive their sin, and will heal their land."

I ask that you take time out now and read "America! America! A Checkup For The Body Of Christ The Church." After you read this work, pray and God will reveal to you the action you should take.

May God Bless You,

Elmore Richmond Jr.
A Prophet of God in the Name of Jesus Christ

ELMORE RICHMOND JR.
A PROPHET OF GOD
3856 W. MARTIN LUTHER KING JR., BLVD. SUITE 102
LOS ANGELES, CALIFORNIA 90008
(323) 239-4564, FAX (323) 294-7368, EMAIL pwrpack@pacbell.net

October 26, 2001

President George W. Bush
The White House
Washington, D. C. 20500

Dear Mr. President:

I am a Prophet of God. I wrote you twenty days ago as God directed me.
However, you have failed to adhere to the word of God. God has commanded me
to write you again. Mr. President, you continue to add sin onto sin. God knows
every one of them. Even the ones that you classify as Top Secret, and God has
revealed some of those secrets to me. Mr. President, if you do not change this
destructive path, terror will continue to visit America. Moreover, America will
experience a plague of national disasters at a level that this nation has not
experienced in its short 200 year history. Many lives will be lost and fear will
continue within the borders of the United States. However, if you should hearken
to the word of God, terror will not come near this nation, and America's peace
will be as a river, and nation's righteousness will be as the waves of the sea.

Mr. President, I am praying that you do not take this communication lightly. I
have enclosed a copy of the letter that I sent you on October 6, 2000. I pray that
this communication will reach your hands. May God have mercy on the
individual that will thwart this communication.

Praying for America's Leaders that they turn to God.

Sincerely yours,

Elmore Richmond Jr.
A Prophet of God in the name of Jesus Christ

Enclosure:
Letter Dated October 6, 2001

ELMORE RICHMOND JR.
A PROPHET OF GOD
3856 W. MARTIN LUTHER KING JR., BLVD. SUITE 102
LOS ANGELES, CALIFORNIA 90008
(323) 239-4564, FAX (323) 294-7368, EMAIL pwrpack@pacbell.net

November 3, 2001

President George W. Bush
The White House
Washington, D. C. 20500

Dear Mr. President:

I am a Prophet of God. On October 6, I sent you a message from God to no avail. Today, I am providing you revelations that God has given me. Please take time and review these revelations of coming events regarding the war in Afghanistan. These revelations are being sent to you so you will know that I am truly a Prophet of God in the name of our Lord and Savior Jesus Christ.

President Bush, please turn and receive the counsel of God.

Sincerely yours,

Elmore Richmond Jr.
Prophet of God
In the Name of Jesus Christ

Enclosure: Summation of Visions Regarding Afghanistan

VISIONS ON NOVEMBER 3, 2001
REGARDING THE WAR ON AFGHANISTAN

On the morning of November 3, 2001, I woke up at 4:45 A.M. after having four visions. I did not wake up between each vision. Below you will find a summation of each of the visions.

Vision I

It was as if I was watching a movie, however it was not a movie. I was watching a situation whereby an individual was in custody and being guarded by two individuals. These guards went into another room. The individual in custody was in what appeared to be an iron cell, however, you could not see through the walls of the cell. It had heavy doors as if it was a vault. Nevertheless, the guards failed to secure the cell. I noticed the cell door opening, but, it was not a man who came out of the door. It was some type of unit that was heavily armored. A man could have been inside of the unit. Next, I noticed one of the guards as he came out of the other room, immediately; this armored unit overpowered and took control of the guard. This was the conclusion of this vision.

Vision II

I observed two birds; they were removing signs from this house. However, this was not a small birdhouse, but a house built for humans. Besides removing signs, they were removing concrete stoppers from the driveway. It appears as if they had just gained possession to this property. More birds came in and it appeared as if they were making resident and guarding the property. This was the conclusion of this vision.

Vision III

Immediately after the vision about the birds, I saw military planes taking to the sky. These planes were not from the United States or England. I noticed one of the planes appeared to have a red tail as the planes took control of the sky. This was the conclusion of this vision.

ELMORE RICHMOND JR.
A PROPHET OF GOD
600 N. Hays Avenue
Jackson, Tennessee 38301
731-421-9066

May 22, 2002

President George W. Bush
The White House
Washington, D. C. 20500

Dear Mr. President:

I am a Prophet of God. I wrote you several times in the past. However, you have failed to adhere to the word of God. God has commanded me to write you again. Mr. President, your directives continue to add sin onto sin. Mr. President, listen closely, God just revealed to me in a vision destruction on a military base. I believe the base located within the United States.

The vision

I observed military planes on display. There was no security around these planes. I observed military people in civilian clothing just having fun; they were young men. Then I noticed some youth playing in another area. I warned the overseer that there was a safety hazard in the area the youth were playing. (This hazard was restricted to where the youth were playing.) Next I noticed a family moving in what appeared to be an apartment. I went inside of the apartment. Then, I heard much commotion outside. After hearing the commotion, I went out side. I saw a man looking out of a window of what appeared to be a military barrack, he said, "They have done it again." Next, I saw many frightened people. The people appeared to be mostly military men, although they were not dressed in military clothing. It appeared they had to run for cover, quickly. Then, I noticed what appeared to be fallout from a blast or fire falling from the sky.

Mr. President, I am praying that you do not take this communication lightly. Mr. Bush, God wants you to know that if we do not change our current course of action, this nation will be faced with calamity after calamity. I pray that this communication will reach your hands. May God have mercy of the individual that will thwart this communication.

Praying for America's Leaders that they turn to God.

Sincerely yours,

Elmore Richmond Jr.
A Prophet of God in the name of Jesus Christ

123

ELMORE RICHMOND JR.
A PROPHET OF GOD
600 N. Hays Avenue
Jackson, Tennessee 38301

September 3, 2002

President George W. Bush
The White House
Washington, D. C. 20500

Dear Mr. President:

On September 2, 2002, God gave another vision to me regarding our military. In the vision, I was on a military base and it appeared to me that the troops on the base were being placed on an alert; I noticed some with their deployment bags. Moreover, I noticed the aircraft being placed in an alert status. Then I woke up. Mr. President, this was not a dream because it was as if I was actually on the military base.

Besides the vision on September 2, 2002, during the week of August 25, 2002, I had two other visions regarding our military. On August 25, 2002, I had a vision that I was on a military base; I believe that the base was in Arizona. Nevertheless, in vision, I saw a military man who was under stress and he went on a rampage destroying property. I woke up immediately after the vision. On August 27, 2002, I had another vision, again I was on a military base, and troops were fighting among themselves. They were not engaged in wartime combat fighting with military weapons, however, there were fights. Again, immediately after the vision I woke up.

After these two visions during the week of August 25, 2002, I asked God to explain to me why did the Holy Spirit bring these matters regarding the military to my attention. After receiving the revelations, I drafted a letter to you. However, God wanted me to wait before dispatching the letter because He had something else to show me. Then of course as I first mentioned on September 2, 2002, God gave me another vision.

Mr. President, I have shared several visions with you before. As I have pointed out to you, God showed me the destruction of the World Trade Center

124

and our preparation for war on September 10, 2001. I have three witnesses, they are (1) Willie Mays, (E-9, U. S. Navy Retired) (2) Chuck Howell, (E-7, USAF Retired) and Janice Carter. I told these three on September 10, 2001 what God had revealed to me. They live in Los Angeles and in the surrounding area.

There is a big difference between the vision of September 10, 2001 and the most recent vision regarding our military preparation for war. Last year in the vision the preparation for war was after provocation. This year however, there is no provocation, however, there are conflicts from within. Mr. President, I pray that you will take the following actions and assess the status of readiness of our military force and measure the impact of the various stress factors.

Drawing on my military experience, I clearly understand what is happening on our military bases and within the military structure, at this time. Many of our troops are under undue stress in the military and it is impacting mission accomplishments and it will worsen if these stress factors are not addressed now. Here are some of the factors and impacts: (1) Many are being over worked. (2) Some troops are violating military standards. However, in many cases, first line supervisors are not reporting these infractions to their commanding officers. (3) Some commanders have relaxed their standards on taking disciplinary actions on infractions they would normally take severe actions. (Note: Taking more disciplinary actions will not resolve these problems.) (4) Some troops are concerned about the duration of the war and the course that it will take. (5) The affects on public opinions on the troops (6) The affects of the Executive Branch and Congress' failure to reach a unified direction on the war on terror regarding the issue of Iraq. (7) The appearance of conflict within the Executive Branch on the issue of a war with Iraq. (8) Extended duty for reservists. (9) Reduction in pay for some of the reservists and (10) Normal daily routine stress factors.

To assess the status of readiness of our military force and to measure the impact of various stress factors should be done immediately. This could be done through a rapid assessment of each military base. The assessment should include a comparison analysis of the following area (1) Number of Letter of Counseling (2) Letter of Reprimands (3) Articles 15's (4) Safety incidents on base (5) Complaints formal and informal (6) Racial incidents (7) Hate crime on base and off base (8) Domestic incidents (9) Auto accidents (10) Sick calls (11) Fights on base (12) Reports of destruction of government property (13) Substance Abuse and (14) Complaints from troops that work the flight lines and aircraft maintenance. (Note: Commanders and maintenance division chiefs must listen closely to the informal complaints from the younger troops that work in these positions. People who work the line and repair the planes know the problems and they can prevent many mishaps when they have real opportunity to express their concerns and when their concerns are addressed. Use your experts at the Department of Defense Equal Opportunity Management Institute to study this problem and for specific recommendations.

The recent killings at Fort Bragg are just a mirror of what is to come. Lessons learned will show that there were a number of indicators prior to these incidents; however supervisors and commanders failed to address them. Often leaders make a common mistake by focusing on mission accomplishment and fail to take care of the needs of their people. The key is to address the small concerns; often addressing concerns when they are small will prevent major future problems. The failure to address small concerns was one of the problems that we experience in the 1960's and early 1970's throughout the military. These failures had negative impacts on mission accomplishments.

The last time that I wrote you was on May 22, 2002. On May 22, 2002, I did not share this in the communication with you, however, while I was wide-awake, I closed my eyes and you flashed before me. And each time you flashed before me I saw a massive number of people protesting. Later on that day, I learned of your trip to Europe. Although I did not share this information with you in the communication, I did share with you a vision that God gave me, but I misinterpreted some key aspects of the vision. Consequently, I thought that everything that observed in the vision all happened on a military base, however, the details in the vision took me away from the base to an apartment near Los Angeles. Moreover, another aspect of the vision that I did not mention was the bridge. I saw these men underneath what appeared to be an incomplete bridge; this puzzled me. Now I know that it was the bridge that was destroyed in Interstate 40.

This year God revealed to me the fires and floods that confronted us here in the United States. A month ago God revealed to me the floods in Europe and the surrounding area. I even saw the dam break in India before it occurred. These revelations keep coming.

Mr. President in respect to the War on Terrorism, we cannot win that war with our military might. As I have explained to you in the past, God said if we hearken to His commandments, He would give us peace as a river, righteousness as the waves of the sea, and terror would not come near us. I wrote you regarding this matter on October 6, 2001. However, I realize that it never reached your hands because of the error of one of your staffers. While I was in the military, I

126

advised commanders at every level regarding difficult problems, tough calls. They heard my voice even when what I had to say was unpopular. Nevertheless, I never steered any of them wrong. Mr. President, there is a non military approach to returning peace back to the Middle East and ending the threats of terrorism within the United States and our allies around the world. I know the answers to these problems. I believe this is one of the reasons God has called me out to do this work.

Mr. President, in the book of Amos, chapter 3, verses 6-7 says: "Shall a trumpet be blown in the city, and the people not be afraid? Shall there be evil in a city, and the Lord hath not done it? Surely the Lord God will do nothing, but He revealeth His secret unto his servants the prophets." Although you and your staffers may not believe that God's word is true, nevertheless, I am a living witness, and I am one of God's Prophets. May God bless you, the United States of America, and nations around the world.

Sincerely yours,

Elmore Richmond Jr.
A Prophet of God in the name of Jesus Christ

ELMORE RICHMOND JR.
A PROPHET OF GOD
P. O. Box 7037
Jackson, Tennessee 38302

December 2, 2002

President George W. Bush
The White House
Washington, D. C. 20500

Dear Mr. President:

I am writing you again to let you know that we will continue to experience calamity after calamity, until we adhere to the counsel of God. God revealed to me the destructive winds that we just experienced here in America several weeks prior to the destruction. On Sunday, November 10, God revealed to me floods that will impact this country. On this morning December 2, 2002, God revealed to me again the floods that will impact this country. They will happen shortly. There will be many homes and facilities damaged in these floods. In many places water will be at the house top level. Besides the revelations regarding the floods, God revealed to me the failed missile attack on the airliner the day before it occurred. Moreover, God gave me an opportunity to look at our military. After examining the vision; I concluded that our military forces additional duties are having a negative impact on them accomplishing their primary duties.

Mr. President, these acts of nature that we are experiencing are only examples of what we will experience if we continue to place our trust in oppression and perverseness and continue to study war. Moreover a war on Iraq is not the answer to ending terrorism. We must address root causes to address terrorism. However, this will require America to look at itself. When we earnestly do that then we will realize the impact of some of our oppressive and perverse policies. Moreover, weapons of mass destruction are not the root causes.

In Isaiah, Chapter 30, the Word of God continues to warn His people of the destruction to come. Starting at verse 9, "That this is a rebellious people, lying people, children that will not hear the law of the Lord. (10) Which say to the seers, See not; and to the prophets, Prophesy not unto us right things, speak unto us smooth things, prophesy deceits: (11) Get you out of the way, turn aside out of the path, cause the Holy One of Israel to cease from before us. (12) Wherefore thus saith the Holy One of Israel, because ye despise this word, and

128

trust in oppression and perverseness and stay thereon. (13) Therefore this iniquity shall be to you as a breach ready to fall, swelling out in a high wall, whose breaking cometh suddenly at an instant."

The terrorism that we are experiencing in America is the fruit of our trust in oppression and perverseness. **We must understand this.** I have provided you messages from God over the past year to no avail. Mr. President, I love America and I want America to continue to be a strong nation for another two hundred years. However, our current approach that is out of the counsel of God will cause this nation to fall. Mr. President, I ask that you review the past communications that I have sent you; in those communications you will discover what we must do as a nation. I pray that you will adhere to this message. May God Bless America.

Sincerely yours,

Elmore Richmond Jr.
A Prophet of God in the Name of Jesus Christ

ELMORE RICHMOND JR.
A PROPHET OF GOD
P. O. Box 7037
Jackson, Tennessee 38302

December 20, 2002

President George W. Bush
The White House
Washington, D. C. 20500

Dear Mr. President:

Reference my letter December 2, 2002, in that letter I conveyed to you the floods that would impact America. Today we are experiencing those floods. Besides, reflecting on past revelations, on December 15, 2002, God gave me another revelation. In a vision I saw what appeared to be one of our military aircraft, it appeared to be some type of gunship. Nevertheless, the aircraft took what appeared to be provocative actions over a military site. First it flew very low over some unmanned anti-aircraft weapons. Then the military aircraft made another trip over the area as the men on the ground were manning their weapons. After that the vision ended.

Do not rush to shed innocent blood. Jeremiah Chapter 14 and Chapter 23 speaks about false prophets and their actions. However, I am one of God's prophets. I stand in His counsel. Therefore, I speak to you the truth that is designed to turn the United States Government from its evil ways and evil doings. In Isaiah, Chapter 30, the Word of God continues to warn His people of the destruction to come. Starting at verse 9, "That this is a rebellious people, lying people, children that will not hear the law of the Lord. (10) Which say to the seers, See not; and to the prophets, Prophesy not unto us right things, speak unto us smooth things, prophesy deceits: (11) Get you out of the way, turn aside out of the path, cause the Holy One of Israel to cease from before us. (12) Wherefore thus saith the Holy One of Israel, because ye despise this word, and trust in oppression and perverseness and stay thereon. (13) Therefore this iniquity shall be to you as a breach ready to fall, swelling out in a high wall, whose breaking cometh suddenly at an instant."

The terrorism that we are experiencing in America is the fruit of our trust in oppression and perverseness. **We must understand this.** I have provided you messages from God over the past year to no avail. Mr. President, I love

130

America and I want America to continue to be a strong nation for another two hundred years. However, our current approach that is out of the counsel of God will cause this nation to fall. I pray that you will adhere to this message. May God Bless America and protect innocent people around the world.

Sincerely yours,

Elmore Richmond Jr.
A Prophet of God in the Name of Jesus Christ

ELMORE RICHMOND JR.
A PROPHET OF GOD
P. O. Box 7037
Jackson, Tennessee 38302

January 14, 2003

President George W. Bush
The White House
Washington, D. C. 20500

GOD'S FINAL WARNING

Dear Mr. President:

For many years, God has given me visions and revelations and some of them were regarding our military. Over the past year, I have shared some of them with you as God commanded me to do so. Besides sharing the visions, I have shared the revelation that we were not walking in the counsel of God and I provided you with corrective actions as God revealed them to me. Mr. President, the United States has failed to take the corrective actions. Now consequently, God will remove His covering from around the United States' battlements if you do not receive His counsel. God has revealed this to me in several visions and the Holy Spirit led me to the appropriate scriptures.

On January 3, 2003, God revealed to me in a vision that I was on a military base; it was as if I was performing a commander's walk-through inspection of a barrack. I observed the conditions of the barrack; the barrack was in need of many repairs including painting. After the walk-through of the barrack, I stepped outside the barrack's door and I was met with a mass of flies they were all over the place. Then I woke up. During the same night, God gave me another vision. Again I was on a military base and I observed a structure on fire. Then the fire moved to another structure. Then I awoke from the vision. I asked the Holy Spirit to give me the interpretation of these visions. Here is the interpretation. Our nation will suffer financially and consequently, our military will suffer in maintaining its quality of life and will experience much destruction by fire.

On January 5, 2003, I had another vision that I was on a military base and there was another structure on fire. Moreover, on January 9, 2003, I had a dream that I was on a military base and I was retiring. I turned in my military I. D. card,

132

my security badge, and my ex-wife I.D. card. Then I awoke from the dream. In reality I retired from the military on 1 February 1989. (I believe that this retirement signified that this was the last vision regarding our military that God will give me at this time.)   Nevertheless, in the spirit, God has shown me events in the military as if I had a Top Secret Clearance with a need to know. However, I was able to see these things before they happened. This may sound strange to you, but, according to the word of God, the Holy Spirit will show the ones who believe things to come.

Some of these events include the bombing of our barrack in the Mid East, the ambush of our troops in Central America, the crew on our submarine before it hit the Japanese fishing vessel, the terrorist attack on the trade center, our preparation for war, the prison uprising in Afghanistan, and the recent downing of one of our planes over Iraq. Now, I believe that I have completed this assignment and God will remove His covering from the United States Military if we fail to adhere to His counsel and fail to change our current direction.

The Holy Spirit directed me to the book of Jeremiah, Chapter 5. Mr. President, the United States has refused to receive correction. Consequently as in Jeremiah 5:10, our battlements will be taken away because they are not the Lord's. Does this have to come to past? No. However, to prevent it, the United States must turn from our trust in oppression and perverseness and our rush to shed innocent blood. In other words, we must receive and follow the counsel of God.

I am being obedient to the Lord by bringing you the message from the living God. Mr. President, God is real and His laws regarding His righteousness are still in effect. God said that His righteousness is forever. Therefore, we must learn from the history of great nations of the past when they fail to receive the counsel of God. Today, the United States is walking in error by trusting in oppression and perverseness, like Judah did, as it is recorded in Isaiah Chapter 29 and Chapter 30.

In Isaiah, Chapter 30, the Word of God continues to warn His people of the destruction to come. Starting at verse 9, "That this is a rebellious people, lying people, children that will not hear the law of the Lord. (10) Which says to the seers, See not; and to the prophets, Prophesy not unto us right things, speak unto us smooth things, prophesy deceits: (11) Get you out of the way, turn aside out of the path, cause the Holy One of Israel to cease from before us. (12) Wherefore thus saith the Holy One of Israel, because ye despise this word, and trust in oppression and perverseness and stay thereon. (13) Therefore this iniquity shall be to you as a breach ready to fall, swelling out in a high wall, whose breaking cometh suddenly at an instant."

Moreover, God has poured out the spirit of deep sleep and all has been covered throughout the United States. This is the same spirit of deep sleep that was poured out on Judah prior to the doom of Jerusalem. Reference Isaiah 29:10-13. Besides, the spirit of deep sleep, the United States government seeks deep to hide their counsel from the Lord, and their work is in the dark, and they say, Who seeth Us? And who knoweth Us? The CIA and the control of the media help to hide the truth from the people. However, God knows, God uncovers and reveals. Reference Isaiah 29:15.

President Bush, the United States is trusting in oppression and perverseness and many of the efforts of the CIA are counterproductive and are not within the righteousness of God. I pray that you will not deny the facts that some of the behaviors of the CIA and some of the United States' policies have been destructive and have helped to create many of the problems this nation faces today. There have been many great nations to fall because of these same things. We do not have to fall deeper into the same open pit. Turn to Jesus and seek the counsel of God. God will pardon us and lift us up. Mr. President, God knows your concerns about what took place on September 11, 2001. Moreover, God realizes that you do not want it to happen again.

Nevertheless, God wants you to know that this occurred because of the United States' trust in oppression and perverseness. As long as we continue to trust in oppression and perverseness we will continue to experience calamities. The United States' perverse and oppressive policies and our rush to shed innocent blood have killed hundreds of thousand. And today, these policies cause millions to suffer around the world.

Moreover, as recorded in Jeremiah 5:26-28, God says: "For among my people are found wicked men: they lay wait, as he that setteth snares; they set a trap, they catch men. As a cage is full of birds, so are their houses full of deceit: therefore they are become great, and waxen rich. They are waxen fat, they shine: yea, they overpass the deeds of the wicked: they judge not the cause, the cause of the fatherless, yet they prosper; and the right of the needy do they not judge." When we carefully examine the word of God and our actions we can clearly see how this applies to the United States on a daily basis and our "**war on terrorism**".

134

The terrorism that we are experiencing in America is the fruit of our trust in oppression and perverseness. **We must understand this.** Do not rush to shed innocent blood. Jeremiah Chapter 14 and Chapter 23 speak about false prophets and their actions. However, I am one of God's prophets. I stand in His counsel. Therefore, I speak to you the truth that is designed to turn the United States Government from it evil ways and evil doings. I have provided you messages from God over the past year to no avail. Mr. President, I love America and I want America to continue to be a strong nation for another two hundred years. However, our current approach that is out of the counsel of God, our failure to adhere to the counsel of God will cause this nation to suffer financially and our military will suffer. I pray that you will adhere to this message. **Listen carefully, if there is one that executeth judgment, and seeketh the truth; God will pardon the United States. Be that one!**

Sincerely yours,

Elmore Richmond Jr.
A Prophet of God in the Name of Jesus Christ

ELMORE RICHMOND JR.
A PROPHET OF GOD
600 N. Hays Avenue
Jackson, Tennessee 38301

January 21, 2003

Senator Edward Kennedy
317 Russell
Senate Office Building
Washington, D. C. 20510

Dear Senator Kennedy:

This is my first time writing you, however, I have written the President eight times since "9/11" to no avail. I pray that you will listen carefully. God revealed to me the destruction of the World Trade Center before it occurred. I have three witnesses. Moreover, God continues to reveal his secrets to me. Over the past year I have shared some of them with the President. I have included some of those communications in this package for your information and action. Senator Kennedy, some teach that God does not have prophets today; that teaching is erroneous. (Reference Amos 3:6-7.) Senator Kennedy, God has given me revelation after revelation - with the exception of the revelations in His final warning all have come to fruition.

I am writing you to let you know that we will continue to experience calamity after calamity, until we adhere to the counsel of God. The United States is not walking in the counsel of God. Therefore, we are not following God's laws regarding His righteousness. God says His righteousness is forever. This means that the same standards apply regarding His righteousness today as it did 2500 years ago. We have not learned from lessons learned. Consequently, the United States is rushing to shed innocent blood and trusting in oppression and perverseness. Like God warned Judah as recorded in Isaiah Chapter 30, now God has warned the United States.

In Isaiah, Chapter 30, the word of God continues to warn His people of the destruction to come when they place their trust in oppression and perverseness. Isaiah, Chapter 30:9-13 says, "That this is a rebellious people, lying people, children that will not hear the law of the Lord. Which say to the seers, See not; and to the prophets, Prophesy not unto us right things, speak unto us smooth things, prophesy deceits: Get you out of the way, turn aside out of the path, cause the Holy One of Israel to cease from before us. Wherefore thus saith the Holy One of Israel, because ye despise this word, and trust in oppression and perverseness and stay thereon. Therefore this iniquity shall be to you as a breach ready to fall, swelling out in a high wall, whose breaking cometh suddenly at an instant." Senator Kennedy, we will experience more breaking points, if we continue this course to destruction.

136

The terrorism that we are experiencing in America is the fruit of our trust in oppression and perverseness. We must understand this. We must address root causes to address terrorism, however, this will require America to look at itself. When we earnestly do that, we will realize the impact of some of our oppressive and perverse polices.

Senator Kennedy, God has given me this message to deliver to the leaders here in the United States. "Woe unto the leaders of the United States, if they continue in their wickedness and fail to adhere to the word that I have given My Prophet. Recall your planes, ships, and My people. Remove all unjust sanctions against countries around the world. Rewrite your trade agreements to ensure that they are fair to the workers. End your eagerness to shed innocent blood. Seek out the bad fruit that has now ripened. Apply just laws to all suspects that are still alive, that were involved in the planning and operation of the terrorism attack on America. Do not prosecute the innocent. Bad fruits that have not ripened, treat them with care, love, and understanding, because you helped created them. Change your hearts and take on a new resolve to end oppression and perverseness. Thus, you will end the terrorism in America if you turn to Me. My righteousness is forever." Thus said the Lord. God gave me this message in October 2001 before we sent out any of our troops, planes, or ships. In God's final warning, He showed me how America will suffer financially and our strong military will be reduced to a military that cannot sustain its basic quality of life that we have grown accustomed to.

I ask that you take time out now and read the complete package; then you will clearly see that God has sent me. I ask you to share this complete package with all of our U. S. Senators.
Your actions are critical in changing the nation's path from destruction to peace. Take heed and allow the Holy Spirit to guide you as you work to secure the future of America and make these important decisions that impact the world.

Sincerely yours,

Elmore Richmond Jr.
A Prophet of God in the Name of Jesus Christ

Nine Enclosures

1. Press Release
2. Letter to President Bush, dated, January 14, 2003
3. Letter to President Bush, dated, December 20, 2002
4. Letter to President Bush, dated, December 2, 2002
5. Letter to President Bush, dated, September 3, 2002
6. Letter to President Bush, dated, May 22, 2002
7. Letter to President Bush, dated, November 3, 2001
8. Letter to President Bush, Dated October 26, 2001
9. Letter to President Bush, Dated October 6, 2001

January 31, 2003

Congressman Dennis Kucinich
1730 Longworth
House Office Building
Washington, D. C. 20515

Dear Congressman Kucinich:

This is my first time writing you, however, I have written the President eight times since "9/11" to no avail. I pray that you will listen carefully. God revealed to me the destruction of the World Trade Center before it occurred. I have three witnesses. Moreover, God continues to reveal his secrets to me. Over the past year I have shared some of them with the President. I have included some of those communications in this package for your information and action. Congressman Kucinich, some teach that God does not have prophets today; that teaching is erroneous. (Reference Amos 3:6-7.) Congressman Kucinich, God has given me revelation after revelation - with the exception of the revelations in His final warning all have come to fruition.

I am writing you to let you know that we will continue to experience calamity after calamity, until we adhere to the counsel of God. The United States is not walking in the counsel of God. Therefore, we are not following God's laws regarding His righteousness. God says His righteousness is forever. This means that the same standards apply regarding His righteousness today as it did 2500 years ago. We have not learned from lessons learned. Consequently, the United States is rushing to shed innocent blood and trusting in oppression and perverseness. Like God warned Judah as recorded in Isaiah Chapter 30, now God has warned the United States.

In Isaiah, Chapter 30, the word of God continues to warn His people of the destruction to come when they place their trust in oppression and perverseness. Isaiah, Chapter 30:9-13 says, "That this is a rebellious people, lying people, children that will not hear the law of the Lord. Which say to the seers, See not; and to the prophets, Prophesy not unto us right things, speak unto us smooth things, prophesy deceits: Get you out of the way, turn aside out of the path, cause the Holy One of Israel to cease from before us. Wherefore thus saith the Holy One of Israel, because ye despise this word, and trust in oppression and perverseness and stay thereon. Therefore this iniquity shall be to you as a breach ready to fall, swelling out in a high wall, whose breaking cometh suddenly at an instant." Congressman Kucinich, we will experience more breaking points, if we continue this course to destruction.

The terrorism that we are experiencing in America is the fruit of our trust in oppression and perverseness. We must understand this. We must address root causes to address terrorism, however, this will require America to look at itself. When we earnestly do that, we will realize the impact of some of our oppressive and perverse polices.

Congressman Kucinich, God has given me this message to deliver to the Leaders here in the United States, "Woe unto the leaders of the United States, if they continue in their wickedness and fail to adhere to the word that I have given My Prophet. Recall your planes, ships, and My people. Remove all unjust sanctions against countries around the world. Rewrite your trade agreements to ensure that they are fair to the workers. End your eagerness to shed innocent blood. Seek out the bad fruit that has now ripened. Apply just laws to all suspects that are still alive, that were involved in the planning and operation of the terrorism attack on America. Do not prosecute the innocent. Bad fruits that have not ripened, treat them with care, love, and understanding, because you helped created them. Change your hearts and take on a new resolve to end oppression and perverseness. Thus, you will end the terrorism in America if you turn to Me. My righteousness is forever." Thus said the Lord. God gave me this message in October 2001 before we sent out any of our troops, planes, or ships. In God's final warning, He showed me how America will suffer financially and our strong military will be reduced to a military that cannot sustain its basic quality of life that we have grown accustomed to.

I ask that you take time out now and read the complete package; then you will clearly see that God has sent me. I ask you to share this complete package with House of Representatives and make it a matter of record. Then the House will know from where we have fallen from if we should engage in an unjust war and face calamity after calamity. Your actions are critical in changing the nation's path from destruction to peace. Take heed and allow the Holy Spirit to guide you as you work to secure the future of America and make these important decisions that impact the world.

I have also enclosed a video that clearly explains the terrorism that confronts America and the world and what do to end it. I give you the rights to use this video, as you deem necessary to accomplish this most important task.

Sincerely yours,

Elmore Richmond Jr.
A Prophet of God in the Name of Jesus Christ

Nine Enclosures
1. Press Release
2. Letter to President Bush, dated, January 14, 2003
3. Letter to President Bush, dated, December 20, 2002
4. Letter to President Bush, dated, December 2, 2002
5. Letter to President Bush, dated, September 3, 2002
6. Letter to President Bush, dated, May 22, 2002
7. Letter to President Bush, dated, November 3, 2001
8. Letter to President Bush, Dated October 26, 2001
9. Letter to President Bush, Dated October 6, 2001
10. Video, "America, America: Ending Terrorism - A Word From God"

ELMORE RICHMOND JR.
A PROPHET OF GOD
600 N. Hays Avenue
Jackson, Tennessee 38301

February 3, 2003

Secretary General Kofi Annan
United Nations Headquarters
First Avenue at 46th Street
New York, New York 10017

Dear Secretary General Annan:

This is my first time writing you, however, I have written the President of
the United States of America eight times since "9/11" to no avail. I pray that you
will listen carefully. God revealed to me the destruction of the World Trade
Center before it occurred. I have three witnesses. Moreover, God continues to
reveal his secrets to me. Over the past year I have shared some of them with the
President Bush. I have included some of those communications in this package
for your information. Secretary General Annan, some teach that God does not
have prophets today; that teaching is erroneous. (Reference Amos 3:6-7.)
Moreover, Jesus said that a Prophet is without honor in his own country, I am
truly a witness to this affirmation. God has given me revelation after revelation -
with the exception of the revelations in His final warning all have come to
fruition. I am writing you because God has commanded me to do so. Therefore,
I pray that you will follow the instructions that are contained herein.

I am writing you to let you know that the United States is not walking in
the counsel of God; this error puts nations around the world on the path of
destruction. Today, the United States is like ancient Egypt, a very powerful
nation. Consequently, many nations strengthen themselves in the strength of the
President Bush and trust in the shadow of the United States. Like God warned
nations in Isaiah Chapter 30:3, the strength of Pharaoh would be these nations
shame, and the trust in the shadow of Egypt their confusion. God wants you to
take action that help guide nations around the world to turn to Him and to stop
going to the President of the United States for their strength and trusting in the
shadow of the United States.

God says His righteousness is forever. This means that the same standards
apply regarding His righteousness today as it did 2500 years ago. The United

States has not learned from lessons learned. Consequently, the United States is rushing to shed innocent blood and trusting in oppression and perverseness. Like God warned Judah as recorded in Isaiah Chapter 30, now God has warned the United States. All nations can learn from this warning.

In Isaiah, Chapter 30, the word of God continues to warn His people of the destruction to come when they place their trust in oppression and perverseness. Isaiah, Chapter 30:9-13 says, "That this is a rebellious people, lying people, children that will not hear the law of the Lord. Which say to the seers, See not; and to the prophets, Prophesy not unto us right things, speak unto us smooth things, prophesy deceits: Get you out of the way, turn aside out of the path, cause the Holy One of Israel to cease from before us. Wherefore thus saith the Holy One of Israel, because ye despise this word, and trust in oppression and perverseness and stay thereon. Therefore this iniquity shall be to you as a breach ready to fall, swelling out in a high wall, whose breaking cometh suddenly at an instant." Secretary General Annan, the United States of America will experience more breaking points, if the United States continues this course to destruction. Moreover, if other nations align with the United States on this path of destruction, they will experience calamity after calamity, while in a state of shame and confusion.

The terrorism that the United States of America is experiencing in America is the fruit of the United States' trust in oppression and perverseness. America and nations around the world must understand this. America and other nations must address root causes to address terrorism, however, this will require America and other nations to look at themselves. When nations earnestly do that, those nations will realize the impact of some of their oppressive and perverse polices.

Secretary General Annan, God gave me this message to deliver to the Leaders here in the United States, "Woe unto the leaders of the United States, if they continue in their wickedness and fail to adhere to the word that I have given My Prophet. Recall your planes, ships, and My people. Remove all unjust sanctions against countries around the world. Rewrite your trade agreements to ensure that they are fair to the workers. End your eagerness to shed innocent blood. Seek out the bad fruit that has now ripened. Apply just laws to all suspects that are still alive, that were involved in the planning and operation of the terrorism attack on America. Do not prosecute the innocent. Bad fruits that have not ripened, treat them with care, love, and understanding, because you helped created them. Change your hearts and take on a new resolve to end oppression and perverseness. Thus, you will end the terrorism in America if you turn to Me.

My righteousness is forever." Thus said the Lord. God gave me this message in October 2001 before we sent out any of our troops, planes, or ships. In God's final warning, He showed me how America will suffer financially and our strong military will be reduced to a military that cannot sustain its basic quality of life that we have grown accustomed to.

Now, God has commanded me to share it with you to prevent other nations from falling into the same pit. I ask that you take time out now and read the complete package; then you will clearly see that God has sent me. I ask you to share this complete package with all members of the United Nations and make it a matter of record. Therefore all Nations will know the consequences of walking outside the counsel of God. Your actions are critical in changing the world path from destruction to peace. Take heed and allow the Holy Spirit to guide you as you work for peace around the world and make these important decisions.

I have also enclosed a video that clearly explains the terrorism that confronts America and the world and what we must do to end it. I give you the rights to use this video, as you deem necessary to accomplish this most important task.

Sincerely yours,

Elmore Richmond Jr.
A Prophet of God in the Name of Jesus Christ

Nine Enclosures

1. Press Release
2. Letter to President Bush, dated, January 14, 2003
3. Letter to President Bush, dated, December 20, 2002
4. Letter to President Bush, dated, December 2, 2002
5. Letter to President Bush, dated, September 3, 2002
6. Letter to President Bush, dated, May 22, 2002
7. Letter to President Bush, dated, November 3, 2001
8. Letter to President Bush, Dated October 26, 2001
9. Letter to President Bush, Dated October 6, 2001
10. Book, "America! America! - A Checkup for the Body of Christ the Church"
11. Video, "America, America: Ending Terrorism - A Word From God"

REFERENCE: 12 March, 2003

Dear Mr. Richmond,

On behalf of Secretary-General Kofi Annan, I wish to acknowledge receipt of your recent letter and the enclosed videotape, which have been referred to this office for reply.

Allow me to express thanks to you for so generously sending us a complimentary copy of your videotape, *America, America: Ending Terrorism – A Word From God*, the contents of which have been duly noted.   In return, I am happy to send you a UN fact sheet detailing the Organization's efforts to defeat international terrorism.

Again, thank you for your videotape and for your interest in the United Nations.

Yours sincerely,

Dawn Johnston Britton
Acting Chief, Public Inquiries Unit
Department of Public Information

Mr. Elmore Richmond, Jr.
600 N. Hays Avenue
Jackson, TN 38301

144

ELMORE RICHMOND JR.
A PROPHET OF GOD
600 N. Hays Avenue
Jackson, Tennessee 38301
(731) 421-9066

March 7, 2003

President George W. Bush
The White House
Washington, D. C. 20500

Dear Mr. President:

If you have not received any of the communications that I have sent to you since 9/11, I pray that God will have mercy on the ones who thwart the communications, but woe to the ones who prevent this complete file from reaching your hands. I have written you eight other times as God has directed me. In those communications, I have informed you that the United States was out of the counsel of God and gave you revelations. All revelations have come to past, except the revelations that were in the final warning. God has given us grace with a window of opportunity for this nation to repent from our current rush to shed innocent blood and our trust in oppression and perverseness; I pray that we will take heed. Mr. President, you are the one that has been given by Congress to make the final decision regarding this war. Although Congress has not declared war according to the Constitution of the United States, moreover the majority of America is against this war. Therefore, if we should engage in this war, this war will be known as Bush's war, a war that was waged outside the counsel of God. Mr. President, you have said that you have sought the help of God, but you are still outside of His counsel. Surely, I am one of His prophets, and our Living God reveals his secrets to His servants the prophets. Therefore, it is my calling to help guide you back to the counsel of God.

Mr. President, terrorism is not a new threat to America and since I have heard your explanations it is apparent that you have not learned the real lessons from 9/11. In the early 1970's we experienced terrorism within our military. There were fire bombings, buildings set aflame, U. S. military buildings taken over by our own military members, and we called them militants. Moreover, these so-called militants, members of our armed services waged war from within against the United States. I was in the Air Force at that time; the Air Force created an organization known as Social Actions to address this deadly internal

145

war. In 1976, I was hand picked by Headquarters TAC to go to England Air Force Base, Louisiana on the heels of the fire bombing of the Wing Commander's car, the Base Commander's car, and after an incident whereby a black Staff Sergeant had taken over the Command Post with an M-16. I was assigned there after these incidents to discover root causes, prevent other incidents from reoccurring, and to help to improve the human relations climate. I successfully achieved all objectives. One of the lessons learned was when commanders engaged in oppressive and perverse policies it lead to the creation of these so-called militants.

While in the Air Force, I was quite effective in resolving these types of problems. The problems that the United States is experiencing today has the same foundations. They are the fruits of our trust in oppression and perverseness. These were the roots of the problems that we experienced on our military bases. Moreover, these are the same roots that cause the riots that we experienced during the 1960's in many of our cities throughout the United States. Today, the terrorism that we are experiencing is based on the same roots, however on an international scale. Consequently, if we fail to address the root causes, we will continue to experience terrorism and many breaking points.

Turing your attention back to the word of God, in Isaiah Chapter 30, 12 - 13. "Wherefore thus said the Holy One of Israel, Because ye despise this word, and trust in oppression and perverseness, and stay thereon: Therefore this iniquity shall be to you as a breach ready to fall. Swelling out in a high wall, whose breaking cometh suddenly at an instant. Mr. President, this nation has been trusting in oppression and perverseness, therefore the terrorism that we are experiencing is the fruit of our trust in oppression and perverseness. Mr. President you did not create this problem, however, now since you are the President of the United States your actions and the actions of God's people are being observed by God.

President Bush, you must learn from the word of God. The example of the King of Nineveh is a good example. I ask that you review Jonah Chapter 3. In Chapter 3, it shows how the King of Nineveh humbled himself after he was told by the Prophet of God of God's judgment of his city. The King and the people of Nineveh repented. Chapter 3:10 says, "And God saw their works, that they turned from their evil way; and God repented of the evil, that he had said that he would do unto them; and he did it not." Romans 15:4 reminds us that whatsoever things were written aforetime were written for our learning. Mr. President, learn from the word of God.

146

Mr. President, God has issued you His final warning. This communication is designed to let you know that the communications I have sent you are from Him. The following event provides you even more evidence that God is with me and has sent these messages to you. On March 5, 2003, God revealed to me destruction of a building that had a tower. The destruction was great. The building came down like the World Trade Center, however, it appeared to be in a residential neighborhood because I saw framed houses in the area. Moreover, there were many electrical power lines. These power lines were falling and people in the area were fleeing for their lives. This appeared to be an accident. This will happen shortly. I pray that you will review the enclosed communications and take heed. Your actions will either bless or curse this nation. Remember Mr. President, like God watched the King of Nineveh and the people of that city; the same God is watching us. I pray that you will humble yourself and take action as recorded on page 40 of the enclosed book, which is the same message that God gave me in the first letter that I wrote you on October 6, 2001. The message is below:

"Recall your planes, ships, and My people. Remove all unjust sanctions against countries around the world. Rewrite your trade agreements to ensure that they are fair to the workers. End your eagerness to shed innocent blood. Seek out the bad fruit that has now ripened. Apply just laws to all suspects that are still alive, that were involved in the planning and operation of the terrorist attack on America. Do not prosecute the innocent. Bad fruits that have not ripened treat them with care, love, and understanding, because you helped create them. Change your hearts and take on a new resolve to end oppression and perverseness. Thus, you will end the terrorism in America if you turn to me. … If my people, which are called by my name, shall humble themselves, and pray, and seek my face, and turn from their wicked ways; then will I hear from heaven, and will forgive their sin, and will heal their land."

In God's Final warning, God showed me that if will continue in our rush to shed innocent blood by going to war with Iraq, we will experience much destruction by fire and this nation will suffer economically to point that our standards of living will be lowered and it will affect all. Moreover, the United States of America will no longer be the super power.

Sincerely yours,

Elmore Richmond Jr.
Prophet of God
In the Name of Jesus Christ

Nine Enclosures

1. Letter to President Bush, dated, January 14, 2003
2. Letter to President Bush, dated, December 20, 2002
3. Letter to President Bush, dated, December 2, 2002
4. Letter to President Bush, dated, September 3, 2002
5. Letter to President Bush, dated, May 22, 2002
6. Letter to President Bush, dated, November 3, 2001
7. Letter to President Bush, Dated October 26, 2001
8. Letter to President Bush, Dated October 6, 2001
9. Book, "America! America! - A Checkup for the Body of Christ the Church"

GEORGE ALLEN
VIRGINIA

204 RUSSELL OFFICE BUILDING
WASHINGTON, DC 20510-4604
(202) 224-4024
(202) 224-5432 (FAX)
http://allen.senate.gov/email.html

COMMITTEES:
COMMERCE, SCIENCE, AND
TRANSPORTATION
FOREIGN RELATIONS
SMALL BUSINESS AND
ENTREPRENEURSHIP

United States Senate

April 8, 2003

Mr. Elmore Richmond
600 North Hays Avenue
Jackson, Tennessee 38301

Dear Elmore:

Thank you for contacting me regarding the war in Iraq. I appreciate your input and value the opportunity to respond to your concerns on this important matter.

I stand with our President in his resolve to protect the American people, and with Secretary of State Colin Powell who is providing steady, serious diplomatic leadership. This, literally, is a matter of life and death – for both our military and the Iraqi people.

Despite repeated efforts and warnings, I am disappointed that Saddam Hussein has failed to disarm by destroying his chemical and biological weapons of mass destruction and has chosen the path that none of us wanted – military engagement. The world community's continuous attempts to deal with Saddam Hussein through diplomatic means have been defied. Regrettably, it seems the only way this dangerous dictator will be disarmed is by force of the U.S. military and our willing allies.

The President, CIA, Department of Defense and the State Department have presented clear and convincing evidence that Saddam Hussein and his regime in Iraq are a credible threat to the United States and its allies around the world. In his presentation to the United Nations, Secretary Powell clearly laid out the case against Iraq. The photographs of Iraqi ammunition dumps and intercepted telephone conversations between Iraqi military leaders prove beyond a doubt that Saddam Hussein is hiding his weapons capabilities from the world. The fact is, the Iraqi regime has still not accounted for thousands of liters of anthrax, only one vial of which, if delivered through a terrorist subcontractor, could have a more deadly impact than did the tragic terrorist attacks on September 11, 2001.

☐ CENTRAL VIRGINIA
507 EAST FRANKLIN ST.
RICHMOND, VA 23219
(804) 771-2221
(804) 771-8313 (FAX)

☐ HAMPTON ROADS
222 CENTRAL PARK AVE., #120
VIRGINIA BEACH, VA 23462
(757) 518-1674
(757) 518-1679 (FAX)

☐ WESTERN AND VALLEY
3140 CHAPARRAL DR., #C-101
ROANOKE, VA 24018
(540) 772-4236
(540) 772-6870 (FAX)

☐ SOUTHWEST VIRGINIA
332 CUMMINGS ST., SUITE C
ABINGDON, VA 24210
(276) 676-2646
(276) 676-2588 (FAX)

☐ NORTHERN VIRGINIA
2214 ROCK HILL RD., SUITE 100
HERNDON, VA 20170
(703) 435-0039
(703) 435-9446 (FAX)

Saddam Hussein is a vile dictator, with regard for only his own survival. He compromises the well-being of all Iraqis in his efforts to maintain power and accumulate wealth. History shows that this Iraqi leader only responds when his power is threatened. The Iraqi regime has not fully cooperated with the U.N. inspectors and we must not allow him to continue his shell game of deceptive ploys. We must not allow Saddam Hussein the unchecked opportunity to continue developing and pursuing the world's worst weapons.

The President has taken a reasonable and steady stand for the safety and security of the world, but more specifically, our families here at home. Terrorists worldwide must know that our resolve to win this War on Terrorism is not just one of words and threats but, where it cannot be avoided, one of action as well. We are concerned about understandable fears of reprisal; however, such anxiety cannot paralyze us from the course we must take for our security. Americans and liberated Iraqis will have a safer, more hopeful life if Saddam Hussein is disarmed and gone.

Right now, my prayers are with the courageous men and women in our armed forces, as they will soon enter the unpredictable field of battle. I also want to assure their families back home that they are prepared and as well equipped as possible for their dangerous mission. We all appreciate their character and risk for our security and freedom.

Thank you again for taking the time to contact me. If you would like to receive an e-mail newsletter about my initiatives to improve America, please sign up on my website (http://allen.senate.gov). It is an honor to serve you in the United States Senate, and I look forward to working with you to make Virginia and America a better place to live, learn, work and raise a family.

With warm regards, I remain

Sincerely,

George Allen

George Allen

Elmore Richmond Jr.
Prophet of God
600 N. Hays Avenue
Jackson, Tennessee 38301
(731) 421-9066

March 19, 2003

President George W. Bush
The White House
Washington, D. C. 20500

Solution to the Iraq Crisis - War is not the Answer

Dear Mr. President:

Terrorism is not a new threat to America; therefore, we must learn lessons from our recent past. In the early 1970's, we experienced terrorism within our military. There were fire bombings, buildings set aflame, U. S. military buildings were taken over by our own military members, and we called them militants. Moreover, these so-called militants, members of our armed services waged war from within against the United States. After these incidents, some commanders took a **preemptive approach**, by discharging blacks without any firm foundation; they used a provision of the personnel discharge manuals called, "character behavior disorder". Consequently, these commanders sent many blacks to psychologists for evaluations. These blacks were classified as having "character behavior disorders" consequently they were discharged. The problem was that these blacks were being referred to these psychologists without any manifestation of destructive behaviors. Therefore, these preemptive actions did not resolve the problems, however they planted more bad seeds. From these experiences, we learned that you must address root causes.

I was in the Air Force at that time; the Air Force created an organization known as Social Actions to address this deadly internal war. In 1976, I was hand picked by Headquarters Tactical Air Command (TAC) to go to England Air Force Base, Louisiana on the heels of the fire bombing of the Wing Commander's car, the Base Commander's car, and after an incident whereby a black Staff Sergeant had taken over the Command Post with an M-16. I was assigned there after these incidents to discover root causes, prevent other incidents from reoccurring, and to

151

help to improve the human relations climate. I successfully achieved all objectives. One of the lessons learned was when commanders engaged in oppressive and perverse policies it lead to the creation of these so-called militants.

The problems that the United States is experiencing today have the same foundations that our military experienced; our military engaged in oppressive and perverse policies. We learned that the racial incidents (acts of terrorism) that we experienced were the fruits of our trust in oppression and perverseness. These were the roots of the problems that we experienced on our military bases; moreover, these are the same roots that caused the riots that we experienced during the 1960's in many of our cities throughout the United States. Today, the terrorism that we are experiencing is based on the same roots, however on an international scale. Consequently, if we fail to address the root causes, we will continue to experience terrorism and have many breaking points. This is also what the word of God says about this matter.

In Isaiah, Chapter 30, the word of God continues to warn His people of the destruction to come when they place their trust in oppression and perverseness. Isaiah, Chapter 30:9-13 says, "That this is a rebellious people, lying people, children that will not hear the law of the Lord. Which say to the seers, See not; and to the prophets, Prophesy not unto us right things, speak unto us smooth things, prophesy deceits: Get you out of the way, turn aside out of the path, cause the Holy One of Israel to cease from before us. Wherefore thus saith the Holy One of Israel, because ye despise this word, and trust in oppression and perverseness and stay thereon. Therefore this iniquity shall be to you as a breach ready to fall, swelling out in a high wall, whose breaking cometh suddenly at an instant." Mr. President, we will experience more breaking points, if we continue this path to destruction.

War is not the answer, we must address root causes. God has granted us this short period of grace to give us time to wake up from a spirit of deep sleep. This is the same spirit of deep sleep that was poured out on Judah prior to the doom of Jerusalem. (Isaiah 29:10) However, instead of waking up, some of our leaders have resolved to discuss measures like changing the name of "French Fries" to "Freedom Fries." France is not our enemy, however they are one of our closest allies. We must stop and listen, and see what they are seeing, because we are too close to the destruction and have not took advantage of our problem solving intellect; we have been too busy studying war.

"Thus saith the Lord, Let not the wise man glory in his wisdom, neither let the mighty man glory in his might, let not the rich man glory in his riches. But let

152

him that glorieth glory in this, that he understandeth and knoweth me, that I am the Lord, which exercise lovingkindness, judgment, and righteousness, in the earth: for in these things I delight, saith the Lord." (Isaiah 9:23) In a letter dated January 14, 2003, I revealed that the United States has failed to take the corrective actions, now consequently; God will remove His covering from around the United States' battlements if he did not receive His counsel. Now, God has removed the covering from around the United States military because the battlements are no longer the Lords.

Consequently, if the United States continues to rush to shed innocent blood, the United States will suffer financially and consequently, the military will suffer in maintaining its quality of life and will experience much destruction by fire. (God revealed this to me in several visions, after these visions, the Holy Spirit had me to read, Jeremiah, Chapter 5.) Today, we are witnessing the evidences of God's covering being removed by the long chow lines, accommodations problems, sand storms, problems with equipment, opposition in the United Nations, etc. Stop and listen.

Can this destruction be prevented? How should we respond?

Yes this can be prevented, for some prophecy is conditional. 2 Chronicles 7:14 states, **"If my people,** which are called by my name, shall humble themselves, and pray, seek my face, and turn from their wicked ways; then will I hear from heaven, and will forgive their sin, and will heal their land." The Nineveh Response is a Good Model to follow.

As recorded in Romans 15:4, "For whatsoever things were written aforetime were for our learning, ..." Today we must learn from the King and the people of Nineveh. The lessons are recorded in the book of Jonah, chapter 3. When Jonah cried out to the people that Nineveh would be overthrown in forty days the people believe him. The people humbled themselves. And when the word of the Lord came to the King of Nineveh, the King arose from his throne, and laid his robe from him, and covered him with sack clothe and sat in ashes." In other words, the king humbled himself. (Jonah 3:4-6)

The king and the people of Nineveh repented. When the king and the people humbled themselves, and turned from their evil, this caused **God to repent.** Jonah 3:10 says, "And God saw their works, that they turned from their evil way; **and God repented of the evil, that he had said that he would do unto them; and he did it not.** We must pray that Our Pride will not keep us from repenting from our plan for war on Iraq. If we fail to repent, it will lead to a great destruction. Proverbs 16:18 says, "Pride goeth before destruction, and an haughty spirit before a fall." We must learn the lessons about the pride of Tyrus as recorded in Ezekiel 28 and Egypt's pride and desolation as recorded in Ezekiel 29 - 31.

Ezekiel 25:15, God warns us what would be the affects of pride mixed with a despiteful heart. Listen! There are some very serious consequences for taking vengeance with a despiteful heart, to destroy for old hatred. Ezekiel 25:17, God says, "And I will execute great vengeance upon them with furious rebukes; and they shall know that I am the Lord, when I shall lay my vengeance upon them. Nevertheless, God have no pleasure at all that the wicked should die. However the Lord desire is that the wicked turned from his wicked ways. (Ezekiel 18:23) Ezekiel 18:27 - 28 says, "Again, when the wicked man turneth away from his wickedness that he hath committed, and doeth that which is lawful and right, he shall save his soul alive. Because he considereth, and turneth away from all his transgressions that he hath committed, he shall surely live, he shall not die."

How to end this crisis and bring an end to terror in the United States? - Follow these instructions. "Woe unto the leaders of the United States, if they continue in their wickedness and fail to adhere to the word that I have given My Prophet. Recall your planes, ships, and My people. Remove all unjust sanctions against countries around the world. Rewrite your trade agreements to ensure that they are fair to the workers. End your eagerness to shed innocent blood. Seek out the bad fruit that have now ripened. Apply just laws to all suspects that are still alive, that were involved in the planning and operation of the terrorism attack on America. Do not prosecute the innocent. Bad fruits that have not ripened, treat them with care, love, and understanding, because you helped created them. Change your hearts and take on a new resolve to end oppression and perverseness. Thus, you will end the terrorism in America if you turn to Me. My righteousness is forever." Thus said the Lord. God gave me this message in September 2001 before we sent out any of our troops, planes, or ships. In God's final warning, God has showed me how America will suffer financially and our strong military will be reduced to a military that cannot sustain its basis quality life that we have grown accustomed to.

Finally, Mr. President, I would like to direct your attention to Jeremiah Chapter 18. You will find that you will fail to meet your objective of establishing a democracy in Iraq because you are not the "Potter." God is the "Potter." Jeremiah 18:7 says, "At what instant I shall speak concerning a nation, and concerning a kingdom, to pluck up, and to pull down, and to destroy it; If that nation, against whom I have pronounced, turn from their evil, will repent of the evil that I thought to do unto them. And at what instant I shall speak concerning a nation, and concerning a kingdom, to build and to plant it; If it do evil in my sight, that it obey not my voice, then I will repent of the good, where with I said I would benefit them.

I pray that you will have the courage to do what the people of United States of America are paying you to do. God says if we hearkened to His commandments we would have peace as a river and righteousness as the waves of the sea. (Isaiah 48:18) "In righteousness shalt thou be established; Thou shalt be far from oppression; for thou shalt not fear; and from terror; for it shall not come near thee." (Isaiah 54:14) Mr. President, I pray that we would hearken to the Commandments of God.

Sincerely yours,

Elmore Richmond Jr.
Prophet of God
In the Name of Our Lord and Saviour Jesus Christ

PROPHET ELMORE RICHMOND JR
600 N. HAYS AVE.
JACKSON, TENNESSEE 38301
(731) 421-9066 - Mail to: Richmondpw@aol.com

MESSAGE TO THE PEOPLE OF GOD IN THE UNITED STATES -

REPENT

Prepared by: Prophet Elmore Richmond Jr. under the Power of the Holy Spirit.

Below is a summary of the Word of God that must go forth at this time. All of God's people should take time out and study the following text and men and women of God should preach this text prior to March 17, 2003 or as soon as possible.

Before the Doom of Jerusalem

> Before the doom of Jerusalem, Judah was out of the counsel of God and God poured out the spirit of deep sleep and all were covered. (Isaiah 29:9)

> Therefore the visions of all became as words of a book that were sealed. (Isaiah 29:11)

> The Lord said that the people drew near Him with their mouth and their lips, but their heart was removed from Him and their fear toward God was taught by the precept of men. (Isaiah 29:13)

> Men sought deep in the dark to hide the counsel of God from God's people. (Isaiah 29:15)

> God called the people of Judah a rebellious children - For they took counsel but not of God - They were covered with a covering, but not of God's Spirit - Thus they added sin to sin (Isaiah 30:1)

> God had Isaiah to write in a table, note it in a book, that it may be for the time to come for ever and ever. That this is a rebellious

156

people, lying children, children that will not hear the law of the Lord. (Isaiah 30:9)

- ➢ These people did not want to hear the truth - They said to the prophets - see not - prophesy not unto us right things, speak unto us smooth things, prophesy deceits. (Isaiah 30:10)
- ➢ God said to them - "Because ye despise this word, and trust in oppression and perverseness and stay thereon: Therefore this iniquity shall be to you as a breach ready to fall, swelling out in a high wall, whose breaking cometh suddenly at an instant. (Isaiah 30:12-13)

Judah despised the word of God and Judah trusted in oppression and perverseness - these are the reasons for the doom of Jerusalem, under Judah. Today, the United States finds itself in the same position as Judah. However, unlike Judah, the United States is more like ancient Egypt, whereby other nations turn to the President of the United States for their strength and trust in the shadow of the United States. For those nations, God is saying today, the strength of the President of the United States should be their shame, and the trust in shadow of the United States should be their confusion. (Isaiah 30:2-3)

Blessed is the Nation whose God is Lord ... (Psalm 33:12)

- ➢ For whatsoever things were written aforetime were written for our learning, that we through patience and comfort of the scriptures might have hope. (Romans 15:4)
- ➢ God says His righteousness shall be forever. (Isaiah 51:7) This means that God applies the same standards regarding His righteousness today as He did 2500 years ago.
- ➢ God says if we hearkened to His commandments we would have peace as a river and righteousness as the waves of the sea. (Isaiah 48:18)

157

> "In righteousness shalt thou be established; Thou shalt be far from oppression; for thou shalt not fear; and from terror; for it shall not come near thee." (Isaiah 54:14)

Is the United States of America trusting in Oppression and Perverseness?

To answer this question you do not have to look deep, but, you must take an earnest look at some of our international policies. When you take an earnest look you will conclude surely we trust in oppression and perverseness. For example the sanctions on Iraq, North Korea, Cuba, as result of these sanctions, hundred of thousands have died. We sold arms to Iran and Iraq. We have used our CIA to create turmoil in other countries such as the Soviet Union, Afghanistan, and Iraq. We killed thousands in Nicaragua and the list goes on. Note: One of the first actions we took to gain support on the war on terror was to remove sanctions from nations in the Mid East. On a smaller scale, within the United States, sometimes we have racial riots; the root causes of these riots are oppression and perverseness.

Conclusion: The terrorism that America is experiencing is the fruit of America's trust in oppression and perverseness and our failure to seek the counsel of God. To end terrorism, we must seek the counsel of God and then we must address root causes. War is not the answer.

In Richmond's most recent letter to President Bush, Richmond warned the President that God has removed the covering from around the United States military because the battlements are no longer the Lords. The United States will suffer financially and consequently, the military will suffer in maintaining its quality of life and will experience much destruction by fire. (God revealed this to Richmond in several visions, after these visions, the Holy Spirit had Richmond to visit, Jeremiah, Chapter 5.)

Can this destruction be prevented? How should we respond?

Yes this can be prevented, for some prophecy is conditional. 2 Chronicles 7:14 states, **"If my people,** which are called by my name, shall humble themselves, and pray, seek my face, and turn from their wicked ways; then will I hear from heaven, and will forgive their sin, and will heal their land."

The Nineveh Response is a Good Model to follow

As recorded in Romans 15:4, "For whatsoever things were written aforetime were for our learning, …" Today we must learn from the King and the people of Nineveh. The lessons are recorded in the book of Jonah, chapter 3. When Jonah cried out to the people that Nineveh would be overthrown in forty days the people believed him. The people humbled themselves. And when the word of the Lord came to the King of Nineveh, the King arose from his throne, and laid his robe from him, and covered him with sack cloth and sat in ashes. In other words, the king humbled himself. (Jonah 3:4-6)

The king and the people of Nineveh repented. When the king and the people humbled themselves, and turned from their evil, this caused **God to repent.**   Jonah 3:10 says, And God saw their works, that they turned from their evil way; **and God repented of the evil, that he had said that he would do unto them; and he did it not.**

Will the pride of the President of the United States lead us to destruction?

We must pray that Pride will not keep us from repenting from our plan for war on Iraq. If we fail to repent, it will lead to a great destruction. Proverbs 16:18 says, "Pride goeth before destruction, and an haughty spirit before a fall."

We must learn the lessons about the pride of Tyrus as recorded in Ezekiel 28 and Egypt's pride and desolation as recorded in Ezekiel 29 - 31. Let us take a look at the affects of pride as recorded in Psalm 10.

Psalm 10 - (1) Why standest thou afar off, O Lord? Why hidest, thou thyself in times of trouble? (2) The wicked in his pride doth persecute the poor: let them be taken in the devices that they have imagined. (3) For the wicked boasteth of his heart's desire, and blesseth the covetous, whom the Lord abhorreth. (4) The wicked, through the pride of his countenance, will not seek after God: God is not in all his thoughts. (5) His ways are always grievous; thy judgments are far above out of his sight: as for all his enemies, he puffeth at them. (6) He hath said in his heart, I shall not be moved: for I shall never be in adversity. (7) His mouth is full of cursing and deceit and fraud: under his tongue is mischief and vanity. (8) He sitteth in the lurking places of the villages: in the secret places doth he murder the innocent: his eyes are privily set against the poor. (9) He lieth in wait secretly as a lion in his den: he doth wait to catch the poor: he doth catch the poor, when he draweth him into his net. (10) He croucheth, and humbleth himself, that the poor may fall by his strong ones. (11) He hath said in his heart, God hath forgotten: he hideth his face; he will never see it."

Listen! Reading this was very painful because I could see the President of the United States as I was reading these words. What would be the affects of pride mixed with a despiteful heart? In Ezekiel 25:15, God warns us about taking vengeance with a despiteful heart, to destroy for old hatred. Ezekiel 25:17, God says, "And I will execute great vengeance upon them with furious rebukes; and they shall know that I am the Lord, when I shall lay my vengeance upon them. Nevertheless, God have no pleasure at all that the wicked should die. However the Lord's desire is that the wicked turn from his wicked ways. (Ezekiel 18:23) Ezekiel 18:27 - 28 says, "Again, when the wicked man turneth away from his wickedness that he hath committed, and doeth that which is lawful and right, he shall save his soul alive. Because he considereth, and turneth away from all his transgressions that he hath committed, he shall surely live, he shall not die."

God wants the United States to do the following: Thus said the Lord. "Recall your planes, ships, and My people. Remove all unjust sanctions against countries around the world. Rewrite your trade agreements to ensure that they are fair to the workers. End your eagerness to shed innocent blood. Seek out the bad fruit that have now ripened. Apply just laws to all suspects that are still alive, that were involved in the planning and operation of the terrorism attack on America. Do not prosecute the innocent. Bad fruits that have not ripened, treat them with care, love, and understanding, because you helped created them. Change your hearts and take on a new resolve to end oppression and perverseness. Thus, you will end the terrorism in America if you turn to Me. My Righteousness is forever."

We must pray that the President of the United States and our leaders of this nation hear the word of God and adhere to His counsel. (Note: Several weeks ago while I prayed and lifted up the leaders in this nation, I was moved in the spirit. As I continued to pray in an unknown tongue, I began to weep bitterly until my eyes were sore. I asked God for the revelation - The Holy Spirit immediately lead me to Jeremiah, chapter 13. As I begin to read Jeremiah Chapter 13, I began to weep again. However, when I reached the seventeenth verse, I knew why I was weeping. "But if ye will not hear it, my soul shall weep in secret places for your pride; and mine eye shall weep sore, and run down with tears, because the Lord's flock is carried away captive.") Pray for the President and all the world's leaders.

June 9, 2003

President George W. Bush
The White House
Washington, D. C. 20500

Dear Mr. President:

Reference my letters December 2, 2002 and December 20, 2003, in those letters I conveyed to you that floods and destructive winds that had impacted America were only an example of what we would experience if we continue to place our trust in oppression and perverseness. We are witnessing these revelations, moreover, we will continue to experience calamity after calamity until we hearten to God's word; we must not play with God, for God knows our hearts.

There is a provision in Deuteronomy 18:21-22 that provides a test to see if a prophet speaks for God. The scriptures say, "And if thou say in thine heart, How shall we know the word which the Lord hath not spoken? When a prophet speaketh in the name of the Lord, if the thing follow not, nor come to pass, that is the thing which the Lord hath not spoken, but prophet hath spoken it presumptuously: thou shalt not be afraid of him." Mr. President, commence the test like Pastor Rodgers of Straight Church of Jackson, Tennessee, a city that is now in crisis because of the damages of the destructive winds.

On April 6, 2003, I shared with Straight Way Church in Jackson, Tennessee various revelations that God had revealed to me. After I shared these revelations, Pastor Rodgers asked me to share with him the next revelation that God reveals to me because he wanted to watch for it. On April 7, I sent Pastor Rodgers a copy of the communications that I had sent you. Then on April 9, 2003, God revealed to me the following revelation. (I shared it with Pastor Rodgers on April 9, 2003)

"God showed me people with very little cash in their pockets and youth and adults were competing for the same few jobs. Then a lady in a crowd warned me that the stores owners should secure their goods. I asked her why? She replied look around you. I was in a black community; I saw hundreds of black people standing around looking for something to do. I immediately woke up; it was about 6:00 A.M."

Pastor Rodgers was able to witness this vision come to past in Jackson, Tennessee. Besides this vision, the vision regarding the destructive winds has also come to past. Let us review some tornado facts. The average number of tornadoes that we experience in the month of November is 30. However, over one weekend in November 2002, we experienced 77. Moreover, the average number of tornadoes that we experience in the month of May is 180, however, in the first seven days in May 2003, we experienced 395. These calamities are a measured response from God. (Jeremiah 30:11, Isaiah 27:8) Mr. President, listen carefully and learn from these scriptures. "Woe to the crown of pride, to the drunkards of Ephraim, whose glorious beauty is a fading flower, which are on the head of the fat valleys of them that are overcome with wine! Behold, the Lord hath a mighty and strong one, which as a tempest of hail and a destroying storm, as a flood of mighty waters overflowing shall cast down to the earth with the hand. The crown of pride, the drunkards of Ephraim, shall be trodden under feet:" (Isaiah 28:1-3)

Mr. President, as I have informed you in the pass, God revealed to me the tornadoes in November, weeks before they happened. Moreover, God reveals to me floods when rain is not even in the forecast, fires before the sparks, planes been shot down before they are schedule to fly. If you do no believe that I am one of God's Prophet, I encourage you to follow the provision that is outlined in Deuteronomy 18:21-22. Here is your next opportunity for you to see if I am a prophet of God.

The Visions of the next Tornadoes to hit Jackson

May 31, 2003 - In a dream I received a report that a tornado was headed for Jackson, Tennessee. I woke up immediately. However, after I awoke, I noticed that the television was still on, so I questioned the creditability of the dream.

June 1, 2003 - after studying the word of God and prior to retiring for the night, I asked God to make it clear to me regarding the dream about the tornadoes' warning for Jackson. While asleep, God revealed to me in a vision, tornadoes approaching. The site that I saw the tornadoes approaching reminded me of Muse Park here in Jackson. I recalled watching a large tornado, on the ground; a baseball diamond was between the tornado and my location as I watched the storms. Besides, the tornado on the ground there were another funnel cloud that had not hit the ground. Next while I was still in a vision, I recalled that I tried to determine exact location of the storm. As I surveyed the area, I remember seeing a structure made of sheet metal. Then I woke up immediately. This was more than a dream; it was as if I was actually there. This will come to past shortly, I

163

believe that it will happen here in Jackson, Tennessee within thirty days. After this happens, the people in Jackson, Tennessee will be more willing to hear from God and to make Jackson a "Hub City for God."

On June 2, 2003, I went to Muse Park in Jackson; I have confidence that Muse Park was the sight in the vision where I saw the tornado on the ground and the funnel cloud. Moreover, I believe that the sheet metal structure that I saw in the vision is a church, Jackson Family Worship Center that is near the park on Parkway. I pray that the Lord will have mercy on this place.

I must remind you again; the terrorism that we are experiencing in America is the fruit of our trust in oppression and perverseness. **We must understand this.** I have provided you messages from God over the past year to no avail. Mr. President, I love America and I want America to continue to be a strong nation for another two hundred years. I pray that you will adhere to this message. May God Bless America and protect innocent people around the world.

Sincerely yours,

Elmore Richmond Jr.
A Prophet of God in the Name of Jesus Christ

Elmore Richmond Jr.
Prophet of God
P. O. Box 7037
Jackson, Tennessee 38302
(731) 421-9066

April 17, 2004

President George W. Bush
The White House
Washington, D. C. 20050

Dear Mr. President:

If you have not receive any of the communications that I have sent you since 9/11, I pray that God will have mercy on the ones who thwarted the communications, but woe unto the ones who prevent this communication from reaching your hands. I have warned you that the United States was not taking counsel from God and on January 14, 2003, I warned you that God would remove His covering from around the United States' Battlement if you did not receive this counsel. (God showed me the mass of flies and much destruction by fire. Reference Letter dated January 14, 2003.) God has removed his covering; moreover God has given me another revelation. Listen carefully, at about 4:00 A. M. this morning God revealed germs' warfare attacks or/and chemical warfare attacks. Below is a summary of what was revealed to me.

The dream appeared to be broken down in four segments. First, I saw five women, these women disobeyed a military official to halt. They went into what appeared to be a military barrack for women. The search continued, however these women escaped.

Next, I see people being warned about these women. They were warned that these women had something that was deadly. I thought that it was some type of virus. The search continued for these women, however the scene changed from watching the search for these women to seeing cats going forth to attack dogs.

Finally, I see a man in civilian clothing at an out door event taking over the microphone issuing a warning to the people that they must evacuate the area because there was something that had become airborne that would cut off a persons oxygen supply within thirty minutes after they came in contact with it. I observed people in military clothes and civilian clothes running from the affected area. Then I woke up.

Mr. President, this was not just a bad dream, however these things were revelations from God. There is only one way to prevent these things from occurring and that is to repent immediately from our effort to shed more innocent blood. God knows our record and God knows our heart.

I have no other information regarding this matter. I pray that you will adhere to this warning and repent and seek the counsel of God. In the past, I have shared with you explicit actions that God wants you to take to no avail. This record should be on file.

Sincerely yours,

Elmore Richmond Jr.
    A Prophet of God, In the name of Our Lord and Saviour Jesus Christ

Chapter Nine
Revelation of the Gulf War of 1991

On September 10, 2001, God revealed to me the destruction of the World Trade Center and the United States of America preparing for war. However, this was not the first time that God had revealed His secrets to me regarding war. In 1990, before the war of words between George H. Bush and Saddam Hussein, God showed me the people in Iraq suffering.

It was as if there were a 35mm slide projection in my head. I kept seeing images after images of people suffering. I woke up saying, "What do you want me to do Lord? I will feed the poor. I will do whatsoever you want me to do." In August of 1990, President George H. W. Bush and Saddam Hussein commenced the war of words. I wrote President George H. W. Bush and offered him some suggestions on how to avoid a war. At that time I did not know that I was being led by God. I did not know that I had a calling on my life to do anything like that. However, I knew that I could help resolve the crisis that was at hand because of my problem-solving abilities.

I felt driven to study the crisis closely. In December 1990, I prepared a booklet entitled: "Mid East Crisis: How to Derail The Train, That's on a Fast Track to War?" I believed that I was commissioned by God to get this message out to every member in the House and the Senate. Besides the booklet, I also prepared a tape. I reproduced enough booklets to send to every member in Congress. However, in January 1991, I was sidetracked after attending a peace rally at Cal Tech in Pasadena, California. I spoke at the rally and gave out many copies of the booklets. Then I decided not to send them out. This was a very serious mistake. Consequently, I suffered throughout the war. I was glued to the television. I would not find God anywhere. It appeared that I was all alone. My family was there with me but I could not feel the presence of God. This was a terrible experience for me and I do not ever wish to experience it again. Below is the content of the booklet.

Mid East Crisis

How to Derail the Train That is on a Fast Track to War?

"Hello, my name is Elmore Richmond Jr., - My name is not important in this communication. Of course, I'm not known throughout the land for great accomplishments. But I know, I m known by a power greater than you and I. God was with me when this message was prepared - and all praises go to God. I'm concerned about the Mid East situation because we are on a fast track to war. This train must be derailed. In order to derail this train certain factors must be brought to your attention and certain actions must be taken.

I realize although I'm not known throughout the land, that, when I speak this truth, some will dislike me. Others may even call me a traitor, or even attempt to kill me. Nevertheless, I'm reminded of something the Late Dr. Martin Luther King Jr. once said: - "You must develop the inner-convictions, that there are some things so dear, some things so precious, and some things are so eternally true, they are worth dying for. I submit to you, that what I have to say to you today is so dear, so precious and so eternally true - I'm prepared to die for this cause. Dr. King also pointed out, if a man hasn't discovered something that he will die for, he is not fit to live.

Therefore, I will be quite candid with my thoughts. Firstly, I must address my concerns about President Bush's involvement in the Persian Gulf Crisis. President Bush is busy studying war and has invested little time for reaching a peaceful solution to this crisis. It has been amazing observing President Bush vacillating from his child ego state to his parent ego state throughout this crisis. Unfortunately, other world leaders, for whatever reasons have yielded to him and

168

allowed President Bush to become the Father of the World, or some type of god. Mr. Bush is not "God" and he must be told.

Like God told Ezekiel to tell the Prince of Tyre that he was not God, Mr. Bush must be reminded. It is understandable how one can begin to think he is God in his heart. Sometimes it is because of what others think of him or because of his position, like President of the United States. However, be reminded that no man can be God. God is. For God is God.

It is apparent that President Bush doesn't want a peaceful solution to this crisis. I believe he holds this disposition because of the perceived future threat of Saddam Hussein's military. And now, he is hiding behind a United Nations Resolution. However, if you carefully evaluate the aspect of the U. N. Resolution which he is giving most of his attention to, you will agree that it appears to be an initiative of President Bush.

The following questions puzzle me: (1) Who appointed President Bush to enforce the U. N. Resolutions? Did the U. N. appoint him to call all the shots? Is Mr. Bush responsible to the people of the United States OR can he just tell us to "Read his lips or to read his hips?"

I disagree with the demeanor of Mr. Bush, because the United States is a Democracy - A Government by the people and for the people. The president is responsible to us, the People. Since the government of the United States is not a Dictatorship, the House and Senate must become more effective, and work closely with the President in directing and addressing the affairs of this nation.

Let's discontinue this madness. War can't resolve this situation - it will only lead to more destruction. Eventually, we must sit down and talk about it. Let's not kid ourselves, the countries in the region aren't going to sit back and permit a foreign government to become their sense of security for a prolonged period of time.

Mr. Bush, where is you real world support? The token troops from other

169

countries - is this your real world support? Or is it the promise of token financial Aide? Mr. Bush if we engage in war it will cost billions and we will lose thousands of lives. In addition, I believe it will take much longer than five days and the aftermath will last for years.

I strongly agree with the principle of President Bush and the United Nations - that President Saddam Hussein must not be rewarded for his aggression. However, I must applaud President Saddam Hussein. I do not applaud him for his aggression, nor do I applaud him for the alleged war crimes committed by his troops. However, I must applaud, Saddam Hussein, because of his resolve, which clearly demonstrates that in this day and time you can't just bully a great nation to move at your will.

There must be some meaningful negotiation. Meaningful negotiation should be a trademark of the U. N. and not war. Thank you Saddam Hussein for this lesson to the world.

Nevertheless, I don't believe Saddam Hussein is just going to arbitrarily pull out of Kuwait. His action must not be condone - however, this type of invasion has been the traditional way in gaining new territory. I need not belabor this point, but look at the history of the United States or how England gained Hong Kong through "the Opium War." A war which was fought in order to continue the trade of Opium to the Chinese, even after the clear opposition of the Chinese Government.

Saddam Hussein must be reminded, just because aggression has been the traditional way in gaining new territory, it doesn't make it right.

If we are truly emerging into a new era of nations working together, with stronger pursuit of justice - we must derail this train, that on a fast track to war. If we are truly establishing a new world order, in which the nations of the world, East and West, North and South, can prosper and live in harmony, we must derail this train.

If this proposal is followed, we can derail this train and reach a peaceful solution of the Mid East Crisis. A solution that will be pleasing in God's sight. For it is recorded that God has no pleasure in the death of the wicked, but his pleasure comes when the wicked turns from his way and lives. If in fact, we are to have a new world order, its foundation should be one that's pleasing in God's sight.

We must remember we can't do anything without God, but mess things up. The Lord will lead us to the path of righteousness for his name's sake. On this path of righteousness we will find love. Not the type of love that one finds with affection and emotion, but the type of love, the late Dr. Martin Luther King Jr. spoke of, - "A type of love much deeper than that found with affection and emotion - A type of love that is a sought of understanding, created redemptive goodwill for all men." Yes, we will find this on the pathway of righteousness.

On this pathway we will also find patience. The Qur'an reminds its believers of the importance of patience in the time of adversity - For God is with those who are patient in adversity.

At this junction, I'm reminded of something Jesus said, "Love your enemies, bless than that despitefully use you." Yes we must discover Love, Patience, and the Power of Prayer. In addition to these things the following actions must be taken:

1. The Mid East must awaken to the realization of the false sense of security the West has to offer to the region. For the Qur'an bears witness to the spoils of war. It tells believers to pay heed unto God and his Apostles, and do not (allow yourselves to) be at variance with one another, lest you lose heart and your moral strength desert you. And be patient in adversity: for, verily, God is with those who are patient in adversity.

The Qur'an also instructs believers to: Be not like those (unbelievers) who went forth from their homelands full of self-conceit and a desire to be seen and praised by men: for they were trying to turn others away from the path of God. And the Qur'an reminds believers how Satan made all their doing seem good to them, and said, "No one can overcome you this day, for behold, I shall be your protector! Nevertheless when the two hosts came within sight of one another, he turned on his heels and said, "behold, I am not responsible for you. Likewise, the West cannot be the Mid East Protector. I say to you today, as it is recorded in the Qur'an, he who places his trust in God, knows that, verily, God is almighty, wise. God is your true protector.

2. After, this awareness, King Fahd of Saudi Arabia must order all foreign troops to leave his country, to include the massive build-up of U. S. troops. When this occurs, it will pave the way for real negotiation in the region.

3. Likewise, President Saddam Hussein must order his troops to leave Kuwait. This is the measure it will take to show that President Saddam Hussein wants peace within the region, also.

4. As the foreign troops pull out of Saudi Arabia, President Saddam Hussein must pull his troops out of Kuwait.

5. President Saddam Hussein must find peace with God. This peace will come once he asks for forgiveness and offers to assist in restoring Kuwait.

6. Next, the restoration of Kuwait's' Ruling Family must become a reality.

7. Once law and order are restored in Kuwait, by the Ruling Family the leadership of Iraq and Kuwait must re-address the disputed territory and resolve this issue peacefully.

8. The leadership of the region must work together to establish a strong network of togetherness in the spirit of love and respect. This solidarity will be pleasing in God's sight.

9. The United Nations must work within the region and address the issues pertaining to the PLO homeland. Meaningful negotiation must become the

172

trademark of the United Nations and not war. The U. N. must take action to ensure that the U. N. is never used as a launching pad or war.

10. Moreover, the United States Government must focus on the things that made this country great - a Government for the people and by the people. We must continue our involvement in world affairs; however, we must take a new look at our priorities. As we re-prioritize, let's make sure our internal affairs are on top of the list i.e. the homeless problem, equal opportunity and treatment, the budget deficit, unemployment, quality of education, drug abuse, the balance of trade, crime, quality of life, gang violence, race relations, environmental concerns, AIDS, and the future of this great country.

If we are to remain a great nation, we must take care of our own. With this resolve, we truly will set the stage and will not be seen as "Bullies" or hypocrites, but as leaders. Let's not lose sight of this fact: ineffective leadership is the catalyst of the downfall of great nations in the past.

Once we begin to take care of our own, we will discover that we can master our deficit problem by addressing our internal affairs. At this point, we will find that all of our problems are inter-related. Once this is accomplished, we will be a true leader of the world - a nation that obtains the second to none status and a nation that will be pleasing to God, the almighty.

I say again, let's come together and regain our focus and attack these difficult days with the resolve that we will overcome and pave the way to a great future. Follow these instructions and let's resolve the Mid East Crisis, peacefully.

America, let's redirect our energy and become a Greater Nation, one that all Americans can proudly stand and sing together, "I too, sing America" For I too, Sing America.

May God bless this land and good will to all mankind.

Note: This was first published in January 1991

Chapter Ten
Learning to Fear God

"And I saw another angel fly in the midst of heaven, having the **everlasting gospel** to preach unto them that dwell on the earth, and to every nation, and kindred, and tongue, and people. Saying with a loud voice, Fear God, and give glory to him; for the hour of his judgment is come: and worship him that made heaven, and earth, and the sea, and the fountains of waters." (Revelation 14:6-7) **Everlasting Gospel is only mention once in the Bible, however it is imperative for Christians to adhere to this message today.**

"The fear of the Lord is the beginning of wisdom: and the knowledge of the holy is understanding." (Proverbs 9:10) We must learn to fear God from his word; however like in the past, today we find that many do not fear the Lord because they were never taught to fear God from his word, but they have been taught to fear God from the precepts of men.

"Wherefore the Lord said, Forasmuch as this people draw near me with their mouth, and their lips do honour me, but have removed their heart far from me, and their fear toward me is taught by the precept of men: Therefore, behold, I will proceed to do a marvelous work among this people, even a wonder: for the wisdom of their wise men shall perish, and the understanding of their prudent men shall be hid. Woe unto them that seek deep to hide their counsel from the Lord, and their works are in the dark, and they say, Who seeth us? And who knoweth us?" (Isaiah 29:13-15)

Mark 7:7 says, we can worship the Lord in vain by teaching for doctrines the commandments of men. Christians must understand what happens to Israel and Judah; they did not fear God and did not hearken to his commandments. They were given an opportunity to be redeemed, however, they rejected the Saviour and continued in their wickedness. Many of us can quote John 3:16 by heart, "For God so loved the world, that he gave his only begotten Son, that whosoever believeth in him should not perish, but have everlasting life."

It is good to memorize this scripture, but it is also important to understand what prompted God to do what he did. Isaiah chapter 59 sheds light for all to understand why God and his Spirit sent the Redeemer. Isaiah explains that wickedness abounds. They shed the blood of the innocent. Their thoughts were iniquity, and there was no judgment. Isaiah 59:14-15 says, "And judgment is turned away backward, and justice standeth afar off: for truth is fallen in the street, and equity cannot enter. Yea, truth faileth; and he that departeth from evil maketh himself a prey: and the Lord saw it, and it displeased him that there was no judgment." Remember the Lord loves judgment. (Isaiah 61:8)

There was no judgment in the land and the ones who departed from evil made himself a prey; this did not please God. Isaiah 26:9 says, "...for when thy judgments are in the earth, the inhabitants of the world will learn righteousness." Isaiah 3:13 says, "The Lord standeth up to plead, and standeth to judge the people. 1 Peter 4:17 says, "For the time is come that judgment must first begin at the house of God;" The Lord of host said that he would come near to us to judgment.

Malachi 3:5-7 says, "And I will come near to you to judgment; and I will be a swift witness against the sorcerers, and against the adulterers, and against false swearers, and against those that oppress the hireling in his wages, the widow, and the fatherless, and that turn aside the stranger from his right, and fear not me, saith the Lord of hosts. For I am the LORD, I change not; therefore ye sons of Jacob are not consumed." According to Malachi Chapter 3, the Lord is like a fuller's soap and sits as a refiner and purifier of silver. God wants us to be purged and refined as gold and silver; He wants an offering in righteousness, therefore God sends judgments near to us so we are not consumed at His coming.

Acts 7:56 records how Stephen look up steadfastly into heaven, and saw the glory of God, and Jesus standing on his right hand. Now we realize, Jesus was standing to plead and to judge. Revelation chapter 2 and chapter 3, bear records of Jesus' report cards to the Seven Churches; this is evidence that judgment has begun in the house of God. These report cards, progress reports, or appraisals, were Jesus' assessments of the Church. Jesus gave complete reports to include their strengths, problem areas, the consequences for failing to repent, and Jesus outlined the rewards for enduring until He comes again. We must learn from these reports. It is important to study the word of God and allow the Holy Spirit to teach us. Then and only then we receive understand.

With this understanding, we bring clarity to Daniel 7:26. Daniel 7:26 says, "But the **judgment sit,** and they shall take away his dominion. To consume and to destroy it unto the end." Where did the judgment sit? The answer is judgment sat on earth. Listen carefully. According to Daniel 7:25, this king made war with the saints of God and prevailed against them. The saints of God were given into his hands until a time and times and the dividing of time. Judgment sits to allow the saints of God to make the Bride ready for the marriage of the Lamb. Jesus brings judgments unto the saints of God to refine them and to make them as gold and silver. After the Bride makes herself ready, then the marriage of the Lamb will take place in heaven. Then the Bride will come back with the Lord as part of His army to the battle of the great day of the Lord against the kings of the earth. (Revelation 19:1-14)

Proverbs 8:13 says, "The fear of the Lord is to hate evil: pride, and arrogancy, and evil way, and the froward mouth, I do hate." In Isaiah 45:7, God says, "I form the light, and create darkness: **I make peace, and create evil: I the Lord do all of these things."** God hates evil, yet He creates evil. Evil is created to reward them that do evil in the sight of God. God gave Law; if you obeyed His Law, you did what was right in His sight; but, if you did not keep His Law, you did what was evil in His sight. Psalm 34:16 says, "The face of the LORD is against them that do evil, to cut off the remembrance of them from the earth." 2 Samuel 3:39 says, "...the Lord shall reward the doer of evil, according to his wickedness."

Isaiah 3:8-9 points out how Jerusalem and Judah rewarded evil unto themselves. Let us read: "For Jerusalem is ruined, and Judah is fallen: because their tongue and their doings are against the LORD, to provoke the eyes of his glory. The show of their countenance doth witness against them; and they declare their sin as Sodom, they hide it not. Woe unto their soul! For they have rewarded evil unto themselves." As you read the Appendix 1 to this book, you will notice what happened to the kings who did that which was right in the sight of God and those which did evil in the sight of God. You can clearly see how when they did what was right in the sight of God they received blessings from God. On the other hand, when they did that, which was evil in the sight of God, God brought evil unto them.

God explains in Jeremiah 18:7-10 how He applies this judgment. "At what instant I shall speak concerning a nation, and concerning a kingdom, to pluck up, and to pull down, and to destroy it; if that nation, against whom I have pronounced, turn from their evil, I will repent of the evil that I thought to do unto them. And at what instant I shall speak concerning a nation, and concerning a kingdom, to build and to plant it; if it do evil in my sight, that obey not my voice, then I will repent of the good, wherewith I said I would benefit them."

In this chapter, we have included some of the scriptures that give the scope of the judgment on the house of Judah and Israel. Besides Judah and Israel, we share the prophecies against Mount Seir, Ammon, Edom, Syria, Hazor, Elam, Babylon, Egypt, and Gog and see how God used these other nations to reward nations with evil for the evil that they have committed. Then we will show how God brings evil to the very nations that He had used to bring evil to others, and

178

then rewarded them with evil for the evil that they have done. Romans 15:4 says, "For whatsoever things were written aforetime were written for our learning, that through patience and comfort of the scriptures might have hope." This is our objective in sharing this work in this chapter.

First, we will review the summary of the judgments on the House of Judah and the House of Israel.

Summary of Judgments on House of Judah and the House of Israel

Jeremiah chapter 11 explains the curse on the House of Judah for breaking the covenant that God commanded their fathers in the day that God brought them forth out of the land of Egypt, from the iron furnace. God told them to, "Obey my voice, and do them, according to all which I command you: so shall ye be my people, and I will be your God: That I may perform the oath which I have sworn unto your fathers to give them a land flowing with milk and honey, as it is this day…" (Jeremiah 11:4)

God told Jeremiah to tell the men of Judah, "Cursed be the man that obeyeth not the words of this covenant." (Jeremiah 11:3) Jeremiah 11:10 says, "They are turned back to the iniquities of their forefathers, which refused to hear my words; and they went after other gods to serve them: the house of Israel and the house of Judah have broken my covenant which I made with their fathers." God promised to bring evil upon them that they could not escape. (Jeremiah 11:11)

God was so displeased with the House of Israel, that he refused to receive their offerings: God wanted them to focus on judgment and righteousness. Amos 5:21-24 records what God told the House of Israel. "I hate, I despise your feast days, and I will not smell in your solemn assemblies. Though ye offer me burnt offerings and your meat offerings, I will not accept them: neither will I regard the peace offerings of your fat beasts. Take thou away from me the noise of thy songs; for I will not hear the melody of thy viols. But let judgment run down as waters, and righteousness as a mighty stream." Below is a summary of some of the things they did to break the covenant that God commanded their fathers in the day that God brought them forth out of the land of Egypt, from the iron furnace.

Summary of the Offenses of the House of Israel and the House of Judah

The iniquity of the house of Israel and Judah is exceeding great, and the land is full of blood, and the city full of perverseness: for they say, The LORD hath forsaken the earth, the LORD seeth not. (Ezekiel 9:9)

House of Judah - They committed abominations - filled the land with violence and returned to provoke God to anger. (Ezekiel 8:17)

Their iniquities testified against them. (Jeremiah 7:7)

They forsook God, walked after other gods, worshipped them, and failed to keep God's law at a level that was worse than their fathers and every one walked after the imagination of his evil heart and did not hearken unto God. (Jeremiah 16:11-12)

House of Israel - Men devised mischief and gave wicked counsel - Israel multiplied the slain in this city of caldron and filled the streets thereof with the slain - They did not walk in the statutes of God and they did not execute the judgments of God, but followed after the manners of the heathen that were round about them. (Ezekiel 11:15)

House of Israel - "Thus saith the Lord God; because thy filthiness was poured out, and thy nakedness discovered through thy whoredoms with thy lovers, and with all the idols of thy abominations, and by the blood of thy children, which thou didst give unto them. Behold, therefore I will gather all thy lovers, with whom thou hast taken pleasure, and all them that thou hast loved,

180

with all them that thou hast hated; I will even gather them round about against thee, and will discover thy nakedness unto them, that they may see all thy nakedness. And I will judge thee, as women that break wedlock and shed blood are judged; and I will give thee blood in fury and jealousy." (Ezekiel 16:36-39)

"They will not frame their doings to turn unto their God: for the spirit of whoredoms in the midst of them, and they have not known the Lord. And the pride of Israel doth testify to his face: therefore shall Israel and Ephraim fall in their iniquity; Judah also shall fall with them." (Hosea 5:4-5)

They trusted in man and made flesh their arm and their heart departed from God (Jeremiah 17:5)

They failed to honor the Sabbath day - they did not incline their ear - they made their neck stiff to keep from hearing God's instruction. (Jeremiah 17:23) (Ezekiel 20:13)

Judah - This is a rebellious people, lying children that will not hear the law of the LORD - They despised the word of God, and trust in oppression and perverseness - Therefore this iniquity shall be to you as a breach ready to fall, swelling out in a high wall, whose breaking cometh suddenly at an instance. (Isaiah 30:9-13)

Judah - "Ye have plowed wickedness, ye have reaped iniquity; ye have eaten the fruit of lies; because thou didst trust in thy way, in the multitude of thy mighty men." (Hosea 10:13)

Judah - "Thus saith the Lord God; This is Jerusalem: I have set it in the midst of the nations and countries that are round about her. And she hath changed my judgments into wickedness more than the nations, and my statutes more than the countries that are round about her: for they have refused my judgments and my statutes, they have not walked in them. Therefore thus saith the Lord God; Because ye multiplied more than the nations that are round about you, and have not walked in my statutes, neither have kept my judgments, neither have done according to the judgments of the nations that are round about you; Therefore thus saith the Lord God; Behold, I, even I, am against thee, and will execute judgments in the midst of thee in the sight of the nations. And I will do in thee that which I have not done, and whereunto I will not do any more the like, because of all thine abominations." (Ezekiel 5:5-9)

The Pastors - Woe be unto the pastors that destroy and scatter the sheep of my pastors (Jeremiah 23:1-2) "His watchmen are blind: dogs which can never have enough, and they are shepherds that cannot understand: they all look to their own way, every one for his gain, from his quarter. Come ye, say they, I will fetch wine, and we will fill ourselves with strong drink; and tomorrow shall be as this day, and much more abundant." (Isaiah 56:10-12)

God also brought word to Ezekiel regarding the pastors; here is a quote from Ezekiel 34:2-5 "Son of man, prophesy against the shepherds of Israel, prophesy, and say unto them, Thus said the Lord God unto the shepherds; Woe be to the shepherds of Israel that do feed themselves! Should not the shepherds feed the flocks? Ye eat the fat, and ye clothe you with the wool, ye kill them that are fed: but ye feed not the flock   The diseased have ye not strengthened, neither have ye healed that which was sick, neither have ye bound up that which was broken, neither have ye brought again that which was driven away, neither have ye sought that which was lost; but with force and with cruelty have ye ruled them. And they were scattered, because there is no shepherd: and they became meat to all the beasts of the field, when they were scattered."

The Prophets - "I have seen also in the prophets of Jerusalem an horrible thing: they commit adultery, and walk in lies: they strengthen also the hands of evildoers, that none doth return from his wickedness: they are all of them unto me as Sodom, and the inhabitants thereof as Gomorrah." (Jeremiah 23:14)

"In that day there shall be a fountain opened to the house of David and to the inhabitants of Jerusalem for sin and for uncleanness. And it shall come to pass in that day, saith the Lord of hosts, that I will cut off the names of the idols out of the land, and they shall no more be remembered: and also I will cause the prophets and the unclean spirit to pass out of the land. (Zechariah 13:1-2) (Note – this pertains to the prophets in the land of Judah; according to scriptures, God still has prophets today. Reference Amos 3:6-7 and Acts 2:18)

Summary of Types of Destruction for the House of Judah and the House of Israel

Cast out of the sight for God. Death to death, sword to sword, famine to famine, and captivity to captivity (Jeremiah 15:2)

Four kinds were appointed over them. The sword to slay, dogs to tear, fowls of the heaven and the beasts of the earth, to devour and destroy. (Jeremiah 15:3) Cause them to be removed into all kingdoms of the earth. (Jeremiah 15:4)

They shall die of grievous deaths; they should not be lamented; neither shall they be buried; but they shall be as dung upon the face of the earth: and they should be consumed by the sword, and by famine; and their carcases shall be meat for the fowls of the heaven, and the beast of the earth. (Jeremiah 16:4)

"Woe unto him that buildeth his house by unrighteousness, and his chambers by wrong; they useth his neighbour's service without wages, and giveth him not for his work." (Jeremiah 22:13)

"For thus said the Lord unto the king's house of Judah; Thou art Gilead unto me, and the head of Lebanon: yet surely I will make thee a wilderness; and cities which are not inhabited. And I will prepare destroyers against thee, every one with his weapons: they shall cut down thy choice cedars, and cast them into the fire." (Jeremiah 22:6-7)

"Therefore thus saith the Lord God; because ye are all become dross, behold, therefore I will gather you into the midst of Jerusalem. As they gather silver, and brass, and iron, and lead, and tin, into the midst of the furnace, to blow the fire upon it, to melt it; so will I gather you in mine anger and in my fury, and I will leave you there, and melt you. Yea, I will gather you and blow upon you in the fire of my wrath, and ye shall be melted in the midst thereof. As silver is melted in the midst of the furnace, so shall ye be melted in the midst thereof; and ye shall know that I the Lord have poured out my fury upon you." (Ezekiel 22:19-22) This describes the systematic mass slaughter of six million European Jews in the Nazi concentration camps during World War II.

Judah - "Therefore the fathers shall eat the sons in the midst of thee, and the sons shall eat their fathers; and I will execute judgments in thee, and the whole remnant of thee will I scatter into all the winds. Wherefore, as I live, saith the Lord God; Surely, because thou hast defiled my sanctuary with all thy detestable things, and with all thine abominations, therefore will I also diminish thee; neither shall mine eye spare, neither will I have any pity. A third part of thee shall die with the pestilence, and a third part shall fall by the sword round about thee; and I will scatter a third part into all the winds, and I will draw out a sword after them. Thus shall mine anger be accomplished, and I will cause my fury to rest upon them, and I will be comforted: and they shall know that I the Lord have spoken it in my zeal, when I have accomplished my fury in them." (Ezekiel 5:10-13)

Prophecy of Israel – The Future Glory

God is a merciful God and faithful to all of His promises. God cast Israel out of his sight because of their sin; nevertheless, In Jeremiah 23:5-8, Jeremiah writes, "Behold, the days come, saith the LORD, that I will raise unto David a righteous Branch, and a King shall reign and prosper, and shall execute judgment and justice in the earth. In his days Judah shall be saved, and Israel shall dwell safely: and this is his name whereby he shall be called, THE LORD OUR

RIGHTEOUSNESS. Therefore, behold, the days come, saith the LORD, that they shall no more say, The LORD liveth, which brought up the children of Israel out of the land of Egypt; But, the LORD liveth, which brought up and which led the seed of the house of Israel out of the north country, and from all countries whither I had driven them; and they shall dwell in their own land."

Ezekiel prophesizes about these days in 36:33-36, "Thus saith the Lord God; In the day that I shall have cleansed you from all your iniquities I will also cause you to dwell in the cities, and the wastes shall be builded. And they shall say, This land that was desolated is become like the garden of "Eden; and the waste and desolate and ruined cities are become fenced, and are inhabited. Then the heathen that are left round about you shall know that I the Lord build the ruined places, and plant that that was desolate: I will do it."

In Ezekiel 37:22-23 the Lord says, "And I will make them one nation in the land upon the mountains of Israel, and one king shall be king of them all: and they shall be no more two nations, neither shall they be divided into two kingdoms any more at all: Neither shall they defile themselves any more with their idols, nor with their detestable things, nor with any of their transgressions: but I will save them out of all their dwelling-places, wherein they have sinned, and will cleanse them: so shall they be my people, and I will be their God."

According to Ezekiel 38:14, a day will come when Israel will dwell in safety. Israel has been working to that end ever since 1948 after returning to their own land. In 1948, the new nation was invaded by neighboring Arab League countries; fighting ended in 1949. At the end of the conflict, Israel occupied part of Jerusalem and part of Arab Palestine. They refused to leave and expelled the Arabs from the land and there was no treaty signed. Jordan annexed the remainder of Arab Palestine to include east Jerusalem in 1950. At that time, there was continued friction along the Jordan-Israel border that led to numerous clashes.

Israel attacked Egyptian bases on the Sinai Peninsula and advance within 10 miles of the Suez Canal in October 1956. There has been many border clashes, however in June 1967, a full-scale war was fought; the war last six days. Israel quickly inflicted massive destruction on Egypt, Syria, and Jordan, and captured the Gaza Strip, the Sinai Peninsula, the Golan Heights, and Jordanian territory west of the Jordan. In 1973, Egypt and Syria made a full-scale attack against Israel. Before the war concluded, Iraq and Jordan sent troops to assist Egypt and Syria. After 22 days, with the support of the United States, and the Soviet Union, the United Nations effected a cease-fire. There was a war between Israel and Lebanon in 1982. Moreover, there has been continued tension with Jordan, and Palestine.

In July 2006, Israel was fighting on two fronts in Lebanon and Gaza Strip. In August 2006, the United Nations effected a cease-fire on the front of Lebanon. This effort is designed to bring Israel to a place of safety. However, before this safety is realized, according to Isaiah chapter 17, Israel will engage in a war with Syria. According to the scriptures, Damascus will cease from being a city. Isaiah 17:1 says, "...Behold, Damascus is taken away from being a city, and it shall be a ruinous heap."

Listen carefully. "The fortress also shall cease from Ephraim, and the kingdom from Damascus, and the remnant of Syria: they shall be as the glory of the children of Israel, saith the Lord of hosts. And in that day it shall come to pass, that the glory of Jacob shall be **made thin**, and the **fatness of his flesh shall wax lean.**" (Isaiah 17:3-4) Isaiah 17:7-9 says, "At that day shall a man look to his Maker, and his eyes shall have respect to the Holy One of Israel." And he shall not look to the altars, the work of this hands, neither shall respect that which his fingers have made, either the groves, or the images. In that day shall his strong cities be as a forsaken bough, and an uppermost branch, which they left because of the children of Israel: and there shall be desolation." **Why will this**

happen to Syria? Isaiah 17:10 says, "Because thou hast forgotten the God of thy salvation, and hast not been mindful of the rock of thy strength, …"

After this war with Syria, Israel will experience a period of safety, however it will be short lived. Before Isaiah ends chapter 17, he gives a warning to the multitude of many people who will attack Israel next. Isaiah 17:12 says, "Woe to the multitude of many people, which make a noise like the noise of the seas; and to the rushing of nations that make a rushing like the rushing of mighty waters! The nations shall rush like the rushing of many waters: but God shall rebuke them, and they shall flee far off, and shall be chased as the chaff of the mountains before the wind, and like a rolling thing before the whirlwind."

Listen carefully. After reading the above text, some have advised to go forth to war because they have sure victory. However, it is not that simple. Let us read another account of this war as recorded by Ezekiel. Ezekiel chapter 38 identifies the people and gives the specifics of the attack.

At Ezekiel 38:2 says, Son of man, set thy face against Gog, the land of Magog, the chief prince of Meshech and Tubal, and prophesy against him. Besides prophesying against Gog, the following nations are included in this prophecy by Ezekiel: Persia, Ethiopia, Libya, Gomer, and all his bands; the house of Togarmah of the north quarters, and all his bands and many people with thee. They all will participate in this attack. (Ezekiel 38:5-6)

Let us take a closer look at the players.

➤ Gog - The sons of Japheth are as follows: Gomer, Magog, Madai, Javan, Tubal, Meshech, and Tiras.

➤ Gomer, and all his bands (Ezekiel 38:6) Today Gomer is Germany. "All of his bands" appears to be the European Union

➤ Gog, the land of Magog the chief prince of Meshech (Moscow the capital of Russia) and Tubal (The military headquarters of Russia)

➤ Persia (Ezekiel 38:5) Persia is Iran

187

> Ethiopia (Ezekiel 38:5)

> Togarmah is Turkey

Ezekiel 38:8-9 says, "After many days thou (Gog) shalt be visited: In the latter years thou shalt come into land that is brought back from the sword, and is gathered out of many people, against the mountains of Israel, which have been always waste: but it is brought forth out of the nations, and they shall dwell safely all of them.   Thou shalt ascend and come like a storm, thou shalt be like a cloud to cover the land, thou, and all thy bands, and many people with thee."

Ezekiel 38:10-12   says, "Thus saith the Lord God, It shall come to pass, that at the same time shall things come into thy (Gog) mind, and thou (Gog) shalt think an evil thought. And thou (Gog) shalt say, I will go up to the land of unwalled villages; I will go to them that are at rest, **that dwell safely,** all of them dwelling without walls, and having neither bars nor gates, to take a spoil, and to take a prey; to turn thine hand unto the desolate places that are now inhabited and upon the people that are gathered out of the nations which have gotten cattle and goods, that dwell in the midst of the land.

Ezekiel 38:16 says, "And thou shalt come up against my people of Israel, as a cloud to cover the land; it shall be in the latter days, and I will bring thee against my land, that the heathen may know me. When I shall be sanctified in thee, O Gog, before their eyes." Ezekiel 38:18-20 says, And it shall come to pass at the same time when Gog shall come against the land of Israel, saith the Lord God, that my fury shall come up in my face. For in my jealousy and in the fire of my wrath have I spoke, surely in that day **there shall be a great shaking in the land of Israel**; So that the fishes of the sea, and the fowls of the heaven and the beasts of the field, and all creeping things that creep upon the earth, and all the men that are upon the face of the earth, shall shake at my presence, and the mountains shall be thrown down, and the steep places shall fall, and every wall shall fall to the ground."

188

After carefully examining Ezekiel chapters 38 and Revelation chapters 6, 17, and 19, and Zechariah chapters 12, 13, and 14, it is apparent this is the war between the Lamb and the kings of the earth. However, before this war occurs, according to Revelation 17:16, Revelation 16:10, 16:19, and Revelation chapter 18, first Mystery Babylon must be destroyed and according to Revelation 19:7 the bride of the Lamb will make herself ready and the marriage of the Lamb will be realized.

In Matthew 24:7 Jesus says, "For nation shall rise against nation, and kingdom against kingdom, and there shall be famines, and **pestilences** and **earthquakes**, in divers places." This occurs when the sixth and seven seals are opened. Israel will also experience a great earthquake at the time of this battle.

Ezekiel 38:19 says, "…there shall be a **great shaking** in the land of Israel…" Besides, Isaiah and Ezekiel, Zechariah gives an account of this war and earthquake. Zechariah 14:2-5 says, "For I will gather all nations against Jerusalem to battle; and the city shall be taken, and the houses rifled, and the women ravished; and half of the city shall go forth into captivity, and the residue of the people shall not be cut off from the city. Then shall the Lord go forth, and fight against those nations, as when he fought in the day of battle. And his feet shall stand in that day upon the mount of Olives, which is before Jerusalem on the east, and the mount of Olives shall cleave in the midst thereof toward the east and toward the west, and there shall be a very great valley; and half of the mountain shall remove toward the north, and half of it toward the south. And ye shall flee to the valley of the mountains; for the valley of the mountain shall reach unto Azal: yea, ye shall flee, like as ye fled from the earthquake in the days of Uzziah king of Judah: and **the Lord my God shall come, and all the saints with thee**."

God word is complete, however we must search the scriptures. To this end, let us review John's account as outlined in the book of Revelation. In Revelation 19:11, John writes, "And I saw heaven opened, and behold a

189

Whitehorse; and he that sat upon him was called Faithful and True, and in righteousness he doth judge and make war." Revelation 19:14 says, And the **armies which were in heaven followed him upon white horses**, clothed in fine linen, white and clean. And out of his mouth goeth a sharp sword, that with it he should smite the nations: and he shall rule them with a rod of iron; and he treadeth the winepress of the fierceness and wrath of Almighty God. And he hath on his vesture and on his thigh a name written, KING OF KINGS, AND LORD OF LORDS." Zechariah 14:9 says, "And the Lord shall be king over all the earth: in that day shall there be one Lord, and his name one."

Before we go to the next point, let us discuss the armies with the Lamb. Zechariah 14:5 says, "…the Lord my God shall come, and **all the saints with thee**. Revelation 19:7-8 says, "Let us be glad and rejoice, and give honour to him: for the marriage of the Lamb is come and **his wife hath made herself ready**. And to her was granted that she should be arrayed in **fine linen, clean and white: for the fine linen** is the righteousness of saints." Revelation 19:14 says, "And **the armies which were in heaven followed** him upon white horses, **clothed in fine linen, white and clean**. This army includes the bride of Christ, the Church. Before this war, the Bride of Christ will be in heaven. Then they will follow the Lamb to battle the kings of the earth.

Ezekiel 38:21-23 says, "And I will **call for a sword** against him (Gog) throughout all my mountains, saith the Lord God: every man's sword shall be against his brother. And **I will plead against him with pestilence and with blood**; and I will rain upon him, and upon his bands, and upon the many people that are with him, an overflowing rain, and great hailstone, **fire,** and **brimstone**. Thus will I magnify myself, and sanctify myself; and I will be known in the eyes; of many nations, and they shall know that I am the Lord." This plead is made during the seven seal. (Revelation chapter 8 and 9)

In Ezekiel 38:21-23, God says that he would **call for a sword** against

190

Gog. It is important for us to realize **where** God will call for this sword, this will keep us from drawing our own conclusions. In the book of Revelation chapter 9 and chapter 16 clearly explains who God will use. Some have suggested that God will use the United States and England, however the scriptures do not support this conclusion.

Revelation 9:13 – 19, explains the source of the sword, fire, and brimstone. John writes, "And the sixth angel sounded, and I heard a voice from the four horns of the golden altar which is before God, Saying to the sixth angel which had the trumpet, Loose the four angels which are bound in the great river Euphrates. And the four angels were loosed, which were **prepared** for an **hour**, and **a day**, and **a month** and **a year**, **for to slay the third part of men**. And the number of the army of the horsemen was two hundred thousand thousand: and I heard the number of them. And thus I saw the horses in the vision, and them that sat on them, having breastplates of fire, and of jacinth, and brimstone: and the heads of the horses were as the heads of lions; and out of their mouths issued fire and smoke and brimstone. By these three was the third part of men killed, by fire, and by smoke, and by the brimstone, which issued out of their mouths. (Revelation 9:13-18)

Let us recap; this source will kill a third of men kind. God has force of two hundred millions (200,000,000) horsemen, on reserve, to kill a third of men at a predetermined time. The source of the destruction will be by fire, smoke, and brimstone. Revelation 16:12 gives more insight regarding this matter. "And the sixth angel poured out his vial upon the great river Euphrates; and the water thereof was dried up, that the way of **the kings of the east** might be prepared. **This appears to be the affect of a nuclear war from the kings of the east**. Revelation 9:20 refers to these elements: fire, smoke, and brimstones as plagues. Zechariah 14:12 describes the affects of this plague.

Zechariah 14:12 says, "And this shall be the plague wherewith the Lord will smite all the people that have fought against Jerusalem; Their flesh shall consume away while they stand upon their feet, and their eyes shall consume away in their holes, and their tongue shall consume away in their mouth."

It is important to understand how God gather all nations against Jerusalem to battle. Revelation 16:13- 16 says, "And I saw three **unclean spirits like frogs** come out of the **mouth of the dragon**, and out of the **mouth of the beast**, and out of the **mouth of the false prophet**. For they are the **spirits of devils**, working miracles which **go forth unto the kings of the earth** and of the whole world, to **gather them to the battle of that great day of God Almighty**. Behold, I come as a thief. Blessed is he that watcheth, and keepeth his garments, lest he walk naked, and they see his shame. And he gathered them together into the place called in the Hebrew tongue Armageddon."

Listen carefully. This is what is occurring today, **like frogs**, messengers are **carrying messages** from the **mouth of the dragon**, from the **mouth of the beast,** and the from **mouth of the false prophet** unto the **kings of the earth** and of the **whole world**. We must understand unfortunately, in the United States of America, today, we are using the Secretary of State to this end, when the Secretary moves from nation to nation like a frog. As the Secretary of State is being used to this end, representatives from other nations also carry messages from the mouth of dragon, and the mouth of beast, and the mouth of the false prophet. It is imperative that we understand this is design to bring about the battle of Armageddon.

To do what is right and that what is pleasing in the sight of God we must know his word and recognize when messages are coming from the mouth of the dragon, the mouth of the beast, or the mouth of the false prophet. Let examine several messages.

(1) **Is the doctrine of preemptive approach to war, God's approach? Or is the doctrine of preemptive approach to war from the mouth of the**

dragon? This is what the word of God says, "At what instant I shall speak concerning a nation, and concerning a kingdom, to pluck up, and to pull down, and to destroy it; if that nation, against whom I have pronounced, turn from their evil, I will repent of the evil that I thought to do unto them. And at what instant I shall speak concerning a nation, and concerning a kingdom, to build and to plant it; if it do evil in my sight, that obey not my voice, then I will repent of the good, wherewith I said I would benefit them." (Jeremiah 18:7-10) **It is clear that the preemptive approach is not the way of the Lord, however it is a message from the mouth of the dragon.**

Doctrine of unjust sanctions on nations - Sanctions have been placed on North Korea and Cuba because of their forms of government. Two of the consequences of these sanctions on North Korea, many people have starved and recently there have been reports of cannibalism in North Korea. The act of controlling people through these sanctions is words from the mouth of the beast. Effecting this doctrine lend to the state when people cannot buy of sell without the mark of the beast.

Doctrine from the mouth of the false prophet – The message: Jesus Christ is not the Son of God is from the mouth of the false prophet. However, words from the mouth of the false prophet are not limited to this falsehood. Words from the false prophet present conclusions contrary to the word of God.

Jesus says, "Behold, I come as a thief. Blessed is he that watcheth, and keepeth his garments, lest he walk naked, and they see his shame." (Revelation 16:15) Some people do not know that they are naked and desire the day of the Lord. Listen to what Amos says about this desire. "Woe unto you that desire the day of the Lord! To what end is it for you? The day of the Lord is darkness, and not light." (Amos 5:18)

Revelation 19:17-18 says, And I saw an angel standing in the sun; and he cried with a loud voice, saying to all the fowls that fly in the midst of heaven,

193

Come and gather yourselves together unto the supper of the great God. That ye may eat the flesh of kings, and the flesh of captains, and the flesh of mighty men, and the flesh of horses, and of them that sit on them, and the flesh of all men, both free and bond, both small and great."

It is important to know the rest of the story. Revelation 19:19-21 says, "And I saw the beast, and the kings of the earth, and their armies, gathered together to make war against him that sat on the horse, and against his army. And the **beast** was taken, and with him the **false prophet** that wrought miracles before him, with which he deceived them that had received the mark of the beast, and them that worshipped his image. **They both were cast alive into the lake of fire burning with brimstone.** And the remnant were slain with the sword of him that sat upon the horse, which sword proceeded out of his mouth: all the fowls were filled with their flesh." The story does not end here. You are encouraged to read Revelation chapter 20 through Revelation chapter 22 to understand the rest of the story. Praise God.

In Ezekiel 37:26-28 the Lord says, "Moreover I will make a covenant of peace with them (Israel); it shall be an everlasting covenant with them: and I will place them, and multiply them, and set my sanctuary in the midst of them for evermore. My tabernacle also shall be in them: yea, I will be their God, and they shall be my people. And the heathen shall know that I the Lord do sanctify Israel, when my sanctuary shall be in the midst of them for evermore." Revelation 21:3 says, "And I heard a great voice out of heaven saying, Behold the tabernacle of God is with men, and he will dwell with them, and they shall be his people, and God himself shall be with them, and be their God."

Learning From the Prophecies of Other Nations

Have you taken time out to really study the word of God? Have you studied the Old Testament that is written for our learning? Ezekiel Chapter 35 shines light on perpetual hatred that still affects the Mid East today. Ezekiel Chapter 36 prophesied to Israel; today we can see how it has come to fruition. In Jeremiah Chapter 48, Jeremiah prophesies against Moab, it has come to pass. (The Moabites are the children of Lot's first daughter; and the children of Lot. Reference Genesis 19:37) Besides, this captivity, Jeremiah prophesies another captivity for Moab at Jeremiah 48:47, **"Yet will I bring again the captivity of Moab in the latter days, said the Lord. Thus far is the judgment of Moab."**

Besides Moab, the Old Testament covers prophecies of other nations to include what will happen in the latter days. However, if you do not read the Old Testament and if it is not preached to you, you will never know the truth that is written in the words of God. In this chapter, we will not just repeat what is written in the Old Testament; but, we are encouraging you to study the word of God. Our aim is to share enough to help you to learn to fear God and to learn more about His ways.

Mount Seir Condemned for Perpetual Hatred and Shedding Blood

In Ezekiel Chapter 35, Ezekiel prophesies against Mount Seir. This prophecy is about the doom of Edom because of their perpetual hatred, they shed the blood of the children of Israel by the force of sword in the time of their calamity, in the time that their iniquity had an end. The book of Obadiah also covers what happened to Edom.

Besides, Ezekiel and Obadiah, in Jeremiah Chapter 49, Jeremiah also prophesies against Edom, Ammon, Syria, Hazor, and Elam. Jeremiah prophesied that Nebuchadnezzar, the king of Babylon, would conquer these nations. This has come to pass. Besides, the captivity of these nations by Babylon let us look at some of the specific things that God said he would do.

Prophecy Against Edom

The children of Edom are the children of Esau. (Genesis 25:30) "Edom shall be a desolation: every one that goeth by it shall be astonished, and shall hiss at all the plagues thereof. As in the overthrow of Sodom and Gomorrah and the neighbour cities thereof, saith the LORD, no man shall abide there, neither shall a son of man dwell in it." (Jeremiah 49:17-18) In Ezekiel 25:14 says, "And I will lay my vengeance upon Edom by the hand of my people Israel: and they shall do in Edom according to my fury; and they shall know my vengeance, saith the Lord God."

Prophecy Against Damasus

Damascus – Hamath is confounded. Damascus is waxed feeble, and turned herself to flee, and fear hath seized on her, anguish and sorrows have taken her as a woman travail. Her young men shall fall in her streets, and all the men of war shall be cut off in that day, saith the Lord of hosts. I will kindle a fire in the wall of Damascus, and it shall consume the palaces of Ben-hadad. (Jeremiah 49:23-27)

Isaiah also prophesies against Damascus. Isaiah 17:1-4 says, "The burden of Damascus. Behold, Damascus is taken away from being a city, and it shall be a ruinous heap. The cities of Aroer are forsaken: they shall be for flocks, which shall lie down, and none shall make them afraid. The fortress also shall cease from Ephraim, and the kingdom from Damascus, and the remnant of Syria: they shall be as the glory of the children of Israel, saith the Lord of hosts." According to Isaiah 17:9, "In that day shall his strong cities be as a forsaken bough, and an uppermost branch, which they left because of the children of Israel: and there shall be desolation."

According to the word of God, Israel will make Syria desolate. Destruction comes to Damascus. Isaiah 17:10-11 says, "Because thou hast forgotten the God of thy salvation, and hast not been mindful of the rock of thy strength, therefore shalt thou plant pleasant plants, and shalt set it with strange slips: In the day shalt thou make thy plant to grow, and in the morning shalt thou make thy seed to flourish: but the harvest shall be a heap in the day of grief and of desperate sorrow."

Prophecy Against Philistines

"Thus saith the Lord God; Because the Philistines have dealt by **revenge**, and have taken **vengeance** with a **despiteful heart**, to destroy it for the **old hatred**; therefore thus said the Lord God; Behold, I will stretch out mine hand upon the Philistines, and I will cut off the Cherethims, and destroy the remnant of the sea coast. And I will execute great vengeance, upon them with furious rebukes; and they shall know that I am the Lord, when I shall lay my vengeance upon them." (Ezekiel 25:15-17) Here we can clearly see how **old hatred** led to vengeance, but vengeance is the Lord. (Deuteronomy 32:35, Psalm 94:1, and Hebrews 10:30) Lesson learned: Vengeance belongs to the Lord; if we should take vengeance, God will bring vengeance back to us. Today, Philistines is Palestine.

Prophecy Against Ammon

Ammon are the children of Lot's younger daughter; and the children of Lot, reference Genesis 19:38. In Ezekiel 25:2-4, the word of the Lord came to Ezekiel saying, "Son of man, set thy face against the Ammonites, and prophesy against them; And say unto the Ammonites, Hear the word of the Lord God; Thus saith the Lord God; because thou saidst, Aha, against my sanctuary, when it was profaned; and against the land of Israel, when it was desolate; and against the house of Judah, when they went into captivity; Behold, therefore I will deliver thee to the men of the east for possession, and they shall set their palaces in thee and make their dwellings in thee: they shall eat thy fruit, and they shall drink thy milk." Ezekiel also prophesied that Ammonites would not be remembered among nations. (Ezekiel 25:8-10) This has come to pass.

Besides, Ezekiel, the word of the Lord came to Jeremiah. Jeremiah 49:1-2 says, "Concerning the Ammonites, thus said the LORD, Hath Israel no sons? Hath he no heir? Why then doth their king inherit Gad, and his people dwell in his cities? Therefore, behold the days come, saith the Lord, that I will cause an alarm of war to be heard in Rabbah of the Ammonites; and it shall be a desolate heap, and her daughters shall be burned with fire: then shall Israel be heir unto them that were his heirs, saith the LORD."

As prophesied, Nebuchadnezzar conquered Ammon. As you study the history of Judah, you find that God sent bands of the children of Ammon against Judah to destroy it. (2 King 24:2-4) The foregoing shows how God used Ammon to bring evil unto Judah, and then God used Nebuchadnezzar to bring evil unto Ammon.

Besides, Ammon going into captivity of Nebuchadnezzar, Jeremiah prophesied that Ammon would go into captivity again. Jeremiah 49:6 says, "And afterward I will bring again the captivity of the children of Ammon, saith the LORD. (Ref. Jeremiah 48:47 and 49:39) This has come to pass; The children of Ammon went into captivity again in the early twentieth century when Western Europe conquered this portion of the Middle East. They were part of the colonization process. Today many live in Jordan.

Prophecy Against Elam

The children of Elam are the children of Shem, the son of Noah. (Genesis 10:1 and 10:22) Jeremiah 49:37-39 goes beyond this captivity by Babylon, it says, "And Elam will bring the four winds from the four quarters of heaven, and will scatter them toward all those winds; and there shall be no nation whither the outcasts of Elam shall not come. For I will cause Elam to be dismayed before their enemies, and before them that seek their life: and I will bring evil upon them, even my fierce anger, saith the LORD; and I will send the sword after them, till I have consumed them: **But** it shall come to pass **in the latter days**, that I will bring again the captivity of Elam, saith the LORD. This too has come to pass; Elam went into captivity again in the early twentieth century when Western Europe conquered this portion of the Middle East. They were part of the colonization process.

Prophecy Against Egypt and All Nations Which Came Against Jerusalem

Zechariah 14:16-19 says, "And it shall come to pass, that every one that is left of all the nations which came against Jerusalem shall even go up from year to year to worship the King, the Lord of hosts, and to keep the feast of the tabernacles. And it shall be, that whoso will not come up of all the families of the earth unto Jerusalem to worship the King, the Lord of hosts, even upon them shall be no rain. And if the family of Egypt go not up, and come not, that have no rain; there shall be the plague, wherewith the Lord will smite the heathen that come not up to keep the feast of tabernacles. This shall be the punishment of Egypt, and the punishment of all nations that come not up to keep the feast of tabernacles."

Prophecy Against Gog and the Kings of the Earth

Ezekiel Chapter 38 and Ezekiel 39 cover the prophecy against Gog, the chief prince of Meshech and Tubal. Who is Gog? In Genesis 10:2, we find the sons of Japheth who is the son of Noah. The sons of Japheth are as follows: Gomer, Magog, Madai, Javan, Tubal, Meshech, and Tiras. Why is it important to us today?

It is important today because part of the prophecies against Gog was for the latter years to include before the one-thousand-year reign of Christ on earth as King of Kings and Lord of Lords and after the one-thousand-year reign. We will turn our attention back to why we should fear God by reviewing the prophecies against Gog and other nations as recorded in Ezekiel chapters 38 and 39. You are encouraged to read Ezekiel Chapter 38 and Chapter 39. After carefully examining Ezekiel chapters 38 and Revelation Chapter 19, it is apparent this is the war between the Lamb and the kings of the earth. However, before this war occurs, according to Revelation 17:16 and Revelation chapter 18, Mystery Babylon must be destroyed and a according to Revelation 19:7 the bride of the Lamb will make herself ready and the marriage of the Lamb will be realized. Below is part of the prophecy against Gog and other nations as recorded in Ezekiel Chapter 38.

"(14) Therefore, son of man, prophesy and say unto Gog, Thus saith the Lord God; In that day when my people of Israel **dwelleth safely**, shalt thou not know it? (15) And thou shalt come from thy place out of the north parts, thou, and many people with thee, all of them riding upon horses, a great company, and a mighty army: (16) And thou shalt come up against my people of Israel, as a cloud to cover the land; it shall be in the latter days, and I will bring thee against my land, that the heathen may know me, when I shall be sanctified in thee, O Gog, before their eyes. (17) Thus saith the Lord God; Art thou he of whom I have spoken in old time by my servants the prophets of Israel, which prophesied in those days many years that I would bring thee against them? (18) And it shall come to pass at the same time when Gog shall come against the land of Israel, saith the Lord God, that my fury shall come up in my face.

At Ezekiel 38:21-22, God says, "And I will call for a sword against him throughout all my mountains, saith the Lord: every man's sword shall be against his brother. And I will plead against him with **pestilence** and with **blood**; and I will rain upon him, and upon his bands, and upon the many people that are with him, **an overflowing rain**, and **great hailstones**, **fire**, and **brimstone**. Thus will I magnify myself, and sanctify myself; and I will be known in the eyes of many nations, and they shall know that I am the LORD. Revelation 19:17-21 gives more details.

Revelation 19:17-18 says, And I saw an angel standing in the sun; and he cried with a loud voice, saying to all the fowls that fly in the midst of heaven, Come and gather yourselves together unto the supper of the great God. That ye may eat the flesh of kings, and the flesh of captains, and the flesh of mighty men, and the flesh of horses, and of them that sit on them, and the flesh of all men, both free and bond, both small and great."

Revelation 19:19-21 says, "And I saw the beast, and the kings of the earth, and their armies, gathered together to make war against him that sat on the horse, and against his army. And the beast was taken, and with him the false prophet that wrought miracles before him, with which he deceived them that had received the mark of the beast, and them that worshipped his image. These both were cast alive into the lake of fire burning with brimstone. And the remnant were slain with the sword of him that sat upon the horse, which sword proceeded out of his mouth: all the fowls were filled with their flesh."

Listen carefully. Eighty-three percent of the people of Gog will perish in this war. Ezekiel 39:1-2 says, "Therefore, Thou son of man, prophesy against Gog, and say, Thus saith the Lord God; behold, I am against thee, O Gog, **the chief prince** of Meshech and Tubal: and I will turn thee back, and **leave but the sixth part of thee**, and will cause thee to come up from the north parts and will bring thee upon the mountains of Israel:" The sixth part of Gog is left for a battle in the future, at least a thousand years, after Christ reigns here on earth, as King of Kings and Lord of Lords. Revelation chapter 20 explains how this battle will occur and gives the results.

Revelation 20:1-3 says, "And I saw an angel come down from heaven, having the key of the bottomless pit and a great chain in his hand. And he laid hold on the dragon, that old serpent, which is **the Devil, and Satan, and bound him a thousand years,** And cast him into the bottomless pit, and shut him up, and set a seal upon him, that he should deceive the nations no more, till the thousand years should be fulfilled: and after that he must be loosed a little season.

In the book of Revelation, Chapter 20:7-9 says, "And **when the thousand years are expired, Satan** shall be **loosed out of his prison,** and shall go out to deceive the nations which are in the four quarters of the earth, **Gog and Magog,** to gather them together to battle: the number of whom is as the sand of the sea. And they went up on the breadth of the earth, and compassed the camp of the saints about, and the beloved city: and fire came down from God out of the heaven, and devoured them.

The best ways to discuss this would be to have a bible study with active participation; God has allowed me to prepare a teaching plan for pastors and ministers to facilitate this teaching. The teaching plan is titled: "Revelation Up To the Minute and Beyond."

It is important to realize Ezekiel chapter 38 covers what happens before Christ 1000-year reign here on earth as King of Kings and Lord of Lords. However, the focus of Ezekiel chapter 39 covers what happens to the dragon and Gog after Christ 1000-year reign. Nevertheless, you were able to see what is to come and how God loves Israel and the people that do what is right in His sight. Nations around the world will understand that there is only one True God. Before we conclude this discussion with the prophecies on the United States, it is important that we discuss the prophecy against Tyrus and a lamentation to the princes of Israel as recorded in Ezekiel chapter 19. First, let us review a prophecy against Tyrus.

Prophecy Against Tyrus

In studying prophecy against Tyrus as recorded in Ezekiel Chapter 26, 27, and 28, it was noticed how God focused on the mariners: the wise men, the pilots of Tyrus. It is very important to note that it was the wise men and the proud ruler that caused the destruction of Tyre. The leaders of United States must also learn from the experiences of the wise men and the proud ruler of Tyre. Let us read Ezekiel Chapter 28 from the New King James Version of the Holy Bible.

(1) The word of the LORD came to me again, saying, (2) "Son of man, say to the prince of Tyre, Thus says the Lord God: "Because your heart is "lifted up, And you say, 'I am god, I sit in the seat of gods, In the midst of the seas,' Yet you are a man, and not a god, Though you set your heart as the heart of a god (3) (Behold, you are wiser than Daniel! There is no secret that can be hidden from you! (4) with your wisdom and your understanding you have gained riches for yourself, And gathered gold and silver into your treasuries; (5) By your great wisdom in trade you have increased your riches, And your heart is lifted up because of your riches)," (6) 'Therefore thus says the Lord GOD: "Because you have set your heart as the heart of a god, (7) Behold, therefore, I will bring strangers against you, The most terrible of the nations; And they shall draw their swords against the beauty of your wisdom, and defile your splendor. (8) They shall throw you down into the Pit, and you shall die the death of the slain in the midst of the seas. (9) "Will you still say before him who slays you, 'I am a god'? But you shall be a man, and not a god, In the hand of him who slays you. (10) You shall die the death of the uncircumcised by the hand of aliens; For I have spoken," says the Lord God.'"

As God gave Ezekiel to deliver the following lamentation to the prince of Tyre, God wants the President, the leaders, and people, in the United States of America to learn from this lamentation to Tyre. The lamentation is found in Ezekiel 28:11-19.

(11) Moreover the word of the Lord came to me saying, (12) Son of man, take up a lamentation for the king of Tyre, and say to him, Thus says the Lord God: "You were the seal of perfection, Full of wisdom and perfect in beauty. (13) You were in Eden, the garden of God; every precious stone was your covering; the sardius, topaz, and diamond, beryl, onyx, and jasper, sapphire, turquoise, and emerald with gold. The workmanship of your timbrels and pipes was prepared for you on the day you were created. (14)You were the anointed cherub who covers; I established you; You were on the holy mountain of God; you walked back and forth in the midst of fiery stones. (15) **You were perfect** in your ways from the day you were created, **till iniquity was found in you**. (16) **"By the abundance of your trading you became filled with violence within**; And you sinned; therefore I cast you as a profane thing out of the mountain of God; and I destroyed you, O covering cherub, from the midst of the fiery stones. (17) Your heart was lifted up because of your beauty; You corrupted your wisdom for the sake of your splendor; I cast you to the ground, I laid you before kings, that they might gaze at you. (18) You defiled your sanctuaries by the multitude of your iniquities, by the iniquity of your trading; Therefore I brought fire from your midst; it devoured you, and I turned you to ashes upon the earth in the sight of all who saw you. (19) All who knew you among the people are astonished at you; You have become a horror, And shall be no more forever."

Israel, What Is Your Mother? Ezekiel Chapter 19

Before we examine the prophecy against the United States of America, it is very important for us to carefully review the lamentation for the princes of Israel as recorded in Ezekiel chapter 19.   Israel is asked the following question: **"What is thy mother?"** It shows how Israel trusted in their own strength and later trusted in another country and fails to trust in God. Consequently, they were not able to defend themselves by their own might, and in the end, the nation that Israel trusts in will not be able to help them. This lamentation shows how Israel fails to trust in God. Consequently, Israel will go in captivity again because this nation has not learned this important message from the Redeemer, "O that thou hadst hearkened to my commandments! Then had thy peace been as a river, and the righteousness as the waves of the sea." (Isaiah 48:18) Let us review Ezekiel chapter 19.

(1) Moreover take thou up a lamentation for the princes of Israel,

(2) And say, **What is thy mother**? A lioness: she lay down among lions, she nourished her whelps among young lions.

(3) And she brought up one of her whelps: it became a young lion, and it learned to catch the prey; it devoured men.

(4) The nations also heard of him; he was taken in their pit, and chains unto the land of Egypt.

(5) Now when she saw that she had waited, and her hope was lost, then she took another of her whelps, and made him a young lion.

(6) And he went up and down among the lions, he became a young lion, and learned to catch the prey, and devoured men.

(7) And he knew their desolate palaces, and he laid waste their cities; and the land was desolate, and the fullness thereof, by the noise of his

roaring.

(8) Then the nations set against him on every side from the provinces, and spread their net over him: he was taken in their pit.

(9) And they put him in ward in chains, and brought him to the king of Babylon: they brought him into holds, that his voice should no more be heard upon the mountains of Israel.

(10) **Thy mother** is like a vine in thy blood, **planted by the waters:** she was **fruitful** and **full of branches by reason of many waters.**

(11) And she had **strong rods for the scepters** of them that bare rule, and her stature was **exalted among the thick branches**, and she **appeared in her height with the multitude of her branches.**

(12) **But she was plucked up in fury**, she was cast down to the ground, and the **east wind dried up her fruit: her strong rods were broken and withered**; the **fire consumed them.**

(13) And **now she is planted in the wilderness,** in a dry and thirst ground.

(14) And fire is gone out of a rod of her branches, which hath devoured her fruit, so that she hath no strong rod to be a scepter to rule **This is** a lamentation, and **shall be for** a lamentation.

Let us carefully review this message. This is a lamentation for the princes of Israel and it **shall be for** a lamentation **not for a prince but for a place**. A review of history shows:

(1) Jehoahaz did that which was evil in the sight of the Lord and Pharaoh-nechoh put him in bands at Riblah in the land of hamath, that he might not reign in Jerusalem, eventually Jehoahaz was taken to Egypt, and died there. (2 Kings 23:31-34)

(2) Babylon came up against Jerusalem, and the city was besieged when

206

Jehoiachin was king of Judah. Jehoiachin was carried away to Babylon, besides the king, his mother, and the king's wives, and his officers, and the mighty of the land. (2Kings 24:8-16)

A quick review of scriptures we can clearly see that Ezekiel 19:2-9 is a lamentation written for Jehoahaz and Jehoiachin. However, Ezekiel 19:10-14 is not written for a person, however it covers a future lamentation for a place that acts as she is Israel's mother. Let us take a close look at this place.

(1) Thy mother is like a vine in thy blood

(2) Planted by the waters

(3) She was fruitful full of branches by reason of many waters

(4) She had strong rods for scepters of them that bare rule

(5) Her stature was exalted among the thick branches

(6) She appeared in her height with the multitude of her branches

This place is like a vine in Israel blood, planted by the waters, became fruitful, had a strong rods for the scepters of them that bare rule, her stature was exalted among the branches. This place acts as if she is Israel's mother, but something happens to this place, like something happened to the young lions. Let us see what happen to this place.

(1) She was plucked up in fury

(2) She was cast down to the ground

(3) The east wind dried up her fruit

(4) Her strong rods were broken and withered

(5) Fire consumed her strong rods

(6) In the end she will be planted in the wilderness, in a dry and thirst ground

(7) The fire will go out of a rod of her branches, which hath devoured her fruit

(8) Then she will have no strong rod to be a scepter to rule

207

Today, we need to as this question: Is the United States of America this place that acts as if she is Israel's mother? The United States is a nation that was planted my many waters, full of branches, (states) our stature is exalted among the thick branches, and we have many cities. The United States has prospered because of the many waters. Surely, the United States of America acts as if she is Israel's mother. Hold your thoughts; we will revisit this matter later.

Prophecy Against the United States of America

Proverbs 28:5 says, "Evil men understand not judgment; but they that seek the LORD understand all things." Today, as many look back on 9/11 asking why this happened to us in the United States, they fail to understand judgment. Evil came unto us because of our past actions. God brought it to us; we rewarded evil unto ourselves, as Judah and Israel did.

The United States must learn before this nation is destroyed. God is faithful to all of his promises. We must learn to fear God. Most who study the prophecies have concluded that at the end of this age the United States will not be a super power. They have reached the correct conclusion. Unless the United States of America repents and returns to God, the nation will be destroyed, as ancient Babylon was destroyed.

The leaders of the United States must understand that God knows all things. Many work deep in the dark to hide the counsel of God from His people; however, today as recorded in the book of Psalm 85:10-11, "Mercy and truth are met together: righteousness and peace have kissed each other. Truth shall spring out of the earth; and righteousness shall look down from heaven."

Truth is springing out of the earth, but the people of God must have love for the truth to receive it. In January 2007, I requested a copy of a book titled,

"Rogue Nation", by Clyde Prestowitz from the Madison County Library in Jackson, Tennessee. The Madison Library did not carry the book, however, the were able to obtain it for me through their interlibrary loan program. After reading the book, I was saddened to find the overwhelming evidences of failed policies, deceitfulness, corruption, misguided, and hypocritical activities in nearly every aspect in policies pertaining to our international relations. I love America, but I love God more and I have love for the Spirit of Truth. The leaders of this land must understand that God knows the desires of their hearts. There is nothing hidden from God and today God has individuals, like Clyde Prestowitz uncovering truths. Moreover, today God truly reveals His secrets to His prophets and prophetess.

Some of the men of God have proclaimed that God showed them that President George W. Bush was going to become President of the United States before he was elected; that prophecy came to fruition. However, God did not reveal to them the negative affects of his presidency on this nation and on the world. God revealed this to me, some of this nation's secrets, and the destruction to come. These revelations have come to pass.

God says that He created Evil; some cannot believe that God created evil because God hates evil. Some writers of the various translations of the Holy Bible have change the word "evil" in Isaiah 45:7 to "calamity" or another word. Listen carefully. Hurricane Katrina, Rita, and many of these storms were not merely storms passing through taking heat to the north. God calls them "destroying winds." They were evil and they were created by God to destroy, rewarding us for the evil that we had done. God has showed me we will experience calamity after calamity until we repent.

We need to learn lessons from the words of God; the rationale from men is not enough. As you search the scriptures, you find how God has used the destroying wind in the past, the present, and God will use destroying winds in the

209

future. Jeremiah 51:1-2 says, "Thus saith the LORD; Behold, I will raise up against Babylon, and against them that dwell in the midst of **them** that rise up against me, a **destroying wind**; And will send unto Babylon **fanners**, that shall fan her, and shall empty her land: for in **the day of trouble they shall be against her round about.**"

On April 9, 2003, in the spirit, God took me to Iraq and showed me the destruction. And in the spirit, God brought me back to the United States, to my hometown, Jackson, Tennessee, and showed me the destruction to come there. The destruction to Jackson, Tennessee happened on May 4, 2003 when two tornadoes hit the city. The message is simple. As we do evil to Iraq, God is bringing evil to us. This is how God works; God has a mighty and strong one that controls the storms. Isaiah 28:2 says, "Behold, the Lord hath a mighty and strong one, which as a tempest of hail and a destroying storm, as a flood of mighty waters overflowing, shall cast down to the earth with the hand." In other word, God has a force that controls the storm as a man would by hands.

In Jeremiah 50:2, a standard was established, published, and declared among the nations. God did not conceal this standard. This standard was not only established for ancient Babylon, but for the images of Babylon. Therefore, it applies to nations today. Jeremiah 50:12, refers to Babylon as the **hindermost** of nations will be a wilderness, a dry land, and a desert.   In Isaiah 47:1 it becomes clear that the writing goes beyond ancient Babylon. Isaiah writes, "COME DOWN, and sit in the dust, **O virgin daughter of Babylon,** sit on the ground: there is no throne, O daughter of the Chaldeans: for thou shalt no more be called tender and delicate." Today, we can clearly see at the time of our trouble destroying winds are round about the United States; they continue to come from every front.

We recommend that you read the prophecy against Babylon as recorded in Isaiah chapter 47 and Jeremiah chapter 50 and 51. A careful reading of the referenced word of God clearly shows some of the text was for when Nebuchadrezzar was king of Babylon and some for the latter days. However, the standard was established, published, and declared for Babylon at the time of publication and Babylon (s) in the future to include the Mystery, Babylon the Great.

Revelation Chapter 18 covers the desolation of Babylon; surely, this is not ancient Babylon of the Old Testament. This is MYSTERY, BABYLON THE GREAT, THE MOTHER OF HARLOTS AND ABOMINATIONS OF THE EARTH, the woman that rides on the beast, with seven heads and ten horns. The beast that was, that is not, and yet is; this beast is in fact the image of the beast, that was. Listen carefully to what God has planned for the woman that the beast carries. **Note: In the days of her trouble "destroying winds" will be round about her.**

God does not want us to guess about the messages that he gave to the prophets to deliver to us. God has given us his word and the Spirit of Truth. However, to understand and receive his word, it is imperative that you have love for truth. Nevertheless, God uses symbols. Let us examine the ten horns.

Revelation 17:12 says, "And the ten horns which thou sawest are ten kings, which have received no kingdom as yet; but receive power as kings one hour with the beast." "And the **ten horns** which thou sawest upon the beast, these **shall hate the whore**, and shall **make her desolate and naked**, and shall **eat her flesh**, and **burn her with fire. For God hath put in their hearts to fulfill his will, and to agree, and give their kingdom unto the beast, until the words of God shall be fulfilled."** (Revelation 17:16-17)

Let us examine how this unfolds in the scriptures. Revelation 16:10 says, "And the fifth angel poured out his vial upon the **seat of the beast**; and **his kingdom was full of darkness**; and they gnawed their tongues for pain, and blasphemed the God of heaven because of their pains and their sores, and repented not of their deeds.   Mystery Babylon was riding on the seat of the beast.

It is imperative that you understand this, MYSTERY BABYLON is a nation that is riding on the back of nations and at God's direction these ten kingdoms will give their strength to this beast (the empire or system) that the woman (MYSTERY BABYLON) is riding. These ten kingdoms will hate MYSTERY BABYLON and will destroy her. **HINT: MYSTERY BABYLON IS NOT THE BEAST, BUT THE WOMAN THAT RIDES THE BEAST.**

Listen. Revelation 18:23 says, "And the <u>light of a candle</u> shall shine no more at all in thee; and the <u>voice of the bridegroom</u> and of the <u>bride</u> shall <u>be heard no more at all in thee</u>: for thy merchants were great men of the earth; for by thy sorceries were all nations deceived.**" Let us make it plain. The "candle" is one of God's Churches.** (Revelation 1:20) **"<u>The light of a candle</u>" is the <u>light of God's Church</u>. This means, <u>God has a Church</u> in Mystery Babylon the Great.**

Let us take a closer look at this revelation. Remember the story about the ten virgins in Matthew chapter 25! Jesus says, "Then shall the kingdom of heaven be likened unto ten virgins, which took their lamps, and went forth to meet the bridegroom. And five of them were wise, and five were foolish. They that were foolish took their lamps, and took no oil with them: but the wise took oil in their vessels with their lamps. While the bridegroom tarried, they all slumbered and slept. And at midnight there was a cry made, Behold, the bridegroom cometh; go ye out to meet him. Then all those virgins arose, and trimmed their lamps. And **the foolish** said unto the wise, Give us of your oil; for **our lamps are gone out.**" The wise virgins were ready with their lamps shining went with the bridegroom to the marriage. The foolish virgins light had gone out and they were left behind.

Listen. Fifty percent of the church of God in Mystery Babylon will not be ready to meet Jesus when he comes back. Their light will have gone out. Many Christians do not realize that there is a church of God in Mystery Babylon because their pastors and teachers do not understand doctrine.

The purpose of this chapter is to learn to fear God from the precepts of God. We must remember this is one of God's mysteries therefore the intellect of men is not sufficient to resolve this mystery. "It is the glory of God to conceal a thing: but the honour of kings to search out a matter." (Proverbs 25:2) The standard that was established regarding the judgments of God against Babylon and the images were not concealed. However, "Mystery Babylon" has been concealed in the word of God. God has directed me to reveal the full mystery of Mystery Babylon through this work. After this revelation, a call will be made to come out of her; however first we must learn to fear God from His precepts, this is the objective of this work.

Some of the teachers of prophecy have concluded Papal Rome is Mystery Babylon. However, this teaching is in error because they did not consider all factors. It is true that Papal Rome is the beast identified in Revelation 13:11 that came up out of the earth with two horns like a lamb, and spake as a dragon, but this beast is not Mystery Babylon.

Mystery Babylon is one of God's mysteries; God wants all to be saved. However, before the call is made "to come out of her," first she must be revealed. The people of God must know who she is. The revelator of Mystery Babylon must have love for truth and love truth more that he or she loves the world and the pleasures of this life.

To unlock this mystery, we will use the following scriptures: (1) Isaiah chapter 47, Jeremiah chapters 50 and 51, and Revelation chapters 17 and chapter 18. Let us explore the factors required to unlock this mystery.

(1) **A Standard published for dealing with ancient Babylon and her images.** Jeremiah 50:1-2 says, "Declare ye among the nations, and publish, and set up a standard; publish, and conceal not: say Babylon is taken, Bel is confounded, Merodach is broken in pieces; her idols are confounded, her images are broken in pieces." A standard has been declared and published how God deals with Babylon and all the images of Babylon to include the daughter of Babylon identified in Isaiah chapter 47 and Jeremiah chapters 50 and 51.

(2) **An assembly of great nations from the north to come up against Babylon.** For, lo, I will raise and cause to come up against Babylon an assembly of great nations from the north country: and they shall set themselves in array against her; from thence she shall be taken: their arrows shall be as of a mighty expert man; none shall return in vain. (Jeremiah 50-9) Revelation 17:16-17 says, "Ten horns (kings) which thou sawest upon the beast, these shall hate the whore, and shall make her naked, and shall eat her flesh, and burn her with fire. For God hath put in their hearts to fulfil his will, and to agree, and give their kingdom unto the beast, until the words of God shall be fulfilled." Jeremiah 50:3 says, "Out of the north there cometh a nation against her, which shall make her land desolate and none shall dwell therein: they shall remove, they shall depart. Both man and beast."

(3) **Mystery Babylon has a mother and is the hindermost of nations;** Ancient Babylon did not have a mother. This conclusion is based on the following scriptures: Jeremiah 50:12-13 and Revelation 17:1-3. Jeremiah 50:12-13 says, "Your **mother shall be sore confounded**; she that bare you shall be ashamed: behold, the **hindermost of the nations** shall be a **wilderness**, a dry land, and a desert. Because of the wrath of the Lord it shall not be inhabited, but it shall be wholly desolate: every one that goeth

214

by Babylon shall be astonished, and hiss at her plagues." Revelation 17:1-3 says, "…Come hither; 'I will show unto thee the judgment of the great whore that sitteth upon many waters: with whom the kings of the earth have been made drunk with the wine of her fornication. So he carried me away in the spirit into the **wilderness:** and I saw a woman sit upon a scarlet coloured beast, full of names of blasphemy, having seven heads and ten horns." Hint: The hindermost of nations means this Babylon is the youngest of nations.

(4) **Judgment against the daughter of Babylon as recorded in Isaiah chapter 47:3** says, "Thy nakedness shall be uncovered, yea, thy shame shall be seen: I will take vengeance, and **I will not meet thee as a man**." This supports Revelation 17:16-17 and Jeremiah 50:9.

(5) **Mystery Babylon will be at a time when Israel is brought again to his own land.** (Jeremiah 50:19) Jeremiah 50:20 says, "In those days, and in that time, saith the Lord, the iniquity of Israel shall be sought for, and there shall be none; and the sins of Judah, and they shall not be found: for I will pardon them whom I reserve."

(6) **Babylon is called the hammer of the whole earth.** Jeremiah 50:23 says, "How is the hammer of the whole earth cut asunder and broken! How is Babylon become a desolation among the nations!"

(7) **The attack on the Daughter of Babylon -** Jeremiah 50:41-42 says, "Behold, a people shall come from the north, and a great nation, and many kings shall be raised up from the coasts of the earth. They shall hold the bow and the lance: they are cruel, and will not show mercy: their voice shall roar like the sea, and they shall ride upon horses, every one put on array like a man to the battle, against thee, O daughter of Babylon.

(8) **The attack on Babylon moves the earth**. Jeremiah 50:46 says, at the noise of the taking of Babylon the earth is moved, and the cry is heard

among the nations.

(9) **A Destroying Wind Will Fan Her At Time of Her Trouble**. Jeremiah
51:1-2 says, "Thus saith the Lord; Behold, I will raise up against Babylon,
and against them that dwell in the midst of them that rise up against me, a
destroying wind; and will send unto Babylon fanners, that shall fan her,
and shall empty her land: for in the day of trouble they shall be against her
round about."

(10)   **Babylon hath been a golden cup in the Lord's hand**. Jeremiah
51:7 says, "Babylon hath been a golden cup in the Lord's hand, that made
all the earth drunken of her wine; therefore the nations are mad."
Revelation 17:4 says, And the woman was arrayed in purple and scarlet
colour, and decked with gold and precious stones and pearls having a
golden cup in her hand full of abominations and filthiness of her
fornication: And upon her forehead was a name written, MYSTERY,
BABYLON THE GREAT, THE MOTHER OF HARLOTS AND
ABOMINATIONS OF THE EARTH.

(11)   **Babylon dwellest upon many waters and is abundant in
treasures**. Jeremiah 51:13 says, "O thou that dwellest upon many waters,
abundant in treasures, thine end is come, and the measure of they
covetousness."   Revelation 18:3 says, "For all nations have drunk of the
wine of the wrath of her fornication, and the kings of the earth have
committed fornication with her, and the merchants of the earth are waxed
rich through the abundance of her delicacies.

(12)   **Babylon is called a destroying mountain** (Jeremiah 51:25)
The Daughter of Babylon is like a threshingfloor. (Jeremiah 51:33)
God used this destroying mountain to bring evil to other nations that had
done evil. God knows the evil heart of the destroying mountains. Listen
carefully. Jehoiakim (King of Judah) did that which was evil in the sight

216

of the LORD. (2 King 23:37) Jehoiakim became a servant to Nebuchadnezzar (King of Babylon) for three years. Jehoiakim rebelled against him. (2 Kings 24:1) Then the LORD sent against Jehoiakim bands of the Chaldees, and bands of the Syrians, and bands of the Moabites, and bands of the children of Ammon, and sent them against Judah to destroy it. (2 King 24:2-4) Nevertheless, God says in Jeremiah 51:25, "Behold, I am against thee, O destroying mountain, saith the LORD, which destroyest all the earth: and I will stretch out mine hand upon thee, and roll thee down from the rocks, and will make thee a burnt mountain." The Daughter of Babylon is also a destroying mountain.

(13) **Her sins have reached unto heaven.** Revelation 18:5-6 says, "For her sins have reached unto heaven, and God hath remembered her iniquities. Reward her even as she rewarded you, and double unto her double according to her works: in the cup which she hath filled fill to her double."

(14) **God avenged on her the death of holy apostles and prophets.** Revelation 18:20 says, "Rejoice over her, thou heaven, and ye holy apostles and prophets; for God hath avenged you on her." Revelation 18:24, says, "In her was found the blood of the prophets, and of saints, and all that were slain upon the earth."

(15) **She glorified herself and lived deliciously.** Revelation 18:7 says, "How much she hath glorified herself, and live deliciously, so much torment and sorrow give her: for she saith in her heart, I sit as a queen, and am no widow, and shall see no sorrow. Therefore shall her plagues come in one day, death, and mourning and famine; and she shall be utterly burned with fire: for strong is the Lord God who judgeth her." Isaiah 47:10 says, "For thou hast trusted in thy wickedness: thou hast said, None seeth me. Thy wisdom and thy knowledge, it hath perverted thee; and

thou hast said in thine heart, I am, and none else beside me. Therefore shall evil come upon thee; thou shalt not know from whence it riseth; and mischief shall fall upon thee; thou shalt not be able to put it off: and desolation shall come upon thee suddenly, which thou shalt not know."

(16)   **Mystery Babylon is the woman who sits on the Beast that was, and is not, and yet is.** (Revelation 17:7-8) The woman is not the beast, however she sits on the beast that was, and is not, and yet is. The beast that was, and is not, and yet is, is not the beast, however it is the image of the beast that was. The beast that was, was Rome and Papal Rome. Rome made war with the saints and overcome them and the saints of God were given to him for a time, and time and division of time. However, that beast is not under discussion because Mystery Babylon is the woman who sits of the Beast that was, and is not, and yet is.

Mystery Babylon sits on the beast that was, and is not, even he is the eighth, and is of the seven, and goeth into perdition. Ten kings have given their power to this beast for God hath put in their hearts to fulfill his will. Therefore, the woman sits upon peoples, multitudes, and nations, and tongues. The woman sits on them or controls them. These kings will hate her and shall make desolate and naked, and shall eat her flesh, and burn her with fire. After Mystery Babylon is destroyed, these kings will make war with the Lamb, and the Lamb shall overcome them: for he is Lord of lords, and King of kings. (Revelation chapter 17)

When you examine these factors closely, you will find: (1) The United States of America is the hindermost of nations (2) Has a mother who is confounded (England) (3) Has a golden cup that if full of abominations (4) Is a destroying mountain (5) A proud nation (6) Glorified herself and lives deliciously (7) Experiencing destroying wind at the time of our trouble (8) And the nation dwells on many waters (9) Is the hammer of the whole earth (10) A nation at the time when Israel has been brought back to his habitation (11) Today many nations hate the United States (12) Today there are nations that are capable of waging such an attack on the United States as described in these scriptures.

Before we conclude this discussion let us, take a closer look at Isaiah chapter 47. This chapter pertains to the virgin daughter of Babylon.   Isaiah 47:3-7 says, "**Thy nakedness shall be uncovered**, yea thy shame shall be seen: I will take vengeance, and I will not meet thee as a man. As for our redeemer, the Lord of hosts is his name, the Holy One of Israel. Sit thou silent, and get thee into darkness, O daughter of the Chaldeans: for thou shalt no more be called, the lady of kingdoms. I was wroth with my people, **I have polluted mine inheritance**, and **given them into thine hand**; upon the ancient hast thou **very heavily laid thy yoke**. And thou sadist, I shall be a lady for ever: so that thou didst not lay these things to thy heart, **neither didst remember the latter end of it.**"

Let us continue to read. "Therefore hear not this, thou that art given to pleasures, that dwellest carelessly, that sayest in thine heart, I am, and none else besides me; I shall not sit as a widow, neither shall I know the loss of children: But these two things shall come to thee in a moment in one day, the loss of children and widowhood: they should come upon thee in their perfection for the multitude of thy sorceries and for the great abundance of thine enchantments. For thou hast trusted in thy wickedness: thou has said, None seeth me. Thy wisdom and thy knowledge, it hath perverted thee; and thou has said in thine heart, I am, and none else beside me." (Isaiah 47:8-10)

God says the nakedness of the daughter of Babylon will be uncovered. Let us uncover this nakedness. When God was wroth with Israel, God gave Israel to the hands of the daughter of Babylon. The daughter of Babylon did not have mercy on Israel, however she laid her yoke on her. Listen, Israel became a mule for the daughter of Babylon; doing things for the daughter of Babylon; things that the daughter of Babylon did not want to do personally, but wanted someone else to do for her. **Do you have love for truth?**

The United States of America acts as Israel's mother. Israel was given into the hands of the United States. We have given Israel financial support to help build their military, trained their pilots and support personnel on the various aircrafts and weapons. On the surface, it appears that we have great love for the people of Israel, however Israel has been fighting some of our battles, and acting as one of our mules to protect our interest in the Middle East. Consequently, instead of having mercy on them they were polluted and carrying out our hidden agendas. This is a sad, sad revelation. However, as we have used Osama bin Laden to fight against Russia, the United States has used Israel to protect our interests in the Middle East.

Like God called Isaiah, Jeremiah, and Ezekiel to be His prophets, the same God has called me to prophesy to the United States of America. This nation has done that which is evil in the sight of God. In the sight of God, the United States of America is a "destroying mountain" and trusts in oppression and perverseness. Is the United States of America Mystery Babylon? That depends on our actions, if we fail to repent from evil, then pray, and turn to God, surely the lamentation for the United States of America has already been written in Ezekiel chapter nineteen. God must see us repenting, as God saw the king and the people of Nineveh, as recorded in the book of Jonah.

Amos 3:6-7 says, "Shall a trumpet be blown in the city, and the people not be afraid? Shall there be evil in a city, and the Lord hath not done it? Surely the Lord God will do nothing, but he revealeth his secret unto his servants the prophets." Jesus says in Luke 4:24, "Verily I say unto you, No prophet is accepted in his own country." Most of the kings of Judah and of Israel did not hearken to the words of God that He gave to His prophets. However, today Christians call these men of God, Major and Minor Prophets and marvel at their works.

Christians who have love for the truth will receive this truth. However, those who do not have love for truth, for them Satan has all power, signs, and lying wonders. They are in the state of mind whereby they are most gullible to be deceived, and they will continue to take **pleasure in unrighteousness**. Besides this, God will continue to send them strong delusions so they will continue to believe the lie, and consequently they will be damned. (2 Thessalonians 2:7-12)

How have we in America taken pleasure in unrighteousness? Again, here we can learn from the scriptures that are written for our learning. In Jeremiah 50:10-11 explained what happened to Chaldea after they celebrated. They were glad and they rejoiced after they brought destruction unto Judah. Note: God brought Chaldea to Judah to destroy it for the sin of Judah. Yet, God says, "And Chaldea shall be a spoil; all that spoil her shall be satisfied, saith the LORD. Because ye were glad, because ye rejoiced, O ye destroyers of mine heritage…" Now let us examine what happened after the Gulf War in 1991.

In June of 1991, it is reported that about five millions Americans lined the streets of New York and had a victory parade after the war with Iraq, celebrating after we had killed thousands of innocent people in Iraq. Besides killing these innocent people, we destroyed Iraq's infrastructure and helped to establish policies that in effect denied food and medicine to dying children. Consequently, hundreds of thousands died. We took the lead to bomb Iraq daily for ten years enforcing no-fly zones. (It is reported that the bombing in the no fly zones was without the United Nation's sanctions.) Then ten years later after we celebrated in New York City, God rewarded us with evil in the very city that we held our major celebration. God brought this evil unto us; then the ones that God used to bring this evil to us, they too were satisfied and then they rejoiced as we celebrated when we brought destruction unto Iraq. We must learn the ways of the LORD.

Then in 2002, the leadership deceived the people, and in 2003, we went to war in Iraq without provocation. God showed me our preparation for war without provocation in September 2002; on September 3, 2002, I shared this revelation with the President of the United States. Then in December 2005, the proud wise men deceived many Americans again, by claiming that we had bad intelligence when we went to war. **What is bad intelligence**?

Was the bad intelligence the lack of capacity for learning, reasoning, and understanding; aptitude in grasping truths, relationships, facts, meanings, etc. Was the bad intelligence the lack of mental alertness or quickness of understanding? On the other hand, was the bad intelligence the inability to properly evaluate and draw conclusions from secret information about an enemy or potential enemy? On the other hand, was the statement made about "bad intelligence" one of the recommendations from one of the wise men or women to deceive the people? God knows.

I love America and our troops. I am an American and I am a military fighting man with twenty years of honorable service. Now I am retired from active duty from the military of the United States. Now I am in the army of the Lord; I know who is my true Commander In Chief. **Now hear this**.

My Commander in Chief, who is King of kings, and Lord of lords says, if we hearken to His commandments, we would have peace as a river and righteousness as the waves of the sea. We would be far from oppression. We should not fear; terror will not come near us, and no weapon that forms against us should prosper. In addition, He will show us how to profit. (Isaiah 48:16-18, Isaiah 54:14, and Isaiah 54:17)

If America repents and turn to God, pray, and then God will heal this land. Listen. Until leaders in the United States repent, "destroying winds" will be round about us in our time of trouble. God declared this standard for Babylon and her images.

222

This book was copyright in 2005, however funds were not available for publishing. Now it is May 2007, as I make the last entry in this book, I realize today, our leaders are trying to address the problem in Iraq; however, they still do not understand the base problem regarding terrorism or the predicament this nation is in.

Jesus said that there is no prophet accepted in his own country, surely, this is true. The answer to this problem and predicament is not the democrats' or republicans' position. First, let us give light to the understanding the problem by the counsel of God.

Understanding The Problem: As Judah despised the word of God the leaders of the United States have done the same thing. They have put their trust in oppression and perverseness. Isaiah 30:4 says, "Because ye despise this word, and trust in oppression and perverseness and stay thereon: Therefore this iniquity shall be to you as a breach ready to fall, swelling out in a high wall, whose breaking cometh suddenly at an instant." Hosea 10:13 say, "You have plowed wickedness; you have reaped iniquity. You have eaten the fruit of lies, because you trusted in your own way, in the multitude of your mighty men." In their hearts, some leaders of the United States despise this word of God and they continue to trust in oppression and perverseness. **Plain-Talk:** The terrorism that we are experiencing is the fruit of our trust in oppression and perverseness.

The Predicament or Box! Isaiah 33:1 says, "Woe to thee that spoilest, and thou wast not spoiled; and dealest treacherously, and they dealt not treacherously with thee! when thou shalt cease to spoil, thou shall be spoiled; and when thou shalt make an end to deal treacherously, they shall deal treacherously with thee." We cannot just withdraw our troops and we cannot win with our military might! However, we must withdraw our troops and do much, much more.

223

In Malachi chapter three, God promises to come near to us in judgment and He would be a swift witness against the following: (1) Sorcerers, (2) The adulterers (3) The false swears (4) Those that oppress the hireling in his wages (This includes the hireling within the United States and the ones employed through out sourcing.) (5) Those that oppress the widow and the fatherless (6) those that turn aside the stranger from his right and (7) those that do not fear God.

The Solution: Hosea 10:12, "<u>Sow for yourselves righteousness</u>; <u>Reap in mercy</u>; <u>Break up your fallow ground</u>, <u>for it is time to seek the LORD</u>, **till He comes and rains righteousness on you**." Listen as God speaks. "If my people, which are called by my name, shall humble themselves, and pray, and seek my face, and turn from their wicked ways; then will I hear from heaven, and will forgive their sin, and will heal their land." America, America needs healing!

At Appendix One of this book, there are more lessons to learn as we review how God applied His judgments to the Kingdom of Judah and the Kingdom of Israel. Let us review again, how God applies his judgments to nations.

God explains in Jeremiah 18:7-10 how He applies His judgments to nations. "At what instant I shall speak concerning a nation, and concerning a kingdom, to pluck up, and to pull down, and to destroy it; if that nation, against whom I have pronounced, turn from their evil, I will repent of the evil that I thought to do unto them. And at what instant I shall speak concerning a nation, and concerning a kingdom, to build and to plant it; if it do evil in my sight, that obey not my voice, then I will repent of the good, wherewith I said I would benefit them."

Policies makers must understand **"THE EARTH is the Lord's, and the fullness thereof; the world, and they that dwell therein." (Psalm 24:1)**

APPENDIX ONE

Review of the History of the Kings of Israel and Judah: Learning to Fear God

The purpose of this review is to show the blessings for hearkening to the commandments of God and the consequences for failing to adhere to God's commandments by carefully examining the history of the kings of Israel and Judah. One of the desired outcomes is to show why we must fear God, because God is faithful to all of his promises. God will bless us if we follow his commandments and we are cursed if we fail to follow his commandments. It is important that we remember, "For whatsoever things were written aforetime, that we through patience and comfort of the scriptures might have hope." (Romans 15:4) I pray that the leaders of this nation, leaders of other nations, people around the world will learn to fear God.

First, we will review Israel before it was split into two kingdoms. Then we will review the two kingdoms simultaneously.

Saul was the first earthly king of Israel. (1 Samuel Chapter ten and eleven)
➢ He did not hearken to the commandments of God
➢ The Lord repented that he had made Saul king over Israel (1 Samuel 15:35)
➢ Saul died for his transgression which he committed against the Lord and for asking counsel of one that had a familiar spirit. (1 Chronicles 10:13
➢ Saul died, and his three sons, and all his house died together. (1 Chronicles 10:6)

David – God made him the second king of all of Israel **(1 Chronicles 10:14, 11:3 and 2 Samuel 5:3)**
➢ David hearkened to the commandments of God
➢ David reigned for 40 years (1 Kings 2:11)
➢ David's last words, "The spirit of the Lord spake by me, and his word was in my tongue. **The God of Israel said to me, He that ruleth over men must be just, ruling in the fear of God.** …. (2 Samuel 23:2-3)
➢ David's charge to Solomon: "I go the way of all the earth: be thou strong therefore, and show thyself a man; And keep the charge of the LORD thy God, to walk in his ways, to keep his statutes, and his commandments, and his judgments, and his testimonies, as it is written in the law of Moses, that thou doest, and whithersoever thou turnest thyself. That the LORD

may continue his word which he spake concerning me, saying, "If thy children take heed to their way, to walk before me in truth with all their heart and with all their soul, there shall not fail thee (said he) a man on the throne of Israel." (1 Kings 2:2-4)

➢ David reigned over Israel forty years: seven years reigned he in Hebron, and thirty and three years reigned he in Jerusalem. Then sat Solomon upon the throne of David his father; ...(1 Kings 2:11-12)

Solomon, the son of David, was the third king of all of Israel

➢ Solomon built an house unto the name of the LORD. David was not able to build this house because of the wars that were at all sides. But God gave Solomon rest on every side so that there was neither adversary nor evil occurrent. (1 Kings 5:3-4)

➢ **God made a covenant with Solomon** (1 King 9:3-9) "And the LORD said unto him, I have heard thy prayer and thy supplication, that thou hast made before me: I have hallowed this house, which thou hast built, to put my name there for ever; and mine eyes and mine heart shall be there perpetually. **And if thou wilt walk before me, as David thy father walked**, in integrity of heart, and in uprightness, to do according to all that I have commanded thee, and wilt keep my statutes and my judgments: Then I will establish the throne of thy kingdom upon Israel for ever, as I promised to David thy father, saying, There shall not fail thee a man upon the throne of Israel. **But if ye shall at all turn from following me**, ye or your children, and will not keep my commandments and my statutes which I have set before you, but go and serve other gods, and worship them: Then will I cut off Israel out of the land which I have given them; and this house, which I have hallowed for my name, will I cast out of my sight; and Israel shall be a proverb and a byword among all people: ..."

➢ King Solomon exceeded all kings of the earth for riches and for wisdom. (1 King 10:23)

➢ **King Solomon's heart turns from God** (1 Kings 11:4) "For it came to pass, when Solomon was old that his wives turned away his heart after other gods.

➢ **Solomon did evil in the sight of the Lord**, and went not fully after the LORD as did David his father. (1 Kings 11:6) The LORD was angry with Solomon. (1 King 11:9-13)

God Splits The Kingdom Because of The Sins of King Solomon
(1 Kings 11:31-32)

Kingdom of Judah

Rehoboam reigned in Judah (1 Kings 12:17)
> He was 41 years old; he reigned for 17 years (1 Kings 14:21)
> **Judah did evil in the sight of the Lord,** and they provoked him to jealousy with their sins which they had committed, above all that their fathers had done. (1 Kings 14:22)

Abijam
> Reigned King of Judah (1 Kings 15:1)
> He reigned three years in Jerusalem (Jeroboam was still king over Israel) (1 Kings 15:2)
> **He walked in all the sins of his father. For David's sake, the Lord gave him a lamp in Jerusalem.** (1 Kings 15:3-4)
> There was war between Rehoboam and Jeroboam all the days of his life. (1 Kings 15:6)

Asa
> Asa the son of Abijam reigned in his stead. (1 Kings 15:8) (Jeroboam was still king of Israel)
> He reigned in Jerusalem for 41 years and **he did what was right in the sight of the Lord** as his father, David. (1 Kings 15: 10-12)
> He took away the Sodomites out of the land and removed all idols that his fathers had made. (1 Kings 15:12)

Kingdom of Israel

Jeroboam was made king of Israel (1 Kings 12:20)
> He reigned for 22 years (1 Kings 14:20)
> **He did not hearken to the commandments of God** – he **did evil above all that were before him** – made other gods, and molten images to provoke God to anger. (1 Kings 14:9) **God shall give Israel up because of the sins of Jeroboam, who did sin, and made Israel to sin.** (1 Kings 14:16)

> In the eighteenth year of King Jeroboam's reign, Abijam began to reign over Judah (1 Kings 15:1)

Nadab
> Nadab the son of Jeroboam began to reign over Israel in the second year of Asa, King of Judah. (1 Kings 15:25)
> He **did evil in the sight of the Lord.** (1 Kings 15:26)
> He walked in the way of his father, and in his sin - he made Israel to sin. (1Kings 15:26)
> In the third year of reign of Asa, King of Judah, Baasha did slay him, and reigned in his stead. (1 Kings 15:28)

Kingdom of Judah	Kingdom of Israel

Asa (cont.)

Baasha

➢ He removed his mother from being queen because she made an idol in the grove. But, he failed to remove the high places – **yet his heart was perfect with God.** (1 Kings 15:13-14)

Asa and **Baasha**, the King of Israel was at war all their days. (1 Kings 15:16)

➢ Baasha was the son of Ahijah, of the house of Issachar. (1 Kings 15:27)
➢ He smote all the house of Jeroboam; he left not to Jeroboam any that breathed… (1Kings 15:29)
➢ There was war between Asa, King of Judah and Baasha all their days. (1 Kings 15:32)
➢ In the third year of Asa, Baasha began to reign over all of Israel in Tirzah, twenty and four years. (1 Kings 15:33)
➢ **He did evil in the sight of the Lord**, and walked in the way of Jeroboam. (1 Kings 15:34)
➢ **The word of the Lord** came to Jehu, the son of Hanani against Baasha, saying, Forasmuch as I exalted thee out of the dust, and made thee prince over my people Israel; and thou hast walked in the way of Jeroboam, and hast made my people Israel to sin, …(1 Kings 16:1-7) (Baasha was killed, like Jeroboam)

Elah
➢ Elah the son of Baasha began to reign over Israel in Tirzah in the 26th year of Asa's reign over Judah.
➢ Elah reigned for two years
➢ His servant Zimri, conspired against him and killed him. (1 Kings 16:8-10)

➢ In the 26th year of Asa's Reign over Judah, Elah began to reign over Israel. (1 Kings 16:8)

Kingdom of Judah	Kingdom of Israel

Asa (cont.)

Elah (Cont.)

Zimri his servant killed him in the 27th year of Asa, King of Judah, and reigned in his stead. (1 Kings 17:10)

Asa was still king of Judah

Zimri
He slew all the house of Baasha. (1 Kings 16:11)

➤ Zimri destroyed all the house of Baasha, according to the word of the Lord, which he spake against Baasha by Jehu the prophet. For all the sins of Elah his son, by which they made Israel to sin, in provoking the Lord God of Israel to anger with their vanities. (1 Kings 16:12-13)

➤ In the 27th year of Asa king of Judah did Zimri reign seven days in Tirzah. And the people encamped against Gibbethon, which belonged to the Philistines. (1 Kings 16:15)

➤ The people that were encamped said, Zimri hath conspired, and slain the king. Israel made Omri, the captain of the host, king over Israel that day in the camp. Omri and all Israel with him besieged Tirzah. (1 Kings 16:16-17)

➤ When Zimri saw that the city was taken, he went into the palace of the king's house, and burnt the king's house over with fire, and died, for his sins which he sinned in doing evil in the sight of the LORD,

Kingdom of Judah	Kingdom of Israel
Asa (cont.)	**Zimri** (cont.)

in walking in the way of Jeroboam, and in his sin which he did, to make Israel to sin. (1 Kings 16:18-19)

Kingdom of Israel divides in two parts

After the death of Zimri, the Kingdom of Israel divided in two parts: half of the people followed Tibni **the son of Ginath to make him King and half followed** Omri. **(1 Kings 16:21-22)**

> **Tibin** – half of the people followed him
> **Omri** – half of the people followed him.

Omri reigned after the death of Tibin. This occurred during the 31st year of Asa's reign over Judah. (1 Kings 16:23)

➤ Omri reigned for twelve years, he reigned for six years in Tirzah.
➤ **He wrought evil in the eyes of the Lord, and did worse than all that were before him.** (1 Kings 16:25)
➤ After Omri's demise, his son Ahab reigned in his stead. (1 Kings 16:28)

Asa was still king of Judah when Omri began his reign over the Kingom of Israel.

Kingdom of Judah

Asa had reigned as king of Judah for 38 years when Ahab began to reign over the kingdom of Israel. (1 Kings 16:29)

> In the 39th year of Asa's reign, he was diseased in his feet, until his disease was exceeding great: yet in his disease **he sought not to the LORD**, but to the physicians. (2 Chronicles 16:12)

Asa died at an old age. He was buried in the City of David. Jehoshaphat his son reigned in his stead. (1 Kings 15:23-24)

Jehoshaphat

> He began his reign of Judah in the fourth year of Ahab king of Israel. (1 Kings 22:41)
> He was 35 years old when he began to reign; and he reigned 25 years in Jerusalem. (2 Kings 22:42)
> **He walked in all the ways of Asa his father**; he turned not aside from it, **doing that which was right in the eyes of the Lord.** (1 Kings 22:43)
> But, the high places were not taken away; for the people offered and burnt incense yet in the high places and Jehoshaphat made peace with the king of Israel. (1 Kings 22:43-44)

Kingdom of Israel

Ahab
> **Ahab, the son of Omri did evil in the sight of the Lord above all that were before him.** (1 Kings 16:25)
> It came to pass, as if it had been a light thing for him to walk in the sins of Jeroboam the son of Nebat. (1 Kings 16:31)
> He took his wife Jezebel and went and served Baal, and worshipped him. (1 Ki 16:31)
> **Ahab did more to provoke the Lord God of Israel to anger than all the kings of Israel that were before him.** (1 Ki 16:33)
> The Lord sent Prophet Elijah, the Tishbite to Ahab. The Lord brought evil upon Ahab, took away his posterity and made Ahab's house like the house of Jeroboam, and like the house of Baasha for the provocation. (1 Kings 21:22)

Ahaziah began to reign king of Israel in Samaria the seventeenth year of Jehospaphat king of Judah. Ahaziah reigned for two years over Israel. (1 Kings 22:51)

> **He did evil in the sight of the Lord**, and walked in the way of his father, and in the way of his mother, and the way of Jeroboam the son of Nebat, who made Israel to sin. He served Baal, and worshipped him, and provoked to anger the Lord God of Israel. (1Kings 22:52-53)

Kingdom of Judah	Kingdom of Israel

Kingdom of Judah

Jehoshaphat continues to reign as king over Judah.

Note: Before Jehoshaphat went to war he sought a prophet of the Lord. (1 Kings 22:7 and 2 Kings 3:11)

Jehoshaphat continues to reign as king of Judah. Jehoram began to reign as king over Israel in the eighteenth year of Jehosphaphat's reign over Judah. (2 Kings 3:1)

Note: Both kings, Jehoshaphat and Ahab had sons named "Jehoram." At times, the name Jehoram is written "Joram." According to 2 Kings 8:16, In the fifth year of **Joram** the son of Ahab king of Israel, Jehospahat being then King of Judah, **Jehoram** the son of **Jehospahat** king of Judah begin to reign.

Jehoram

 ➤ He was 32 years old when he began to reign; and he reigned eight years **in Jerusalem**. And he walked in the way of the kings of Israel, **as did the house of Ahab**: for the daughter of Ahab was his wife: and he did **evil in the sight of the Lord**. (2 Kings 8:17-18)

Kingdom of Israel

Ahaziah (Cont.)

 ➤ Ahaziah became sick and sent messengers to inquire of Baal–zebub the god of Ekron whether he would recover of the disease. (2 Kings 1:2)

 ➤ Prophet Elijah met the messengers and said, "Is it not because there is not a God in Israel, that ye go to inquire of Baal-zebub the god of Ekron? Now therefore thus said the Lord, thou shall not come down from that bed ..., but shalt surely die." (2 Kings 1:3-4)
 ➤ Ahaziah died according to the word of Prophet Elijah. (2 Kings 1:17)

Jehoram reigned in Ahaziah's stead because he had no son in the second year of **Jehoram the son of Jehospahat.** (2 Kings 1:17)
 ➤ **Jehoram** the son of **Ahab** began to reign over Israel in Samaria the **eighteenth year of Jehoshaphat** king of Judah, and reigned twelve years. (2 Kings 3:1) **(See note this page)**

House of Judah	House of Israel
Jehoram, son of Jehospahat, (Cont.)	**Jehoram, son of Ahab. (Cont.)**

House of Judah

Jehoram, son of Jehospahat, (Cont.)

➤ After Jehoram began to reign, he strengthened himself, and slew all his brethren with the sword, and divers also the princes of Israel. (2 Chronicles 21:4)

➤ "Howbeit the Lord would not destroy the house of David, because of the covenant that he had made with David, and as he promised to give a light to him and to his sons for ever." (2 Chronicles 21:7)

➤ He made high places in the mountains of Judah, and caused the inhabitants of Jerusalem to commit fornication, and compelled Judah thereto. (2 Chronicles 21:11)

➤ Elijah the prophet wrote him and pointed out his transgressions and told him that the Lord would smite his people with a great plague, his children, his wives, and all his goods. In the communication, Elijah also told him that he would have great sickness by disease of his bowels, until his bowels fall out by reason of the sickness day by day. (2 Chronicles 21:12-15)

➤ And the Lord stirred up against Jehoram the spirit of the Philistines, and of the Arabians, that were near the Ethiopians: And they came up into Judah, brake into it, and carried away all the substance that was found in the king's house, and his sons also, and his wives; so

House of Israel

Jehoram, son of Ahab. (Cont.)

➤ He wrought evil in the sight of the Lord; but not like his father, and like his mother:

➤ For he put away the image of Baal that his father had made.

➤ But he cleaved unto the sins of Jeroboam. (2 Kings 3:3)

Kingdom of Judah

that there was never a son left him, save Jehoahaz, the youngest of his sons. As Elijah prophesied, it all came to pass. (2 Chronicles Chapter 21)

Ahaziah (Jehoahaz), the son of Jehoram began to reign. The people of Jerusalem made him king. (2 Chronicles 22:1) The following is taken from the 2 Chronicles, chapter 22.

➢ He was 42 years old when he began his reign; he reigned one year in Jerusalem. (22:2)

➢ He also walked in the way of Ahab: for his mother was his counselor to do wickedly. (22:3)

➢ He did evil in the sight of the Lord like the house of Ahab: for they were his counselors after the death of his father to his destruction: (22:4)

➢ He went with Jehoram the son of Ahab king of Israel to war against Hazael king of Syria at Ramoth-gilead: and the Syrians smote Joram (Jehoram) (22:5)

➢ His going to Joram was God's occasion for Ahaziah's downfall; for when he arrived, he went out with Jehoram against Jehu the son of Nimshi whom the Lord had anointed to cut off the house of Ahab. (22:7)

➢ Ahaziah was caught and brought to Jehu. He was killed and buried by them. (2 Chronicles 22:9)

Kingdom of Israel

Joram (Jehoram) was still king of Israel when Ahaziah began to reign in Judah; this was in the eleventh year of Joram the son of Ahab's reign over Israel. (2 King 9:29)

➢ Joram the son of Ahab went to war against Hazael King of Syria in Ramoth-gilead; and the Syrians wounded him. Ahaziah assisted Joram in this war. (2 Kings 8:28)

➢ Joram went back to Jezreel to be healed of his wounds.

➢ While Joram was healing in Jezreel, Ahaziah went down to see him. (2 Kings 8:29)

➢ Elisha the prophet sent one of the children of the prophets to Jehu the son of Jehoshaphat the son of Nimshi. The young prophet followed Elisha's instructions and poured oil on the head of Jehu and said unto him, "Thus said the LORD God of Israel, I have anointed thee king over the people of the Lord, even over Israel." Jehu was charged to smite the house of Ahab to avenge the blood of the prophets and the blood of all the servants of the Lord, at the hand of Jezebel. (2 Kings chapter 9)

➢ Joram king of Israel was killed by Jehu. (2 Kings 9:24) Jehu also ordered Ahaziah to be killed. Besides, the killing of Joram and Ahaziah Jehu' horses trode Jezebel under their feet. (2 Kings 9:33)

Kingdom of Judah

Athaliah, the mother of Ahaziah began to reign over the land. (2 King 11:3)

> When **Athaliah** the mother of Ahaziah saw that her son was dead, she arose and destroyed all the seed royal of the house of Judah, except for Joash, the son of Ahaziah who was stolen by his daughter. Joash was given to the wife of Jehoida the priest, who hid him from Athaliah, so she slew him not.

> **Athaliah, the mother of Ahaziah reigns over the land.**

> In the seventh year of Athaliah's reign, Jehoiada, the priest strengthened himself. The priest had been caring for and protecting Joash, the son of Ahaziah in the house of God. (2 Chronicles 22:12 and 23:1)

> Jehoiada organized, gathered the Levites out of all the cities of Judah, and the chief fathers of Israel. They all came to Jerusalem. They made a covenant with Joash, the king in the house of God. Jehoiada said unto them, Behold, the king's son shall reign, as the Lord hath said of the sons of David. (2 Chronicles 23:2-3)

Joash, the son of Ahaziah, at the age of seven was crowned king of Judah. (2 Chronicles 23:11) (2 Chronicles 24:1) (This was the 7th year of Jehu's reign. 2 Kings 12:1)

> **Athaliah** was slain after **Joash** was crowned king. (2 Chronicles 23:14-15)

Kingdom of Israel

Jehu (son of Jehosphaphat) was anointed by God to be king of Israel. (2 Kings 9:3)

> Jehu reigned over Israel 28 years. (2 Kings 10:36)

> Besides the killing of Joram, Ahaziah and Jezebel, seventy sons of the king Ahab were killed and all that remained of the house of Ahab in Jezreel, and all his great men, and his kinsfolks, and his priests, until he left him none remaining. (2 Kings chapter 10)

> Jehu proclaimed a solemn assembly for Baal. All the worshippers of Baal came to the assembly. **This was a ploy**, Jehu ordered all of the worshippers to be killed. Then he ordered his guard and captains to tear down the house of Baal. Thus **Jehu destroyed Baal out of Israel**. (2 Kings 10:20-28)

> Jehu did not turn away from the sins of Jeroboam, who made Israel sin. That is, from the golden calves that were at Bethel and Dan. (2 Kings 10:29)

> **God said** to Jehu, "Because you have done well in doing what is right in My sight, and have done to the house of Ahab all that was in My heart, your sons shall sit on the throne of Israel to the fourth generation." But Jehu **did not**

Kingdom of Judah

> Jehoiada, the priest made a covenant between him, and between all the people and between the king, that they should be the Lord's people. (2 Chronicles 23:16)

> All the people went to the temple of Baal, and tore it down, and killed Mattan the priest of Baal before the altars. (2 Chronicles 23:17)

> **Joash did what was right in the sight of the Lord** all the days of Jehoiada the priest. (2 Chronicles 24:2)

> He was minded to repair the house of the Lord. Under his direction this was accomplished. (2 Chronicles 24:4-14)

> Jehoiada, the priest died, Jehoida was an hundred and thirty years old when he died.

> Joash hearkened to the princes of Judah after the death of Jehoida, then they left the house of the Lord God of their fathers, and served groves and idols: and wrath came upon Judah and Jerusalem for this their trespass. (2 Chronicles 24:17-18)

> Prophets were sent to them and testified against them, but they would not give ear. (2 Chronicles 24:19)

> The Spirit of God came upon Zechariah the son of Jehoiada the priest, which stood above the people, and said unto

Kingdom of Israel

turn away from the sin of Jeroboam. (2 Kings 10:29-30)

> In those days the Lord began to cut off parts of Israel; And Hazael concurred them in all the territory of Israel. (2 Kings 10:32)

> **Jehoahaz** the son of Jehu began to reign over Israel in the 23rd year of Joash's reign over Judah. He reigned over Israel in Samaria for seventeen years. (2 Kings 13:1)

> **He did what was evil in the sight of the Lord**, and followed the sins of Jeroboam the son of Nebat, which made Israel to sin; he departed not therefrom. (2 Kings 13:2)

> The **anger of the Lord** was kindled against Israel, and God delivered them into the hand of Hazael, all their days. (2 Kings 13:3)

> **Jehoahaz besought the Lord,** and **the Lord hearkened unto him**: for he saw the oppression of Israel, because the king of Syria oppressed them. (2 Kings 13:4)

> God gave Israel a saviour. So they went from under the hand of the Syrians: And the children of Israel dwelt in their tents, as beforetime. But they departed not from the sins of Jeroboam. The king of Syria had destroyed them and made them like the dust by threshing.

Kingdom of Judah

Joash (son of Ahaziah. cont.)

(The name "Joash" same as "Jehoash")

them, "Why transgress ye the commandment of the Lord, that ye cannot prosper? Because ye have forsaken the Lord, he hath also forsaken you." (They conspired against Zechariah, and stoned him with stones at the commandment of the king.) (2 Chronicles 24:20-21)

➤ Joash did not remember kindness of Jehoiada the father of Zechariah; he commanded the killing of Zechariah. When Zechariah died he said, "The Lord look upon it, and require it." (2 Chronicles 24:21-22)

➤ It came to pass at the end of the year, that the host of Syria came up against him: and they came to Judah and Jerusalem, and destroyed all the princes of the people from among the people, and sent all the spoil to them unto the king of Damascus.

➤ The army of Syria came with a small company of men, and the Lord delivered a very great host into their hand because they forsook the Lord God of their fathers.

➤ Joash had great diseases when the army of Syria left. Then his own servants conspired against him for the blood of the sons of Jehoiada the priest, and slew him on his bed. He was not buried in the sepulchers of the kings. (2 Chronicles 24:25)

Kingdom of Israel

➤ **Jehoash, the son of Jehoahaz** began to reign over Israel in Samaria and he reigned for 16 years. (Joash was king of Judah for 37 years when Jehoash began to reign over Israel.) (2 Kings 13:9-10)

➤ **Jehoash did that which was evil in the sight of the LORD;** he departed not from all the sins of Jeroboam. (2 Kings 13:11)

➤ Joash the King of Israel went to visit Elisha, after Elisha had fallen ill. Before Elisha died, he gave Joash instructions on how they would be delivered from the Syrians. Hazael king of Syria, oppressed Israel all the days of Jehoahaz. The Lord was gracious unto them, and had compassion on them, because of his covenant with Abraham, Isaac, and Jacob, and would not destroy them, neither cast he them from his presence as yet. (2 Kings 13:14-23)

➤ Jehoash after Hazael king of Syria died, took again Israel out of the hand of Ben-hadad the king of Syria, the son of Hazael. Joash beat Ben-hadad three times and recovered the cities of Israel. (2 Kings 13:25)

Kingdom of Judah

➤ **Amaziah king of Judah** began to reign the second year of Joash's reign over Israel. (2 Kings 14:1)

➤ He was twenty-five years old when he began to reign, and reigned twenty-nine years in Jerusalem. (2 Kings 14:2)

➤ He did what was right in the sight of the Lord, yet not like David his father: he did according to all things as Joash his father did. But the high places were not taken away: as yet the people did sacrifice and burnt incense on the high places. (2 Kings 14:3-4)

➤ He slew his servants which had slain the king his father as soon as he was confirmed king of Judah. (2 Kings 14:5)

➤ Amaziah strengthened himself in battle against the children of Seir and it came to pass that he brought the gods of the children of Seir, and set them up to be his gods, and bowed down to them. The anger of the Lord was kindled against Amaziah. God sent a prophet to Amaziah and told him that God was determined to destroy him. (2 Chronicles 25:11-16)

➤ **Amaziah** sent messegers to **Jehoash** the king of Israel, saying, "Come, let us look one another in the face." Amaziah and Jehoash went to war. (2 Kings 14:8-12)

Kingdom of Israel

➤ **Jehoash (Joash), the son of Jehoahaz** (Cont.)

➤ **Jehoash took Amaziah** King of Judah, the son of Jehoash the son of Ahaziah, at Beth-shemesh, and came to Jerusalem, and brake down the wall of Jerusalem from the gate of Ephriam unto the corner gate, four hundred cubits. He took all the gold, silver, and vessels that were found in the house of the Lord and treasures of the king's house and returned to Samaria. (2 Kings 14:13-14)

238

Kingdom of Judah

➢ **Amaziah** the son of Joash King of Judah lived after the death of Jehoash son of Jehoahaz king of Israel fifteen years. (2 Kings 14:17)

➢ After the time that Amaziah turned away from following the LORD, they made a conspiracy against him in Jerusalem, and he fled to Lachish; but they sent after him to Lachish and killed him there. He was brought back and buried with his fathers in the City of Judah. (2 Chronicles 25:27-28)

Uzziah, the son of Amaziah began to reign in his stead. (2 Chronicles 26:1) In the twenty-seventh year of Jeroboam II king of Israel began **Azariah** son of Amaziah king of Judah to reign. (2 Kings 15:1) **Note**: The name Azariah is used for Uzziah.

➢ He was sixteen years old when he became king, and he reigned fifty-two years in Jerusalem. (2 Chronicles 26:3)

➢ Uzziah did what was right in the sight of the LORD. (2 Chronicles 26:4)

➢ He sought God in the days of Zechariah, who had understanding of visions of God; and as long as he sought the LORD, God made him prosper. (2 Chr. 26:5)

➢ God helped him against the Philistines, the Arabians, the Meunites and the Ammonites. (2 Chronicles 26:7-8)

Kingdom of Israel

Jeroboam II, the son of Jehoash reigned in his father's stead. (2 Kings 14:16)

➢ In the fifteenth year of Amaziah the son of Joash king of Judah Jeroboam II the son of Joash king of Israel began to reign in Samaria, and he reigned forty-one years. (2 Kings 14:23)

➢ Jeroboam II did that which was **evil** in the sight of the LORD: he departed not from all the sin of Jeroboam the son of Nebat, who made Israel to sin. (2 Kings 14:24)

➢ Jeroboam II slept with his Fathers, even with the kings of Israel; Zachariah his son reigned in his stead. (2 Kings 14:29)

Zachariah, son of Jeroboam II reigned over Israel in Samaria six months. His reign began in the thirty-eighth year of Azariah king of Judah. (2 Kings 15:8)

➢ **He did that which was evil in the sight of the Lord** as his fathers had done: he departed not from the sins of Jeroboam the son of Nebat, who made Israel to sin. (2 Kings 15:9)

➢ Shallum the son of Jabesh conspired against him, and smote him before the people, and slew him, and reigned in his stead. (2 Kings 15:10)

Shallum, the son of Jabesh began to reign in the thirty-ninth year of

Kingdom of Judah

Uzziah (Cont.)

➤ Uzziah's fame spread as far as the entrance of Egypt, for he became exceedingly strong. He prepared and equipped a mighty power. **When he was strong his heart lifted up** to his destruction, for **he transgressed against the LORD his God** by entering the temple of the Lord to burn incense on the altar of incense. (2 Chronicles 26:9-16)

➤ After Uzziah went into Temple of the Lord, Azariah the priest and eighty priests of the LORD went in after him. They told him, "It is not for you, Uzziah, to burn incense to the LORD, but the priests, the sons of Aaron, who are consecrated to burn incense. Get out of the sanctuary, for you have trespassed! You shall have no honor from the LORD God." Uzziah became furious; and had a censer in his hand to burn incense. **While he was angry with the priests, leprosy broke out on his forehead.** (2 Chronicles 26:17-19)

➤ Uzziah was a leper until the day of his death. He dwelt in an isolated house, because he was a leper; for he was cut off from the house of the LORD. (2 Chronicles 26:21)

Kingdom of Israel

Uzziah king of Judah; he reigned a full month in Samaria. (2 Kings 15:13)

➤ Menahem the son of Gadi went up from Tirzah, and smote Shallum the son of Jabesh in Samaria, and slew him, and reigned in his stead.

➤ Menahem smote Tiphsah, and all that were therein, and the coasts thereof he smote it; and all the women therein that were with child he ripped up. (2 Kings 15:16)

Menahem began to reign over Israel in the thirty-ninth year of Azariah king of Judah. He reigned ten years in Samaria. (2 Kings 15:17)

➤ **He did that which was evil in the sight of the LORD**: he departed not all his days from the sins of Jeroboam the son of Nebat, who made Israel to sin. (2 Kings 15:18)

➤ Pul the king of Assyria came against the land: and Menahem gave Pul a thousand talents of silver, that his hand might be with him to confirm the kingdom in his hand. Menahem exacted the money of Israel, even of all the mighty men of wealth, of each men fifty shekels of silver to give to the king of Assyria. So the king of Assyria turned back, and stayed not there in the land. (2 Kings 15:20)

Kingdom of Judah

Uzziah (Cont.)

Jotham

> Uzziah was a leper when he died; Jotham his son reigned in his stead. (2 Chronicles 26:23)
> He was twenty-five years old when be began to reign, and he reigned sixteen years in Jerusalem. (2 Chronicles 27:1)
> **He did that which was right in the sight of the LORD**, according to all that his father Uzziah did (Although he did not enter the temple of the LORD). But still the people acted corruptly. (2 Chronicles 27:2)
> Jotham became mighty, because he prepared his ways before the LORD his God. (2 Chronicles 27:6)

Ahaz

> After Jotham died, his son Ahaz reigned in his stead. (2 Chronicles 27:9) This was in the seventeenth year of Pekah's reign in Israel. (2 Kings 16:1)
> Ahaz was twenty years old when he began to reign. He reigned in Jerusalem: **but he did not that which was right in the sight of the LORD**, like David his father: for he walked in the ways of the kings of Israel, and made also molten images for Baalim. (2 Chronicles 28:1-2)

Kingdom of Israel

Pekahiah

> Pekahiah, son of Menahem began to reign over Israel in Samaria in the fiftieth year of Azariah king of Judah. Pekahiah reigned for two years. (2 Kings 15:23)
> **He did that which was evil in the sight of the LORD**: he departed not from the sins of Jeroboam the son of Nebat, who made Israel to sin. (2 Kings 15:24)
> Pekah the son of Remaliah, a captain of his, conspired against him, and smote him in Samaria, in the palace of the king's house. Pekah killed him and reigned in his room. (2 Kings 15:25)

Pekah

> Pekah the son of Remaliah began to reign over Israel in Samaria in the fiftieth and two year of Azariah King of Judah. Pekah reigned for twenty years. (2 Kings 15:27)
> **He did that which was evil in the sight of the LORD**: he departed not from the sins of Jeroboam the son of Nebat, who made Israel to sin. (2 Kings 15:28)
> Hoshea the son of Elah made a conspiracy against Pekah the son of Remaliah and smote him, and slew him, and reigned in his stead, in the twentieth year of Jotham the son of Uzziah. (2 Kings 15:30)

Kingdom of Judah

Ahaz (Cont.)

➢ The LORD brought Judah low because of Ahaz king of Israel; for he made Judah naked, and transgressed sore against the LORD.

➢ He sacrificed unto the gods Damascus, which smote him. (2 Chronicles 28:23)

➢ Ahaz gathered together the vessels of the house of God, and cut in pieces the vessels of the house of God, and shut up the doors of the house of the LORD, and made him altars in every corner of Jerusalem. (2 Chronicles 28:24)

➢ In every city of Judah, Ahaz made high places, to burn incense unto other gods, and provoked to anger the LORD God of his fathers. (2 Chronicles 28:25)

➢ When Ahaz died, he was buried in Jerusalem, but he was not brought into the sepulchers of the kings of Israel. Hezekiah his son reigned in his stead. (2 Chronicles 28:27)

Hezekiah

➢ Hezekiah began to reign when he was twenty-five years old, and he reigned twenty-nine years in Jerusalem. (2 Chronicles 29:1)

➢ He did that which was right in the sight of the LORD, according to all that David his father had done. (2 Chronicles 29:2)

Kingdom of Israel

Hoshea

➢ In the twelfth year of Ahaz king of Judah began Hoshea the son of Elah to reign in Samaria over Israel nine years. (2 Kings 17:1)

➢ He did that which was **evil in the sight of the LORD**, but not as the kings of Israel that were before him. (2 Kings 17:2)

➢ Against Hoshea came up Shalmaneser king of Assyria: and Hoshea became his servant, and gave him presents. (2 Kings 17:3)

➢ The king of Assyria found conspiracy in Hoshea: for he had sent messengers to So king of Egypt, and brought no present to the king of Assyria, as he had done year by year: **therefore the king of Assyria shut him up, and bound him in prison.** (2 Kings 17:4)

➢ The king of Assyria came up throughout all the land, and went up to Samaria, and besieged it three years. (2 Kings 17:5)

➢ In the ninth year of Hoshea the king of Assyria took Samaria, and carried Israel away to Assyria, and placed them in Halah and in Habor by the river of Gozan, and in the cities of the Medes.

➢ For so it was the children of Israel that had sinned against the LORD their God, which had brought them up out of the land of Egypt, from under the hand of Pharaoh king of Egypt, and feared other gods,

Kingdom of Judah	Kingdom of Israel

Kingdom of Judah

Hezekiah (Cont.)

➢ Hezekiah in the first year of his reign, in the first month, opened the doors of the house of the LORD, and repaired them. (2 Chronicles 29:3)

➢ Hezekiah realized that the wrath of God was upon Judah and Jerusalem because their fathers had trespassed, and done evil in the eyes of the LORD. Therefore, it was in Hezekiah's heart to make a covenant with the LORD God of Israel, that his fierce wrath may turn away from them. (2 Chronicles 29:4-10)

➢ Hezekiah took concrete actions to effect this covenant. And the LORD hearkened to Hezekiah, and healed the people. (2 Chronicles Chapter 29:3 through Chapter 30:20 – **Recommended reading**)

➢ He did that which was **good** and **right** and **truth** before the LORD his God. And in every work that he began in the service of the house of God, and in the law, and in the commandments, to seek his God, he did it with all his heart, and prospered. (2 Chronicles 31:20-21)

➢ He trusted in the LORD God of Israel; so that after him was none like him among all the kings of Judah, nor any that were before him. (2 Kings 18:5)

Kingdom of Israel

God Moved Them Out of His Sight

➢ The children of Israel walked in the statutes of the heathen, whom the LORD cast out from before the children of Israel, which they had made. (2 Kings 17:7-8)

➢ The children of Israel did secretly those things that were not right against the LORD their God, and they built them high places in all their cities, from the tower of the watchmen to the fenced city. (2 Kings 17:9)

➢ They set them up images and groves in every high hill, and under every green tree:

➢ And there they burnt incense in all the high places, as did the heathen whom the LORD carried away before them; and wrought wicked things to provoke the LORD to anger:

➢ For they served idols, whereof the LORD had said unto them, Ye shall not do this thing. (2 Kings 17:10-12)

➢ Yet the LORD testified against Israel, and against Judah, by all the prophets, and by all the seers, saying, Turn ye from your evil ways, and keep my commandments and my statutes, according to all the law which I commanded your fathers, and which I sent you by my servants the prophet. (2 Kings (17:13)

Kingdom of Judah

Hezekiah (Cont.)

> God added fifteen years to Hezekiah's life. (2 Kings 20:6) After Hezekiah died, Manasseh his son reigned in his stead. (2 Kings 20:21)

Manasseh

> Manasseh was twelve years old when he began to reign, and reigned fifty-five years in Jerusalem. (2 Kings 21:1)
> He did that which was evil in the sight of the LORD, after the abominations of the heathen, whom the LORD cast before the children of Israel. (2 Kings 21:2)
> He built up again the high places which Hezekiah his father had destroyed; and reared up altars for Baal, and made grove, as did Ahab king of Israel; and worshipped all the host of heaven, and served them. (2 Kings 21:3)
> He built altars in the house of the LORD, of which the LORD said, In Jerusalem will I put my name. (2 Kings 21:4)
> He built altars for all the host of heaven in the two courts of the house of the LORD. (2 Kings 21:5)
> He made his sons pass through the fire, and observed times, and used enchantments, and dealt with familiar spirits and wizards: he wrought much wickedness in the

Kingdom of Israel

God Moved Them Out of His Sight

> Notwithstanding they would not hear, but hardened their necks, like to the neck of their fathers, that did not believe in the LORD their God. (2 Kings 17:14)
> And they rejected his statutes, and his covenant that he made with their fathers, and his testimonies which he testified against them; and they followed vanity, and became vain, and went after the heathen that were round about them, concerning whom the LORD had charged them, that they should not do like them. (2 Kings 17:15)
> And they left all the commandments of the LORD their God, and made them molten images, even two claves, and made a grove, and worshipped all the host of heaven, and served Baal. (2 Kings 17:16)
> And they caused their sons and their daughter to pass through the fire, and used divination and enchantments, and sold themselves to do evil in the sight of the LORD, to provoke him to anger. (2 Kings 17:17)
> **Therefore the LORD was very angry with Israel, and removed them out of his sight: there was none left but the tribe of Judah only.** (2 Kings 17:18)

Kingdom of Judah	Kingdom of Israel

Manasseh cont.

God Moved Them Out of His Sight

sight of the LORD, to provoke him to anger. (2 Kings 21:6)

➢ He set graven images of the grove that he had made in the house, of which the LORD said to David, and to Solomon his son, "In this house, and in Jerusalem, which I have chosen out of all tribes of Israel, will I put my name fore ever: Neither will I make the feet of Israel move any more out of the land which I gave them, and according to all the law that my servant Moses commanded them." (2 Kings 21:8)

➢ Manasseh seduced the people of Judah and Jerusalem to do more evil than did the nations whom the LORD destroyed before the children of Israel.

➢ The LORD by the Servants the prophets saying:

➢ Because Manasseh king of Judah hath done these abominations, and hath done wickedly above all that the Amorites did, which were before him, and hath made Judah also to sin with his idols: (2 Kings 21:11)

➢ Therefore thus saith the LORD God of Israel, Behold, I am bringing such evil upon Jerusalem and Judah, that whosoever heareth of it, both his ears shall tingle. (2 Kings 21:12)

➢ For God rent Israel from the house of David; and they made Jeroboam the son of Nebat king: and Jeroboam drove Israel from following the LORD, and made them sin a great sin.

Kingdom of Judah	Kingdom of Israel

Manasseh cont.

> The LORD said, I will stretch over Jerusalem the line of Samaria, and the plummet of the house of Ahab: I will wipe Jerusalem as a man wipeth a dish, wiping it, and turning it upside down. (2 Kings 21:13)

> The LORD said, I will forsake the remnant of mine inheritance, and deliver them into the hand of their enemies; because they have done that which was evil in my sight and provoked me to anger, since the day their fathers came forth out of Egypt even unto this day.

> Moreover Manasseh shed blood very much, till he had filled Jerusalem from one end to another; beside his sin wherewith he made Judah to sin, in doing that which was evil in the sight of the LORD.

> Manasseh died; Amon, his son reigned in his stead. (2 Kings 21:18)

Amon

> Amon was twenty-two years old when he began to reign, and he reigned two years in Jerusalem. (2 Kings 21:19)

> He did that which was evil in the sight of the LORD, as his father Manasseh did. (2 Kings 21:20)

God Moved Them Out of His Sight

Kingdom of Judah	Kingdom of Israel

Kingdom of Judah

Amon cont.

❯ He walked in all the way that his father walked in and served idols that his father served, and worshipped them: (2 Kings 21:21)

❯ He forsook the LORD God of his fathers, and walked not in the way of the LORD. (2 Kings 21:22)

❯ The servants of Amon conspired against him, and slew the king in his own house. And the people of the land made Josiah, his son king in his stead. (2 Kings 21:23)

Note: Manasseh reigned for fifty-five years and his son Amon reigned for two years, therefore it had been fifty-seven years since Judah did what was right in the sight of the LORD.

Josiah

❯ Josiah was eight years old when he began to reign, and he reigned thirty-one years in Jerusalem. (2 Kings 22:1)

❯ He did what was **right** in the sight of the LORD, and walked in all the ways of David his father, and turned not aside to the right hand or to the left. (2 Kings 22:2)

Kingdom of Israel

God Moved Them Out of His Sight

Kingdom of Judah	Kingdom of Israel
Josiah cont.	**God Moved Them Out of His Sight**

➤ In the eighteenth year of Josiah's reign, Hilkiah the high priest **found the book** of the law in the house of the LORD. Hilkiah gave the book to Shaphan, the scribe. Shaphan, the scribe read the book before the king. (2 Kings 22:9-10)

➤ Josiah's actions after hearing the reading of the book of Law.

➤ He rent his clothes (2 Kings 22:11)

➤ He commanded the high Priest and others to inquire of the LORD for him regarding the book. (2 Kings 22:12-13)

➤ Hilkiah the high priest and others went unto Huldah the prophetess, the wife of Shallum the son of Tikvah, and they communed with her. She said unto them, Thus saith the LORD God of Israel, Tell the man that sent you to me, Thus said the LORD, Behold, I will bring evil upon this place, and upon the inhabitants thereof, even all the words of the book which the king of Judah hath read: (2 King 22:14-16)

➤ Prophetess Huldah continued to give the word from the LORD, Because they have forsaken me, and have burned incense unto other gods that they might provoke me to anger with all the works of their hands; therefore my wrath shall be kindled against this place, and it shall not be quenched.

248

Kingdom of Judah	Kingdom of Israel

Josiah (Cont.)

God Moved Them Out of His Sight

➢ Prophetess Huldah continued, But to the king of Judah which sent you to inquire of the LORD, thus shall ye say to him, Thus saith the LORD God of Israel, As touching the words which thou hast heard; Because thine heart was tender, and thou hast humbled thyself before the LORD, when thou heardest what I spake against this place, and against the inhabitants thereof, that they should become a desolation and a curse, and hast rent thy clothes, and wept before me; I also have heard thee, saith the LORD.

➢ Behold therefore, I will gather thee unto thy fathers, and thou shalt be gathered into thy grave in peace; and thine eyes shall not see all the evil which I will bring upon this place. (2 Kings 22:18-20)

➢ King Josiah read the words of the book of the covenant to all the people, both small and great. (2 Kings 23:2)

➢ King Josiah made a covenant before the LORD, to walk after the LORD, and to keep his commandments and his testimonies and his statutes will all their heart and all their soul, to perform the words of this covenant that were written in this book. And all the people stood to the covenant. (2 Kings 23:3)

Kingdom of Judah	Kingdom of Israel
Josiah cont.	**God** Moved Them Out of His Sight

➤ Josiah commanded
Hilkiah the high priest and others
that they **remove all the vessels** that
were made to **Baal**, and for the
grove, and for the **host of heaven**:
and he burned them outside of
Jerusalem in the fields of Kidron,
and carried the ashes of them unto
Bethel. (2 Kings 23:4)

➤ **He put down the
idolatrous priests**, whom the kings
of Judah had ordained to burn
incense in the high places in the
cities of Judah, and the places round
about Jerusalem; them also that
burned incense unto Baal, to the sun,
and to the moon, and to the planets,
and to all the host of heavens. (2
Kings 23:5)

➤ He brought out the
grove from the house of the Lord,
without Jerusalem, unto the brook of
Kidron, and stamped it small to
powder, and cast the powder thereof
upon the graves of the children of the
people. (2 Kings 23:6)

➤ **Josiah took other
actions to tear down the high
places.** And he slew all the priests
of the high places that were there
upon the altar, and burned men's
bones upon them, and returned to
Jerusalem. (2 Kings 23:7-20)

➤ **Josiah** commanded all
the people to keep the Passover of
the LORD, as it was written in the
book of the Covenant. (2 Ki 23:21)

Kingdom of Judah	Kingdom of Israel
Josiah (Cont.)	**God Moved Them Out of His Sight**

> In the eighteenth year of King Josiah this Passover was held before the LORD in Jerusalem. Such a Passover surely had never been held since the days of the judges who judged Israel, nor in all the days of the kings of Israel and the kings of Judah. (2 Kings 23:22-23)

> Josiah put away the workers with familiar spirits, and the wizards, and the images, and the idols, and all the abominations that were spied in the land of Judah and in Jerusalem, that he might perform the words of the law which were written in the book that Hilkiah the priest found in the house of the Lord. (2 Kings 23:24)

> **Now before him there was no king like him, who turned to the LORD** with all his **heart**, with all his **soul**, and with all his **might**, according to the Law of Moses; nor did any arise like him. (2 King 23:25)

> Nevertheless, **the LORD turned not from the fierceness of his great wrath,** wherewith his anger was kindled against Judah, because of all the provocations that Manasseh had provoked him withal. And the LORD said, **I will remove Judah also out of my sight**, as I cast off this city Jerusalem which I have chosen, and the house of which I said, My name shall be there. (2 Kings 23:26-27)

Kingdom of Judah	Kingdom of Israel
Josiah (Cont.)	**God** Moved Them **Out of His Sight**

➢ In Josiah's days Pharaoh-
nechoh king of Egypt went up
against the king of Assyria to the
river Euphrates: and king Josiah
went against him; and he slew him at
Megiddo, when he had seen him.
His servants carried him in a chariot
dead from Megiddo, and brought
him to Jerusalem, and buried him in
his own sepulchre. And the people
of the land took Jehoahaz the son of
Josiah, and appointed him, and made
him king in his father's stead. (2
Kings 23:29-30)

Jehoahaz
➢ The people appointed
Jehoahaz as king in his father's
stead. (2 Kings 23:30)
➢ He was twenty-three
years old when he began to reign;
and he **reigned three months** in
Jerusalem. (2 Kings 23:31)
➢ He did that which was
evil in the sight of the LORD,
according to all that his fathers had
done.
➢ Pharaoh-nechoh **put
Jehoahaz in bands at Riblah in the
land of Hamath, that he might not
reign** in Jerusalem; and put the land
to a tribute of an hundred talents of
silver, and a talent of gold.

Kingdom of Judah	Kingdom of Israel

Jehoahaz cont.

➤ Pharaoh-nechoh made Eliakin the son of Josiah king in the room of Josiah his father, and turned his name to Jehoiakim, and took Jehoahaz away: and he came to Egypt, and died there. (2 Kings 23:33-34)

Jehoiakim

➤ Jehoiakim was twenty-five years old when he began to reign. (2 Kings 23:36)

➤ Jehoiakim gave the silver and the gold to Pharaoh; but he taxed the land to give the money according to the commandment of Pharaoh: he exacted the silver and the gold of the people of the land, of every one according to his taxation, to give it unto Pharaoh-nechoh. (2 Kings 23:35)

➤ He reigned eleven years in Jerusalem. (2 Kings 23:36)

➤ **He did that which was evil in the sight of the LORD**, according to all that his fathers had done. (2 Kings 23:37)

➤ Jehoiakim became a servant to Nebuchadnezzar King of Babylon for three years. Then Jehoiakim rebelled against him. (2 Kings 24:1)

253

Kingdom of Judah	Kingdom of Israel

Jehoiakim (Cont.)

**God Moved Them
Out of His Sight**

> ➢ The LORD sent against him bands of the Chaldees, and bands of the Syrians, and bands of the Moabites, and bands of the children of Ammon, and sent them against Judah to destroy it, according to the word of the LORD, which he spake by his servants the prophets. Surely at the commandments of the LORD came this upon Judah, to remove them out of his sight, for the sins of Manasseh, according to all that he did; And also for the innocent blood that he shed: for he filled Jerusalem with innocent blood; which the LORD would not pardon. (2 King 24:2-4)

> ➢ Against him came up Nebuchadnezzar king of Babylon, and bound him in fetters, to carry him to Babylon. Nebuchadnezzar also carried of the vessels of the house of the LORD to Babylon, and put them in his temple at Babylon. Jehoiachin his son reigned in his stead. (2 Chronicles 36:6-8)

Jehoiachin

> ➢ He was **eight years old** He began to reign, and he reigned three months and ten days in Jerusalem: and **he did that which was evil in the sight of the LORD**. (2 Chronicles 36:9) **Note.** According to 2 Kings 24:8, Jehoiachin was **eighteen years old** when he began to reign. (See Note this page)

Note: The writers of 2 Kings and the writers of 2 Chronicles give conflicting information regarding the age of Jehoiachin when he began to reign as king.

Kingdom of Judah	Kingdom of Israel
Jehoiachin (Cont.)	**God Moved Them Out of His Sight**

➢ At that time the servants of Nebuchadnezzar king of Babylon came up against Jerusalem, and the city was besieged. And Nebuchadnezzar king of Bablyon came against the city and his servants were besieging it. (2 Kings 24:10-11)

➢ After the city was besieged, Jehoiachin king of Judah, his mother, his servants, his princes, and his officers went out to the king of Babylon; and the king of Babylon, in the eighth year of his reign, took him prisoner. (2 Kings 24:12)

➢ Nebuchadnezzar carried out from there all the treasures of the house of the LORD and the king's house. He cut in pieces all the articles of gold which Solomon king of Israel had made in the temple of the LORD, as the LORD had said. He carried captivity to all Jerusalem, except the poorest people of the land. He carried Jehoiachin captive to Babylon. The king's mother, his wives, his officers, and mighty of the land, all the valiant men, seven thousand, all craftsmen and smiths, one thousand, and all who were strong and fit for war he carried into captivity from Jerusalem to Babylon. The king of Babylon made Mattaniah, Jehoiachin's uncle, king in his place and changed his name to Zedekiah. (2 Kings 24:13-17)

Kingdom of Judah	Kingdom of Israel

Kingdom of Judah

Zedekiah

> Zedekiah was twenty-one years old when he became king, and he reigned eleven years in Jerusalem. (2 Kings 24:18)

> He did that which was **evil in the sight of the LORD** his God, and **humbled not himself before Jeremiah the prophet speaking from the mouth of the LORD.** (2 Chronicles 36:12)

> He also rebelled against King Nebuchadnezzar, who had made him swear by God: but he stiffened his neck, and hardened his heart from turning unto the LORD God of Israel. (2 Chronicles 36:13)

> Moreover all the chief of priests, and the people transgressed very much after all the abominations of the heathen; and polluted the house of the LORD which he had hallowed in Jerusalem

> And the LORD God of their fathers sent to them by his messengers, rising up betimes, and sending; because he had compassion on his people, and on his dwelling place: **But they mocked the messengers of God**, and despised his words, and misused his prophets, until the wrath of the LORD arose against his people, till there was no remedy. (2 Chronicles 36:15-16)

Kingdom of Israel

God Moved Them Out of His Sight

Kingdom of Judah	Kingdom of Israel
Zedekiah (Cont.)	**God Moved Them Out of His Sight**

➤ And it came to pass in the ninth year of his reign, in the tenth month, in the tenth day of the month, that Nebuchadnezzar king of Babylon came, he, and all his host, against Jerusalem, and pitched against it; and they built forts against it round about. And the city was besieged unto the eleventh year of king Zedekiah. (2 Kings 25:1-2)

➤ And on the ninth day of the fourth month, the famine prevailed in the city, and there was no bread for the people of the land. (2 Kings 25:3)

➤ Then the city wall was broken through, and all the men of war fled at night by way of the gate between two walls, which was by the king's garden, even though the Chaldeans were still encamped all around against the city. And Zedekiah went by the way of the plain. But the army of the Chaldeans pursued the king, and they overtook him in the plains of Jericho. All his army was scattered from him. (2 Kings 25:4-5)

➤ They took Zedekiah king of Judah and brought him up to the king of Babylon at Riblah, and they pronounced judgment on him. Then they killed the sons of Zedekiah before his eyes, put out the eyes of Zedekiah, bound him with bronze fetters, and took him to Babylon. (2 Kings 25:6-7)

257

Kingdom of Judah	Kingdom of Israel
Zedekiah (Cont.)	**God Moved Them Out of His Sight**

➢ The LORD brought upon them the king of the Chaldees, who slew their young men with the sword in the house of their sanctuary, and had no compassion upon young man or maiden, old man, or him that stooped for age: he gave them all into his hand. And all the vessels of the house of God, great and small, and the treasures of the house of the LORD, and the treasures of the king, and of his princes; all these he brought to Babylon. (2 Chronicles 36:17-18)

➢ They burnt the house of God, and brake down the wall of Jerusalem, and burnt all the palaces thereof with fire, and destroyed all the goodly vessels thereof. And them that had escaped from the sword carried he away to Babylon; where they were servants to him and his sons until the reign of the Kingdom of Persia. The king of Persia ended their captivity after the land had laid desolate for seventy years. (2 Chronicles 36:20-23)

Making Both Ears Tingle

God said that he would remove Judah out of his sight as he did Israel. (2 King 23:27) Moreover, God said that it would make both ears of the people who heard it tingle.

Kingdom of Judah	Kingdom of Israel
God Moved Judah Out of His Sight	**God Moved Israel Out of His Sight**
Making Both Ears Tingle	**Making Both Ears Tingle**

➢ Because Manasseh king of Judah hath done these abominations, and hath done wickedly above all that the Amorites did, which were before him, and hath made Judah also to sin with his idols: Therefore thus saith the LORD God of Israel, Behold, I am bringing such evil upon Jerusalem and Judah, that whosoever heareth of it, **both his ears shall tingle**. And I will stretch over Jerusalem the line of Samaria, and the plummet of the house of Ahab: and **I will wipe Jerusalem as a man wipeth a dish, wiping it, and turning it upside down.** (2 Kings 21:11-13)

➢ Jeremiah proclaimed these words, Hear ye the word of the LORD, O Kings of Judah, and inhabitants of Jerusalem: Thus saith the LORD of hosts, the God of Israel; Behold, I will bring evil upon this place, the which whosoever heareth, his ears shall tingle. Because they have forsaken me, and have estranged this place, and have burned incense in it unto other gods, whom neither thy nor their fathers have known, nor the kings of Judah, and have filled this place with the blood of innocents. (Jeremiah 19:3-4)

➢ Before Israel had earthly Kings, the LORD was their king and he had judges for them. In the days of Eli, God said to Samuel, Behold I will do a thing in Israel, at which **both the ears of every one that heareth it shall tingle.** In that day I will perform against Eli all things which I have spoken concerning his house: when I begin, I will also make an end. For I have told him that I will judge his house for ever for the iniquity which he knoweth; because his sons made themselves vile, and he restrained them not. And therefore I have sworn unto the house of Eli that the iniquity of Eli's house shall not be purged with sacrifice nor offering for ever. (1 Samuel 3:11-14)

Jeroboam did not hearken to the commandments of God – **he** did evil above all that were before him – **made other gods, and molten images to provoke God to anger. (1 Kings 14:9)** God shall give Israel up because of the sins of Jeroboam, who did sin, and made Israel to sin. **(1 Kings 14:16)** Most of the kings of Israel used Jeroboam as their model.

APPENDIX TWO

SERMON

A CHECK-UP FOR THE BODY OF CHRIST- THE CHURCH

This is the first sermon the Holy Spirit gave me to preach, "A Check-up for the Body of Christ - The Church." This sermon was preached on July 9, 2000 at Pleasant Hill Baptist Church in Los Angeles, California. The pastor of the church was Sylvester Washington. On the morning of July 9, 2000, after praying to Our Heavenly Father in the name of Jesus, the Holy Ghost preached to me for about fifteen minutes. I did not realize it at the time, but this is when I received my commission as a Prophet of God. The message was clear what God wants me to do. Now I realize that it was not only a sermon, however it is a work.

Thank you for allowing me to share this sermon and work with you. I pray that you will also obtain a copy of the Book, titled, "Edifying the Body of Christ: Unbinding the Strong Man which is designed to help effect the edification process of the Body of Christ.

The Sermon: A Check-Up For The Body Of Christ- The Church

CALLING:

LUKE 4:18-19

The spirit of the Lord is upon me, because he hath anointed me to preach the gospel to the poor; he hath sent me to heal the brokenhearted, to preach deliverance to the captives, and recovering of sight to the blind, to set at liberty them that are bruised, and to preach the acceptable year of the Lord.

Ephesians 5:23-32

23   For the husband is the head of the wife, even as Christ is the head of the church: and he is the Saviour of the body.

24   Therefore as the church is subject unto Christ, so let the wives be to their own husbands in every thing.

25   Husbands, love your wives, even as Christ also loved the church, and gave himself for it;

26   That he might sanctify and cleanse it with the washing of water by the word.

27   That he might present it to himself a glorious church, not having spot, or wrinkle, or any such thing; but that it should be holy and without blemish.

28   So ought men to love their wives as their own bodies. He that loveth his wife loveth himself.

29   For no man ever yet hated his own flesh; but nourisheth and cherisheth it, even as the Lord the church:

30   For we are members of his body, of his flesh, and of his bones.

31   For this cause shall a man leave his father and mother, and shall be joined unto his wife, and they two shall be one flesh.

32   This is a great mystery: but I speak concerning Christ and the church.

The subject of today's message is "A Check-Up For The Body Of Christ - The Church"

Today as we look at the world we can clearly see the destruction throughout. However, the condition of the world is not our subject today. Today, we will examine the word of God to see what we must do so God can heal this land. 2 Chronicles 7:14 states,

"If my people, which are called by my name, shall humble themselves, and pray, seek my face, and turn from their wicked ways; then will I hear from heaven, and will forgive their sin, and will heal their land."

These words are written for us in times like these, because we do need a Saviour. Church, it is time for a check-up of the body of Christ.

The Holy Spirit has led me to present this message to you the body of Christ.

1. Today, we will take a look at Who Christ is, the head of the church.
2. Our relationship with Christ
3. Who are we?
4. What are our benefits?
5. What powers do we have?
6. What we should do to get along with one another and why is it important?
7. What should we do now to experience the full joy of God's love?

Today we will integrate teaching and preaching to enhance the activation of the word of God in our personal lives and the life of the church.

The church is defined as the people of God. Those destined to inherit the kingdom of God. Any local group of believers.

Therefore, you could join all the buildings together throughout Los Angeles and you still would not have a church. We the people of God are the church.

You notice that this is a checkup for the body and not the head because Christ is the head and he does not need any check-up.

He is the Saviour of the body and much more.

John 1:1-3

1   "In the beginning was the word, and the word was with God, and the word was God."

2   "The same was in the beginning with God."

3   "All things were made by him; and without him was not any thing made that was made."

John 1:14

"And the word was made flesh, and dwelt among us, (and we beheld his glory, the glory as of the only begotten of the father,) full of grace and truth."

Jesus is the word that was made flesh.

Jesus is the one that had no sin, worked miracles, healed the sick, raised the dead, walked on water, yielded not to any temptation, calmed the seas, stopped the wind, did the will of the father who sent him, took up his cross as the lamb of God. He was crucified on cavalry, He died for our sins, He was buried in a tomb, and descended into hell. The grave could not hold him. He got up on the third day, and appeared before men. He then ascended into the heavens.

He is sitting on the right hand of God.

According to Matthew 28:18, after he was crucified and had risen he appeared before his disciples and others.

Matthew 28:18

" And Jesus came and spake unto them saying, all power is given unto me in heaven and in earth."

Often when people discuss things, they find some controversy.

However, on certain things there is no controversy.

We know that water will freeze at 32 degrees Fahrenheit and at 212 degrees water will boil. And there is not any controversy regarding this.

Though there is no controversy, there still may be some unbelievers who may test the waters at 33 degrees or 211 degrees with their hands or some other instrument.

Lord help them if they should put their hands in water at 211 degrees one degree below boiling point.

Like there is no controversy regarding this matter, there is no controversy regarding Jesus.

According to Timothy 3:16

And without controversy great is the mystery of Godliness. God was manifest in the flesh, justified in the spirit, seen of angels, preached unto the Gentiles, believed on in the world, and received up into glory.

2000 years ago you had some who did not believe. So it does not surprise me to find some people today that do not believe so they can make a use of their time to document their disbelief and then air it on national television.

I am here to tell you today that I am, sent me to tell you that you should hold on to your faith.

According to the word, we are members of his body, of his flesh, and of his bones.

This is a serious relationship with the King of kings and the Lord of lords.

How did we obtain this relationship?

John 3:16

"For God so loved the world, that He gave His only begotten Son, that whosoever believeth in Him should not perish, but have everlasting life."

Why did Jesus die for us? The answer is simply, because he loved us.

We have been bought with the price - Jesus' life on the cross - now we are not our own.

1 Corinthians 6:19

"… Your body is the temple of the Holy Ghost which is in you, which ye have God, and ye are not your own."

1 Corinthians 6:20

"For ye are bought with a price: therefore glorify God in your body, and ye are not your own."

According to John 15:12-14

12   "This is my commandment; that ye love one another, as I have loved you."

13   "Greater love hath no man than this, that a man lay down his life for his friends."

14   "Ye are my friends, if ye do whatsoever I command you "

Are we willing to die for one another?

Are we?

Let me remind you that the doctor is in the house and this is a check up for the body. When a check up is performed questions are asked about your behavior.

If you are willing to die for me, are you also willing to volunteer to help me with my homework so I can improve my grades?

Are you willing to visit me when I am sick?

John 15:7-8

"If ye abide in me, and my words abide in you, ye shall ask what ye will, and it shall be done unto you."

John 15:9

"As the father hath loved me, so have I loved you; continue ye in my love."

John 15:10

"If ye keep my commandments, ye shall abide in my love; even as I have kept my father's commandments, and abide in his love."

I can recall a lawyer asking Jesus what was the greatest commandment.
Jesus said unto him, "Thou shalt love the Lord thy God with all thy heart, and with all thy soul, and with all thy mind. Thou shalt love thy neighbor as thy self."

On these two commandments hang all the law and prophets.
There are conditions that are placed on our relations with Jesus and we must have faith.

Matthew 17:20

"...if ye have faith as a grain of mustard seed, ye shall say unto this mountain, remove hence to yonder place; and it shall remove; and nothing shall be impossible unto you."

Let us stay with this point for a moment

Let's take a close look at this important statement that is often misunderstood. It says, "If you have faith as a grain of mustard seed." It did not say if you have faith as the size of a grain of mustard seed. It says a mustard seed has faith. A grain of mustard like most of God's creations, knows its purpose.

The purpose of a mustard seed is defined in Genesis 1: 12. It says, "And the earth brought forth grass, and herb yielding seed after his kind, and the tree yielding fruit, whose seed was in itself, after his kind: and God saw that it was good." The mustard seed knows its purpose. It produces after its kind and the seed is within itself.

The first test of faith for a mustard is seed is when it is planted into the ground. A mountain is placed on top of it.

The mustard seed asks for water and then receives it.

Next the germination process commences.

Roots go into the soil.

A stem peaks at the top of the grain and the grain of mustard seed is confronted with its first mountain.

The mustard seed says, "I must go through that mountain because there is a light on the other side."

The mustard seed says, "I am coming" and the mountain opens up and lets it through.

Next the stem peaks through the earth and sees the sunlight and then praises the Lord.

The mustard plant receives its daily bread and begins to grow.

It becomes more rooted and grounded because it knows that the more it matures the more responsibilities it would have.

As the mustard plant continues to grow it is faced with the storms of life. The wind begins to blow, and the rain falls. Nevertheless, the mustard plant is rooted and grounded, therefore it just moves backwards and forward, as the storms come. Then the mustard plant provides shelter to the birds; food for insects and man.

Finally, the mustard plant produces it seeds. The mustard seed knows its purpose. If we had faith as a mustard seed, we would move the mountains in our lives.

The faith as a grain of mustard seed

We can see that each one of us that does what Jesus commands us to do. To love the Lord thy God with all our heart, mind, soul, and might, and to love one another as we love ourselves, abide in his word, have faith as a grain of mustard seed, nothing shall be impossible unto you and anything you ask in his name shall be done.

There are other benefits in Christ

Romans 6:23

"Eternal life is Christ"

Roman 8:39

"Love of God which is in Christ"

1 Cor 1:2

"Sanctified in Christ"

Romans 3:24

"Redemption that is in Christ"

Romans 6:11

"Alive to God in Christ"

1Cor 4:10

"You are wise in Christ"

1 Corinthians 15:19

"We have hope in Christ"

2 Corinthians 2:14

" Now thanks be to God, which causes us to always triumph in Christ"

Romans 8:1

"No condemnation to them which are in Christ Jesus, who walk not after the flesh, but after the Spirit"

Ephesians 1:3

"Blessed be the God and Father of our Lord Jesus Christ, who hath blessed us with all spiritual blessings in heavenly places in Christ:

2Timothy 1:9

"Grace which was given to us in Christ"

2 Timothy 2:10

"The salvation which is in Christ Jesus"

"Yes, there are benefits as a member of the body of Christ."

Jesus made us some promises:

"Because I live, you also will live" (John 14:19)

"Never will I leave you; never will I forsake you" (Heb 13:5)

"Remain in me, and I will remain in you" (John 15:4).

"Come to me, all you who are weary and burdened, and I will give you rest" Matt. 11:28).

"You will receive power when the Holy Spirit comes on you."

John 14:12 - "Verily, verily, I say unto you, he that believeth on me, the works that I do shall he do also; and greater works than these shall he do, because I go unto my father."

"As a member of the body of Christ, you have been given power. If you have power as an individual, how much more power are given to the churches working together."

In the church, we find many members.

Romans 12:4

"For as we are many members in one body and all members have not the same office"

Romans 12:5

"So we being many, are one body in Christ and every member one of another."

Now let us take a closer look at how this body of Christ is joined together.

In Ephesians 4:16

Apostle Paul describes how the body is joined together

16   "From whom the whole body fitly joined together and compacted by that which every joint supplieth, according to the effectual working in the measure of every part, maketh increase of the body unto the edifying of itself in love."

Explain example

"Members of the body are given spiritual gifts"

1 Corinthians 12:4

"Now there are diversities of gifts, but the same Spirit."

1 Cor 12:5   "And there are difference of administrations, but the same Lord."

1 Cor 12:6   "There are diversities of operations, but the same God which worketh all."

1 Cor 12:8   "For one is given by the spirit the word of wisdom; to another the word of knowledge by the same spirit."

1 Cor 12:9   "To another the working of miracles; to another prophecy; to another discerning of spirits; to another divers kinds of tongues, to another the interpretations of tongues. But all these worketh that one and the selfsame spirit, by dividing to every man severally as he will."

Now let us look at how we should use these gifts

Romans 12:6

"Prophecy let us prophesy according to the proportion of faith"

Romans 12:7

"... Ministry, let us wait on our ministering, or he that teach, on teaching"

Romans 12:8

" ... He that exhorteth, on exhortation:

He that giveth, let him do it with simplicity;

He that ruleth, with diligence;

He that sheweth mercy, with cheerfulness"

Romans 12:9

"Let love be without dissimulation.   Abhor that which is evil, cleave to that which is good."

Romans 12:10

"Be kindly affectioned one to another with brotherly love; in honour preferring one another."

Romans 12:11

"Not slothful in business; fervent in spirit; serving the Lord;"

Romans 12:12

"Rejoicing in hope; patient in tribulation; continuing instant in prayer;"

Romans 12:13

"Distributing to the necessity of saints; giving to hospitality."

Romans 12:14

"Bless them which persecute you; bless, and curse not."

Romans 12:15

"Rejoice with them that do rejoice, and weep with them that weep."

Romans 12:16

"Be of the same mind one toward another. Mind not high things, but condescend to men of low estate. Be not wise in your own conceits."

Romans 12:17

"Recompense to no man evil for evil. Provide things honest in the sight of all men."

Romans 12:18

"If it be possible, a s much as lieth in you, live peaceably with all men

Romans 12:19.

"…Avenge not yourselves, but rather give place unto wrath: for it is written vengenance is mine; I will repay, saith the Lord"

Romans 12:20

"Therefore, if thine enemy hunger, feed him; if he thirst, give him drink: for is so doing thou shalt heap coals of fire on his head."

Romans 12:20

"Be not overcome of evil, but overcome evil with good."

God gave his only begotten Son for us because He loves us so. He sent the Holy Spirit in Jesus' name to give us power and to lead us into all truth. He also has angels encamped around us. They listen to our prayers to hear the desires of our hearts - they respond as they are directed.

We have reviewed the word of God straight from the Master - The question now is do you believe that God will do what he said he would.

This brings us to our final point.

What should we do now to experience the full joy of God's love?

Repent

For give others.

Let it go.

Totally, surrender yourself to God.

Receive the Holy Spirit and receive power.